Macs For Seniors
FOR
DUMMIES®

by Mark L. Chambers

WILEY

Wiley Publishing, Inc.

Macs For Seniors For Dummies®

Published by
Wiley Publishing, Inc.
111 River Street
Hoboken, NJ 07030-5774

www.wiley.com

Copyright © 2009 by Wiley Publishing, Inc., Indianapolis, Indiana

Published by Wiley Publishing, Inc., Indianapolis, Indiana

Published simultaneously in Canada

For general information on our other products and services, please contact our Customer Care Department within the U.S. at 877-762-2974, outside the U.S. at 317-572-3993, or fax 317-572-4002.

For technical support, please visit www.wiley.com/techsupport.

Wiley also publishes its books in a variety of electronic formats. Some content that appears in print may not be available in electronic books.

Library of Congress Control Number: 2009923968

ISBN: 978-0-470-43779-7

Manufactured in the United States of America

10 9 8 7 6 5 4 3 2

WILEY

About the Author

Mark L. Chambers has been an author, a computer consultant, a BBS sysop, a programmer, and a hardware technician for 25 years — pushing computers and their uses far beyond "normal" performance limits for decades now. His first love affair with a computer peripheral blossomed in 1984 when he bought his lightning-fast 300 bps modem for his Atari 400. Now he spends entirely too much time on the Internet and drinks far too much caffeine-laden soda.

With a degree in journalism and creative writing from Louisiana State University, Mark took the logical career choice: programming computers. After five years as a COBOL programmer for a hospital system, however, he decided that there must be a better way to earn a living — and he became the documentation manager for Datastorm Technologies, a well-known communications software developer. Somewhere between designing and writing software manuals, Mark began writing computer how-to books. His first book, *Running a Perfect BBS*, was published in 1994 — and after a short decade or so of fun (disguised as hard work), Mark is one of the most productive and best-selling technology authors on the planet.

Along with writing several books a year and editing whatever his publishers throw at him, Mark has branched out into Web-based education, designing and teaching online classes (called WebClinics) for Hewlett-Packard.

His favorite pastimes include collecting gargoyles, watching St. Louis Cardinals baseball, playing his three pinball machines and the latest computer games, supercharging computers, and rendering 3D flights of fancy with TrueSpace. And, during all that activity, he listens to just about every type of music imaginable. Mark's worldwide Internet radio station, MLC Radio (at www.mlcbooks.com), plays only CD-quality classics from 1970 to 1979, including everything from Rush to Billy Joel to the *Rocky Horror Picture Show* soundtrack.

Mark's rapidly expanding list of books includes *MacBook For Dummies,* 2nd Edition; *iMac For Dummies,* 5th Edition; *Mac OS X Leopard All-in-One Desk Reference For Dummies; Build Your Own PC Do-It-Yourself For Dummies; Scanners For Dummies,* 2nd Edition; *CD & DVD Recording For Dummies,* 2nd Edition; *PCs All-in-One Desk Reference For Dummies,* 4th Edition; *Mac OS X Tiger: Top 100 Simplified Tips & Tricks; Hewlett-Packard Official Printer Handbook; Hewlett-Packard Official Recordable CD Handbook; Digital Photography Handbook; Computer Gamer's Bible* (co-author); *Recordable CD Bible; Teach Yourself Visually iMac* (all from Wiley Publishing); *Running a Perfect BBS; Official Netscape Guide to Web Animation; Windows 98 Optimizing and Troubleshooting Little Black Book, Microsoft Office v. X for Mac Power User's Guide;* and *Burn It! Creating Your Own Great DVDs and CDs.*

Mark's books have been translated into 16 languages so far — his favorites are German, Polish, Dutch, and French. Although he can't read them, he enjoys the pictures immensely.

Mark welcomes all comments about his books. You can reach him at mark@mlcbooks.com, or visit MLC Books Online, his Web site, at www.mlcbooks.com.

Dedication

This book is proudly dedicated to my Uncle Tuffy and my Aunt Ruby — a couple forever young and forever in love.

Author's Acknowledgments

Leave it to my friends at Wiley to recognize that seniors deserve a well-designed guide to the Apple line of Macintosh computers — and the Mac OS X Leopard operating system to boot! It's time for me to thank the hard-working individuals who were instrumental in placing this book in your hands.

My friend Dennis Cohen (who also happens to be one of the best Mac technical editors anywhere) contributed his expert knowledge of Apple hardware and software, making sure that every step-by-step procedure and every tip is completely accurate. I also owe a huge debt of gratitude to ace copy editor Rebecca Whitney and to Linda Morris and Jodi Jensen for their development work — they all kept each chapter on track, easy to read, and full of the right information. (They should clone themselves — *all* my books need such guidance!)

As with every book I've written, I'd like to thank my wife, Anne, and my children, Erin, Chelsea, and Rose, for their support and love — and for letting me follow my dream!

Finally, two wonderful editors at Wiley deserve a special round of applause: my project editor, Rebecca Huehls, and my acquisitions editor, Bob Woerner. A book like this one simply doesn't become reality without their patience, guidance, and hard work, and I look forward to our next project together!

Publisher's Acknowledgments

We're proud of this book; please send us your comments through our online registration form located at http://dummies.custhelp.com. For other comments, please contact our Customer Care Department within the U.S. at 877-762-2974, outside the U.S. at 317-572-3993, or fax 317-572-4002.

Some of the people who helped bring this book to market include the following:

Acquisitions, Editorial

Project Editor: Rebecca Huehls

Acquisitions Editor: Bob Woerner

Copy Editor: Rebecca Whitney

Technical Editor: Dennis Cohen

Editorial Manager: Leah Cameron

Media Development Project Manager: Laura Moss-Hollister

Media Development Assistant Project Manager: Jenny Swisher

Media Development Assistant Producers: Angela Denny, Josh Frank, Shawn Patrick, and Kit Malone

Editorial Assistant: Amanda Foxworth

Sr. Editorial Assistant: Cherie Case

Cartoons: Rich Tennant (www.the5thwave.com)

Composition Services

Project Coordinator: Patrick Redmond

Layout and Graphics: Joyce Haughey, Sarah Philippart, Mark Pinto

Proofreader: Betty Kish

Indexer: Sherry Massey

Publishing and Editorial for Technology Dummies

> **Richard Swadley,** Vice President and Executive Group Publisher
>
> **Andy Cummings,** Vice President and Publisher
>
> **Mary Bednarek,** Executive Acquisitions Director
>
> **Mary C. Corder,** Editorial Director

Publishing for Consumer Dummies

> **Diane Graves Steele,** Vice President and Publisher

Composition Services

> **Gerry Fahey,** Vice President of Production Services
>
> **Debbie Stailey,** Director of Composition Services

Contents At a Glance

Table Of Contents

Macs For Seniors For Dummies

Introduction

Is the Macintosh the computer for you? I can unequivocally answer Yes! Why am I so sure? Because Apple has been producing the best consumer computers for many years now — including desktops, laptops, and software that surpass anything else now offered on the market. (Yes, that includes companies you've heard of, such as Dell, Microsoft, and Gateway.) You probably know that Macs are designed to be easy to use, and computing beginners will find that Apple has a knack for writing the best personal computer software around.

Let me be honest: I'm not easily impressed when it comes to computers. As a cynical old computer programmer (and curmudgeon), I've used every version of Windows that His Gateness has produced, including the various server versions and Windows Vista. And yes, I've used Mac OS since before the days of System 7, using a Macintosh SE with a 9-inch monitor (and a built-in handle). That takes us back to 1989.

Macintosh computers and their operating system, Mac OS X (now in version 10.5, affectionately called *Leopard*) are now the height of technical sophistication. As I've said, Mac OS X performs like a Ferrari, and (unbelievably) it looks as good, too.

The book you hold in your hands is written especially for seniors, using the classic *For Dummies* design — it provides you with step-by-step instructions (plenty of which my editors agree are humorous) for using the major features of both your computer and Leopard.

What you *don't* find in this book is wasted space. Everything is explained from the ground up, just in case you've never touched an Apple computer.

About This Book

This book is designed to be read in a linear fashion (straight through) — probably not in one session, mind you. (Then again, Diet Coke is cheap, so it *is* possible.) The material is divided into four parts, each of which covers a different area of Mac knowledge. For example, you'll find parts on software, the Internet, and Mac maintenance.

Each self-contained chapter discusses a specific feature, application, connection, or cool feature of your Mac. Feel free to begin reading anywhere or skip chapters at will, although I recommend that you read this book from front to back, like any good mystery novel. (Watch out — oncoming spoiler: For those who want to know right now, Bill Gates did it.)

What's Truly Required

If you have a Mac that's running Mac OS X version 10.5 (Leopard) — or you're ready to buy your Mac — you're set to go. Despite what you might have heard, you *don't* require any of the following:

➡ **A degree in computer science:** Apple designed Leopard and Macs for regular people, and I designed this book for people of every experience level. Even if you've never used a Mac, you'll find no hostile waters here.

➡ **A fortune in software:** Almost everything covered in this book is included with Mac OS X Leopard — and the size of this volume gives you a rough idea of just how complete Leopard is! Heck, many folks buy Macs just because of the free software they get, such as iMovie and iPhoto. ("Tough cookies" to the vast Unwashed Windows Horde.)

➡ **An Internet connection:** Granted, you can't do much with Apple Mail without an Internet connection, but computers *did* exist before the Internet. You can still be productive with Mac OS X without receiving buckets of spam. (Don't worry, if you *do* have an Internet connection, this book helps you connect and become familiar with the best of what's online!)

Conventions Used in This Book

Even *For Dummies* books must get technical from time to time, usually involving commands you have to type and menu items you have to click. If you've read any of my other *For Dummies* books, you know that a helpful set of conventions is used to indicate what needs to be done or what you see onscreen.

Tip icons

 The Tip icons in this book are more than just attractive — they're also important visual cues for information you don't want to miss.

Stuff you type

When I ask you to type a command or enter information (such as your name or phone number) in a text field, the text appears in bold like this: **Type me**.

Press the Return key to process the command or enter the text.

Menu commands

When I give you a specific set of menu commands to use, they appear in the following format: Edit➪Copy.

In this example, you should click the Edit menu and then choose the Copy menu item.

Display messages

If I mention a specific message that you see on your screen, it looks like this on the page: This message is displayed by an application.

In case you're curious about computers

No one expects a book in the *For Dummies* series to contain technojargon or ridiculous computer science semantics — especially a book about the Macintosh, which has always strived for simplicity and user friendliness. I hereby promise that I'll do my absolute best to avoid unnecessary technotalk. When you need to understand a technical term, I explain it clearly and simply so that anyone who's new to Mac computers can understand.

How This Book Is Organized

I did my best to emulate the elegant design of the Mac by organizing this book into four parts, with cross-references where appropriate.

Part I: Buying and Getting Started with Your Mac

This part begins with a chapter that helps you choose the right Mac for your needs, followed by a chapter of instruction in setting up your system. Then I provide an introduction to the basic tasks that you perform — such as copying files, running programs, and the like. You'll also find coverage on customizing Leopard, adding a printer, and using the Mac OS X Help system.

Part II: Having Fun and Getting Things Done with Software

Sweet! This part jumps right in among the crown jewels of Mac software: Pages, Numbers, iPhoto, the DVD Player, iTunes, and the gaming possibilities under Leopard. Get ready to connect your digital camera and MP3 player, too!

Part III: Exploring the Internet

This part contains just what it says. But then again, you can easily become enthusiastic about Apple Mail and iChat (the latest version of the Apple instant messaging application) and the online storage provided by iDisk. I also cover Safari, Apple's hot-rod Web browser.

Part IV: Taking Care of Your Computer

Maintenance may not sound exciting, but it keeps your Mac running smoothly — and the security information in this part of the book helps reduce your risks of identity theft, viral infection, and swindles while connected.

Get Going!

Do you want my recommendations on how to proceed? I just happen to have three:

➡ If you're thinking about buying a new Mac, the box is still unopened in your living room, or you want help with setting things up, start with Part I.

➡ If you've already set up your Mac and you're familiar with Leopard basics, start with Part II.

➡ For all other concerns, use the index or check out the table of contents to jump directly to the chapter you need.

A Final Word

I want to thank you for buying my book, and I hope that you find that *Macs For Seniors For Dummies* answers the questions you have along the way! When you have this fearless guide in hand, I believe that you and your Mac will bond as I have with mine. (That sounds somewhat wrong, but it's really not.)

Now it's time for the first Tip in this book:

 Take your time — after all, finding out how to use your computer isn't a race — and don't worry if you're not a graphic artist, professional photographer, or video editor. With your Mac and its software by your side, you don't have to be!

Part I

Buying and Getting Started with Your Mac

The 5th Wave
By Rich Tennant

"Well, here's your problem. You only have half the ram you need."

Buying a Mac

*S*hopping for a Mac can leave you dazzled by a long list of features, functions, acronyms, and assorted hoohah. This chapter is here to help explain *what* to look for, and *why*, while you're shopping for a Mac.

The best part? I wrote it in common English, with the least amount of technobabble possible. (That's my job!)

In this chapter, I show you

➡ Tasks and work that your Mac can perform

➡ Differences between hardware and software

➡ Differences between the models in Apple's Mac computer line

➡ Features you should look for while shopping for a monitor

➡ Specifications you should look for when comparing the central processing unit (also known as CPU — the computer's brain) and memory

➡ Reasons that ordering online may save you money

Know What Your Mac Can Do

I would bet that you already know why you want a computer — you have an idea what you want to do with a Mac. But you may not know all the things you can do with a computer.

To help get you excited about owning a Mac, here's a (very) short list of only a few of the more popular uses for a computer these days. See whether any of these uses reflects what you want to do and whether you see any tasks that you want to learn more about:

➡ **The Internet:** (You knew I would start with the Web and e-mail.) Now you can also add online games, chat rooms, and Internet radio to the mix. The Internet literally expands in front of your eyes, and your Mac can be your doorway to the online world.

➡ **Digital media:** Whether your interest is in photography, video, or music (making it or listening to it), your Mac comes with everything you need to get started.

➡ **Data collection:** Just in case genealogy is your passion — or collecting baseball cards or cataloging your DVD library — your Mac can help you enter, organize, and present your data.

➡ **Productivity stuff:** Oh, yes — your Mac can work hard as well, with productivity programs such as Microsoft Office and iWork. Compose documents, create spreadsheets, and build professional-looking presentations on your Mac with ease.

As I said, this list offers only a few high points — the more time you invest in learning about your Mac and the software that's available, the more you get out of it.

Understand Hardware and Software

First-time computer owners often become confused about what consti-
tutes hardware and what should rightly be called software. It's time to
clear things up!

In the computing world, *hardware* is any piece of circuitry or any component of your Mac that has a physical structure. For example, your
Mac's monitor is a piece of hardware, as is your keyboard. Even the
components you normally can't see or touch — the ones buried inside
the case — are considered hardware too, such as your Mac's mother-
board and power supply. (Yes, your computer's case is technically a
piece of hardware, although it's not electrical.)

Figure 1-1 illustrates a common piece of hardware — in this case, an
Internet router that shares your DSL or cable Internet connection with
your home network.

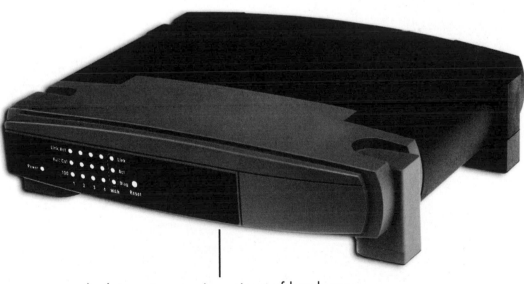

An Internet router is a piece of hardware.

Figure 1-1

The other side of the computing coin is the software you use. *Software* refers to programs you interact with on-screen. Examples include a word processing program that displays your typing or a chess program that enables you to move pieces around on the screen. **Figure 1-2** shows Apple's Aperture image editor, a photo editing program that helps you see and organize digital photos.

Apple's Aperture image editor is a software program.

Figure 1-2

Essentially, computer hardware and software work together so that you can do various tasks on your computer.

 When you hear folks discussing a software *upgrade*, *patch*, or *update*, they're talking about (you guessed it) *another* piece of software! However, the upgrade-patch-update program isn't designed to be run more than once; rather, its job is to apply the latest features, bug fixes, and data files to a piece of software that's already installed and running on your Mac, to update it to a new *version*. (Virtually all software developers refer to successive editions of their software, such as Version 1.5 or Version 3; the later the version, the more features the software includes.) In Chapter 17, you find out how to maintain your Mac with updates.

Choose a Desktop or Laptop

First, let me give you a definition of terms: A *desktop* Mac is designed to sit permanently on your desktop and uses a separate monitor, keyboard, and mouse. (Examples are the iMac, the Mac mini, and the Mac Pro.) On the other hand, a *laptop* Mac is designed to be portable — you can carry it along with you because it has a built-in keyboard, pointing device, and monitor. (MacBooks are laptop computers.)

This leads us to the question "Should I buy a desktop or a laptop Mac?" Naturally, if the portability of a MacBook laptop is a requirement for you — if your job or your lifestyle demands plenty of travel every year — you really have no other choice than a MacBook. Luckily, today's laptops are as powerful as most of the Mac desktop line: MacBooks offer features such as high-resolution graphics, 17-inch wide-screen displays, larger hard drives, and DVD recording.

However, if you're sitting on the fence and portability is a lesser requirement, I generally recommend a Mac desktop system, for these three reasons:

➡ **MacBooks aren't as expandable as desktops.** Although you can hang plenty of *peripheral* (external) devices, such as printers and scanners, from a MacBook, using USB and FireWire ports, the high-end Mac desktops are just plain easier to *upgrade* by adding newer, more powerful hardware inside your computer. For example, you might upgrade the graphics card on a Mac Pro, which is impossible to swap on a laptop.

➡ **MacBooks are more expensive than desktop Macs of similar capability.** My friend, you pay dearly for that portability. If you don't need it, jump to the desktop side of the fence. It's as simple as that.

➡ **Laptops cost much more to repair.** Part of the MacBook portability stems from the Apple practice of shoehorning all hardware onto one circuit board to save space. So, if one piece malfunctions, you have to take apart the whole thing, which isn't an easy task.

If portability isn't important, I would opt for a Mac mini, iMac, or Mac Pro, depending on the power you need, as described in the following section.

Know How Much Power Is Too Much

Take a moment to consider which tasks your Mac will be used for — not only now but also a year or two down the road. If you plan to try your hand at any of the following tasks, feel free to label yourself as a power user:

➡ **High-resolution photography or video editing:** If you want to try your hand at editing today's highest-resolution digital photography (images from a 10-megapixel camera, for example) or any type of video editing, you need a Mac with more horsepower. (Think of serious hobbyists or professional photographers or videographers.)

➡ **Running expensive software:** Examples include Adobe Photoshop and Illustrator, which are programs you use to work with high-resolution images and which usually demand the highest level of horsepower your Mac can deliver.

If the preceding points apply to you, you need a more powerful iMac desktop, Mac Pro desktop, or MacBook Pro laptop.

If you're going to run specific programs, check the requirements for that software on the manufacturer's Web site or directly from the side of the box at your local Apple Store. That way, you gain a better idea of whether you need to make the investment in a Mac Pro or MacBook Pro.

On the other side of the coin, these activities require less power:

➠ Surfing the Web

➠ Sending and receiving e-mail

➠ Keeping track of a large, digital music library

➠ Using programs such as Microsoft Office, iWork, and iLife for tasks such as creating documents

➠ Storing and sharing digital photos of friends, family, and more taken with a point-and-shoot digital camera

If the preceding tasks are more your speed, any Mac in the current product line would suit you, including the basic iMac, the Mac mini, or the standard MacBook.

Choose a Price Range

If you're working on a limited budget and you want a new Mac computer (rather than have to search eBay for a used machine), your choice becomes simpler. The least expensive Mac — the Mac mini — is no pushover, and it handles the Office, iLife, and iWork suite programs that I mention in the previous section (with aplomb, even). The least expensive iMac also fits into a smaller budget, and it includes a built-in monitor. On the laptop side, the standard-issue MacBook provides plenty of punch for those same productivity programs.

Part of the reason that the Mac mini is inexpensive is that it doesn't come with a keyboard, mouse, or monitor. You have to buy those items separately. Or if you're lucky, you can scavenge a flat-panel monitor, keyboard, and mouse from an old computer or from a friend who has spare computer hardware on hand.

Power users have no choice either: If you're going to run top-of-the-line software that requires top-of-the-line performance, you're limited to the most expensive iMac, Mac Pro, or MacBook Pro. 'Nuff said.

Apple controls its hardware prices quite closely, so you don't find a huge price difference between ordering directly from Apple.com (or an Apple Store) and from an online company.

Table 1-1 illustrates price ranges for each model in the Apple line at the time this chapter was written.

Table 1-1	Macintosh Computer Price Ranges		
Computer Model	*Best Suited For*	*Low Price*	*High Price*
Mac mini desktop	Entry level to typical home computing; no monitor or keyboard	$600	$800
iMac desktop	Midrange to power user; built-in monitor	$1200	$2200
Power Mac desktop	Power user; no monitor	$2800	$19700
MacBook laptop	Entry level to typical home computing	$1000	$1600
MacBook Pro laptop	Midrange to power user	$2000	$2800
MacBook Air laptop	Typical home computing; no built-in DVD drive	$1800	$2500

When you order a Mac from Apple.com, you can tweak these prices by a significant amount by using the Configure feature. For example, you might save $200 on the price of an iMac by opting for a smaller-capacity hard drive. (On the other hand, if you're looking to improve the performance of your pick, you might decide to spend more on a faster video card than the standard model sports.) See the later section "Compare Processors, Memory, and Hard Drives" for more information about these options.

Select a Monitor

No matter how powerful your Mac may be, if it's hooked up to a low-quality monitor, you see chunky, slow graphics. Hence this section, where I tell The Truth about the two most important specifications you should consider while shopping for an LCD flat-panel monitor: resolution and size:

 If you decided on an iMac or a MacBook laptop, you can skip this section — those computers have built-in monitors. However, keep in mind that you can hook up external (add-on) monitors to any Mac, so if you expand your system, you may want to return here.

➡ **Resolution:** Your video system's resolution is expressed in the number of pixels displayed horizontally and also the number of lines displayed vertically. (A pixel is a single dot on your monitor.) For example, a 1024 x 768 resolution means that the monitor displays 1024 pixels horizontally across the screen and 768 pixels vertically. (Any resolution lower than 1024 x 768 is barely usable these days. Higher resolutions are 1280 x 1024 and 1600 x 1200.) The more pixels, the higher the resolution.

And the higher the resolution, the more information you can fit on the screen, and the smaller that stuff appears, which I find strains my older (read: wiser and more mature) eyes. But higher resolutions also make graphics look crisper. Only you can determine the best display resolution. The decision is completely personal, like choosing a keyboard that feels "just right." While shopping for a monitor, try a wide range of resolutions to see which one suits your optic nerves.

→ **Size:** You can buy a monitor in one of several different sizes, starting at approximately 17 inches. (All monitors are measured diagonally, just like TVs are.) You can easily find larger monitors, at 24 inches and even larger.

In general, the larger the monitor, the easier it is on your eyes. At the same resolution, a 19-inch monitor displays the same images as a 17-inch model, but the image is physically bigger and the details stand out more clearly.

For general home use, a 17-inch monitor is fine. If you prefer to view larger text and graphics, if you plan to do graphics-intensive work for several hours at a time, or if you're a hard-core gamer, I would point you toward a 19-inch monitor at minimum.

Compare Processors, Memory, and Hard Drives

When you hear Mac owners talk about the speed and performance of their computers, they're typically talking about one of four different components (or all these components as a group):

➡ **System memory, or random access memory (RAM):** The more memory your Mac has (and the faster that memory is), the better your computer performs — especially Mac OS X.

➡ **Central processing unit (CPU):** Macs now use either an Intel Core 2 or its faster cousin, the Xeon. The speed of your processor is measured in gigahertz — and, of course, the faster the speed of your processor, the faster your Mac performs.

 Each core that's built-in to your processor provides a significant performance boost, so a quad-core processor is faster than a dual-core processor.

➡ **Hard drive space:** The higher your hard drive capacity, the more documents, programs, songs, and movies you can store and use.

➡ **Graphics processing unit (GPU):** This item is the graphics chip used on your Mac's video hardware. The more memory allotted to your video chip and the faster it is, the smoother and more realistic your 3D graphics.

For a typical home Mac owner, a minimum of 1GB of RAM and a Core 2 Duo processor should provide all the power you need. Power users shouldn't settle for less than 2GB of RAM and the fastest dual- or quad-core processor that Apple offers for your specific model.

Decide Which Software You Want

When you buy a Mac directly from Apple, you also can immediately purchase a few Apple programs and extras for your new system. These add-ons include the ones in this list:

➡ **iWork:** The Apple productivity suite includes Pages, for word processing; Numbers, for spreadsheets; and Keynote, for creating presentations. I discuss Pages in Chapter 8 and Numbers in Chapter 9.

➡ **MobileMe:** The Apple MobileMe Internet subscriber service includes e-mail and Web site hosting in addition to iDisk (for remote file storage) and the ability to synchronize your data between multiple Macs. You can find more information about MobileMe in Chapter 13.

➡ **AppleCare:** AppleCare is the Apple extended warranty and service plan. I recommend AppleCare for any MacBook owner because your laptop tends to endure quite a bit of road warrior treatment while you're traveling.

Buy Online or at the Apple Store

Should you spend your money online? In my opinion, the short answer is Yes — because of three important advantages to online shopping:

➡ **You may save sales tax.** Depending on your location (and the location of the online store), you may not have to pay any sales tax on your Mac purchase, and that's a hefty advantage.

➡ **You don't need a nearby Apple Store.** Some of us aren't lucky enough to live within easy driving distance of an Apple Store or Apple reseller — but Apple.com is open 24/7.

➡ **Apple.com is a premiere Web store:** You can not only configure your Mac while browsing to save money or increase performance (as I mention earlier in this chapter) but also rest assured that Apple follows a strict privacy statement and offers secure encrypted shopping. That means your credit card information is safe.

You gain two major advantages by shopping in person, however: You can ask questions and receive answers from a trained salesperson before you buy, and you can drive away with that fancy box in your trunk (without having to wait a week).

Setting Up Your Mac

Remember the classic iMac advertisements that touted the one-plug approach to the Internet? The entire campaign was centered on one idea: The Internet was *supposed* to be easy to use.

That's the Mac Way — our good friends at Apple do their best to make sure that hardware and software work together as closely as possible. Their hard work means that you're left with as few configuration and technical details as necessary while setting up your system. In this chapter, I cover the relatively few details you still *do* have to worry about.

Choose a Location for Your New Mac

If you choose the wrong spot to park your new Mac, I can *guarantee* that you'll regret it. Not all domiciles and office cubicles offer a choice — you have one desk at work, for example, and nobody will hand over another one — but if you *can* select a home for your Mac, consider these important points:

➡ **Keep things cool.** Your new Mac is silent, but that superfast Intel Core 2 or Xeon processor generates heat. Make sure that the location you choose is far from heating vents and shielded from direct sunlight. If you're using a laptop, I also recommend a cooling pad, which elevates the base of your laptop to allow air to circulate underneath.

➡ **Outlets are key!** Your computer needs a minimum of at least one nearby outlet, and perhaps as many as three:

- A standard AC outlet (using a current adapter if you're traveling abroad, if necessary)

- A telephone jack (if you have an Apple modem for connecting to the Internet or sending and receiving faxes)

- A nearby Ethernet jack (if you use your Mac's built-in Ethernet port for connecting to a wired Ethernet network)

 If you prefer to send your data over the airwaves, consider wireless networking for your Mac. Your local Apple reseller can offer an AirPort Extreme wireless base station that provides a wireless network with a shared Internet connection among all the computers in your home or office.

➡ **Don't forget the lighting.** In the words of Moms everywhere, "You can't possibly expect to work without decent lighting! You'll go blind!" You need a desk lamp or floor lamp, at a minimum.

➡ **Plan to expand.** Allow an additional foot of space on each side of your Mac on your desk. That way, you have room for external peripherals, more powerful speakers, and an external keyboard and mouse if you need one.

Unpack Your New Mac

You're going to love this section because the configuration of a Mac is a piece of cake. (Sorry about the cliché overload, but this really *is* easy.)

Follow these guidelines when unpacking your system:

⟶ **Check for damage.** I've never had a box arrive from Apple with shipping damage, but I've heard horror stories from other people (who claim that King Kong must have been working for That Shipping Company).

 Check all sides of the box before you open it. If you find significant damage, take a photograph (just in case).

⟶ **Search for all the parts.** When you're removing those chunks o' foam, make certain that you check all sides of each foam block for parts snuggled therein or taped for shipment.

⟶ **Keep all packing materials.** Do *not* head for the trash can with the box and packing materials. Keep your box and all packing materials for at least a year, until the standard Apple warranty runs out. If you have to ship the laptop to an Apple service center, the box, including its original packing, is the only way for your machine to fly.

 Smart computer owners keep their boxes much longer than a year. If you sell your Mac or move across the country, for example, you need that box. *Trust me on this one.*

⟶ **Store the invoice for safekeeping.** Your invoice is a valuable piece of paper indeed. Save the original invoice in a plastic bag, along with your computer's manuals and original software and other assorted hoo-hah. Keep the bag on your shelf or stored safely in your desk and enjoy a little peace of mind.

⟱➡ **Read the Mac manual.** "Hey, wait a minute, Mark. Why do I have to read the manual from Apple along with your tome?" Good question, and here's the answer: The documentation from Apple might contain new and updated instructions that override what I tell you here, including some subtle configuration differences between each Mac model. (For example, "*Never* cut the red wire — cut the blue wire instead" or something to that effect.) Besides, Apple manuals are rarely thicker than a restaurant menu.

 You can always download the latest updated manuals for Apple computers in electronic format from the Apple Web site at `http://support.apple.com/ manuals`. (Adobe PDF format is the standard for reading documents on your computer, and Leopard can open and display any PDF document.) I always keep a copy of the PDF manual for my MacBook Pro on my hard drive, just in case.

Connect Cables

Your Mac makes all its connections simple, but your computer depends on you to place the outside wires and thingamabobs where they belong.

After your new Mac is resting comfortably in its assigned spot (I assume that's a desktop), you need to make that important first required connection: the power cable. Plug the cable into the corresponding socket on the Mac first, and then plug 'er into that handy wall outlet.

If you have Internet access or a local computer network, you need to also make at least one of the connections in this section.

If you get on the Internet by dialing a standard phone number and your laptop has an external USB modem (a little box that makes all kinds of squeaks and skronks when you get on the Internet), you should make three more connections:

1. Plug your USB external modem into one of the USB ports on your Mac. (The connector only goes in one way, which is a Good Thing.)

2. Plug one of the telephone cable's connectors into your external modem.

3. Plug the other telephone cable connector into your telephone line's wall jack.

> Your ISP (Internet service provider), such as AT&T, NetZero, or some other company, should provide you with account information and details on configuring your Internet settings for dialup access.

If you have high-speed Internet service, or if you're in an office or a school with a local computer network, you can probably connect by using your Mac's built-in Ethernet port. You make two connections:

1. Plug one end of the Ethernet cable into the Ethernet port on the Mac. (An Ethernet connector looks like a telephone cable connector, but it's a little wider. If you can't locate the cable, yell for help from your network guru or cable/DSL provider.)

2. Plug the other end of the Ethernet cable into the Ethernet port from your network.

Your network port is probably one of the following: an Ethernet wall jack, an Ethernet hub or switch, or a cable or DSL Internet router (or sharing device).

Setting up your keyboard and mouse is about as simple as can be:

    1. Plug the USB connector from your keyboard into one of the USB ports on your Mac.

    2. Plug the USB connector from your mouse into one of the USB ports on your keyboard.

Apple provides USB ports on the keyboard to prevent you from using up all your USB ports just for necessary gear.

Some Apple models have their monitors built-in, like the iMac and the MacBook line of laptops. If you have one of these models, pat yourself on the back and do the Built-In Technology Dance.

If, however, you need to connect a monitor to your Mac Pro or Mac mini, follow these steps:

    1. Plug your monitor into a wall socket and turn it on.

|◻| *2.* Plug the DVI connector from your monitor into your Mac's DVI port. (DVI stands for Digital Visual Interface, which you don't really need to know, but it makes great coffee-table trivia.)

    ◎ DVI cables are standard equipment with today's flat-panel monitors and TVs, but if you didn't get one with yours, you can pick up a DVI cable at your local Best Buy.

Figure Out Ports

Because we're discussing connections, this is a good spot to cover the *ports* on your Mac. In computer-speak, a *port* is not where the cruise ship docks — ports are those rows of holes on the sides of your computer. Each port connects a different type of cable or device, allowing you to easily add all sorts of functionality to your computer.

Here's a list of what you'll find and a quick rundown on what these ports do. These connections are for external devices and networking:

➠ **FireWire:** This port is the standard in the Apple universe for connecting external hard drives and DVD recorders, but it does double duty as the connector of choice for peripherals such as your digital video (DV) camcorder. (A *peripheral* is another silly technonerd term that means a separate device you connect to your computer, such as a camera or printer.) Depending on the Mac model you chose, you may have one of the older FireWire 400 ports, and you may also have a much faster FireWire 800 port; your Mac's manual lists which FireWire ports it offers.

➠ **USB:** Short for *Universal Serial Bus*, the familiar USB port is the jack-of-all-trades in today's world of computer add-ons. Most external devices that you connect to your Mac (such as a portable hard drive, scanner, and digital camera) use a USB port, and so does the iPod. Depending on the model of laptop, you have either two or three USB 2.0 ports available. USB 2.0 connections are much faster than the old USB 1.1 standard, but they still accept USB 1.1 devices running at the slower speed.

➠ **Ethernet:** All of today's Macs, except the MacBook Air, include a standard gigabit Ethernet port, so your Mac is ready to join your existing wired Ethernet network. (Alternatively, you can go wireless for your network connection.) *Gigabit* indicates the speed of the network connection — today's Macs can handle the fastest network speeds you're likely to encounter at your home or office, so feel free to be smug.

Because the MacBook Air is designed to be completely wireless, it doesn't have a wired Ethernet port — if necessary, you can add a USB Ethernet adapter to have a wired network port on your Air.

Connections for external video and audio are described in this list:

→ **DVI connector:** This port lets you send the video signal from your Mac to a DVI monitor (or, depending on the model, even to S-Video output for your TV and VCR).

→ **Headphone/optical output:** You can send the high-quality audio from your Mac beast to a set of standard headphones or an optical digital audio device, such as a high-end home theater system.

→ **Optical line in:** Last (but certainly not least) is the optical audio Line In jack, which lets you pipe the signal from another audio device into your Mac. This one comes in particularly handy when you record MP3 files from your old vinyl albums or when you want to record loops in GarageBand.

Turn On Your Mac and Run Leopard Setup

After you press the Power button on your Mac — on either the side of the keyboard, or the front or back of the case — you hear the soon-to-be-familiar boot chime, and the Apple logo appears on your screen. A progress bar appears below the Apple logo to indicate that Mac OS X is loading.

In moments, you'll marvel at those beautiful rounded edges, brushed stainless steel surfaces, and liquid colors of the Max OS X interface. But wait — you're not quite done yet. Mac OS X needs to be personalized for you, just like your toothbrush or your car's six-way power seat; therefore, use the Setup Wizard, which automatically appears the first time you boot Mac OS X Leopard.

These wizard screens change periodically — and they're completely self-explanatory — so I don't march you through each one step by step. However, here are a few tips that provide a bit of additional over-the-shoulder help while you're setting things up:

➠ **How rude!** If you're outside the United States or other English-speaking countries, you should know that Mac OS X defaults to U.S. formats and keyboard layouts. Rest assured, though, that Mac OS X does indeed provide full support for other languages and keyboard configurations. To display these options in the list boxes, click the Show All button at the bottom of the keyboard wizard screen.

➠ **Accounts are important.** When Mac OS X asks you to create your account, don't forget your password — oh, and they're case-sensitive, so *THIS* is different from *this* or *ThiS*. Enter a password hint, but don't make the hint easy to guess. For example, *My first dog's name* is probably preferable to *Plays Seinfeld on TV*. Mac OS X uses the name and password you enter to create your account, which you use to log in if you set up a multiuser system for several people. *Never* write down your passwords, either; crib sheets work just as well for others as for you.

➠ **I need to fix that.** You can click the Back button at any time to return to previous wizard screens. Mac OS X, the bright child that it is, automatically saves your choices for you so that when you click Continue to return, everything is as you left it.

➠ **Extra stuff.** Whether you decide to accept the news, offers, and related-product information from Apple is your decision. However, it's only right to point out that you can find this same information on the Apple Web site, so there's no need to engorge your e-mail inbox. (I turned off this option, if you couldn't guess.)

➠ **Local-area network (LAN) connections.** If you're connecting your Mac to an existing network (or you're using an Internet router), click Yes when you're asked whether you should use the configuration supplied by the existing server.

➠ **Create your MobileMe account!** The Apple MobileMe service just plain rocks. Take my word for it. Join up, trooper. (The trial subscription is free, and you can easily upgrade to a full membership if you decide that you like the MobileMe benefits.) I tell you more about the benefits of MobileMe in Chapter 13.

➠ **Have your Mail settings handy.** If you set up your trial MobileMe account, Mail sets up your @me.com address automatically — again, this is A Good Thing. However, if you're setting up an existing account, make sure that you have all the silly settings and numbers and names that your ISP supplied when you signed up. This stuff includes your e-mail address, mail server variety, user account ID, password, and outgoing mail server. (Leopard does the best it can to help you fill out this information automatically, but it can only do so much.)

Use Your Mouse

The Mighty Mouse from Apple (and shown in **Figure 2-1**) is shaped like most mice you've likely used with other computers, but it has two major differences:

➠ **It has no buttons.** The entire surface of the mouse acts as the buttons! Press down on the left edge of the mouse to left-click, and on the right edge to right-click.

➠ **It has a bump in the middle.** That bump is the scroll ball, which you can move with your finger to scroll up, down, left, and right within a window. (For example, if you're reading a long Web page that covers multiple screens, you can move the ball down with a fingertip to display the additional text.)

Unlike older mice that used a ball, the Mighty Mouse uses an advanced laser optical system and doesn't require a mouse pad or special surface to work. However, if you would rather not use your mouse on that expensive desk, a standard mouse pad might come in handy.

When you move your mouse across your desk, you notice that the mouse cursor moves along with it across your screen, in the same direction. Leopard is always aware of what your mouse cursor is on top of at the moment, allowing you to left-click, right-click, and double-click items to launch applications or turn things on and off. (More on this in upcoming chapters.)

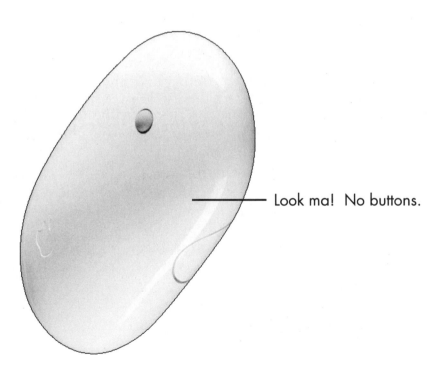

Look ma! No buttons.

Figure 2-1

Change Your Account Password

One task performed by the Leopard Setup Wizard is the creation of your user account, where you enter a username and choose a password.

Many folks like to change their passwords regularly. I should know — I'm one of them. It's especially important to be able to change your password if someone else discovers it — and that includes kids who may not treat your files and documents with the respect they deserve!

You can easily change the password for your personal account. Follow these steps:

1. Move the mouse cursor over the Apple icon in the upper-left corner of your Leopard desktop and click the icon.

2. Click the System Preferences menu item that appears.

   Leopard displays the System Preferences window.

3. Click the Accounts icon to display the settings you see in **Figure 2-2**.

4. Click your account in the list on the left side of the Accounts pane.

5. Click the Change Password button to display the sheet you see in **Figure 2-3**.

6. Type your old password and press Tab on your keyboard to move to the next field.

7. Type a new password in the New Password text box and press Tab to move to the next field.

8. Type your new password a second time in the Verify text box. (This ensures that you didn't accidentally type it wrong the first time.) Press Tab to continue.

Click your account in this list. Click to change your password.

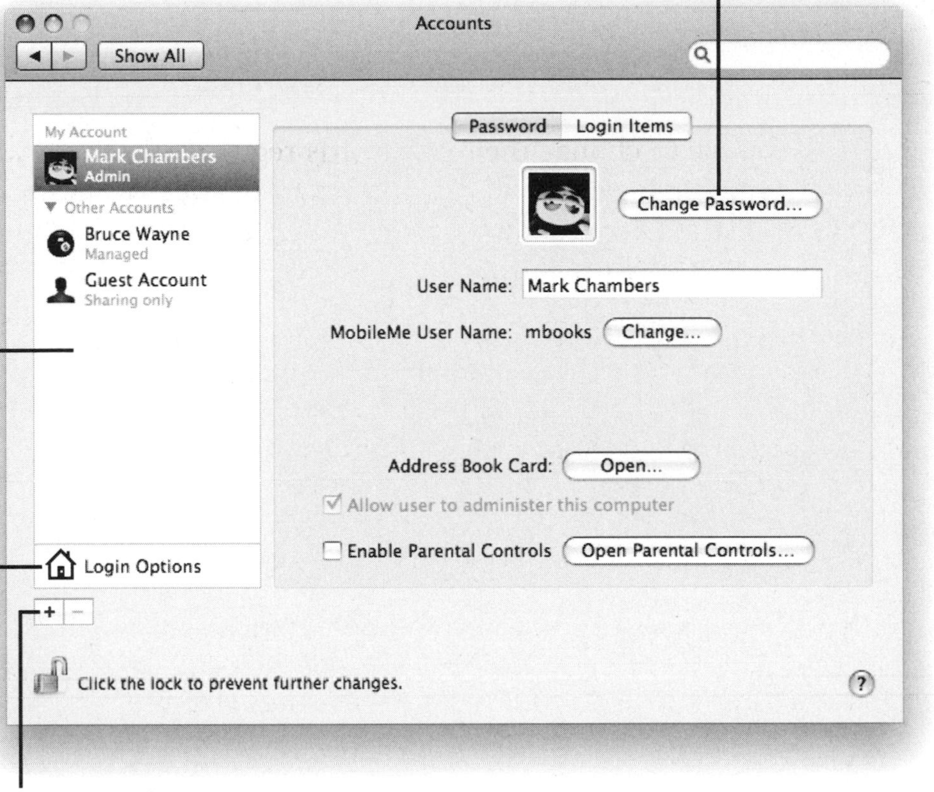

New User button

Login Options button

Figure 2-2

9. Type a short password hint that reminds you of the password you chose (just in case you forget it).

10. Click the Change Password button.

11. Click the red button in the upper-left corner of the System Preferences window to close System Preferences and save your changes.

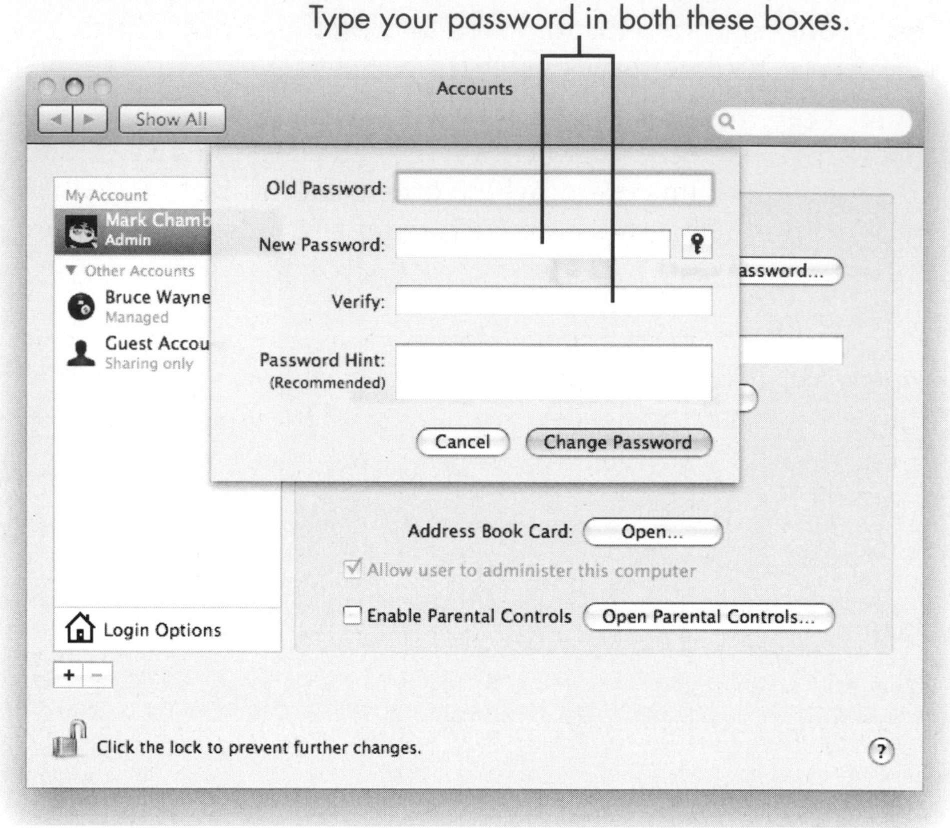

Type your password in both these boxes.

Figure 2-3

Add Another Account to Your System

If you share your Mac with other people, it's time to add one or more accounts. (If you are the only person who uses your Mac, you can guilt-lessly skip over this task.) If a person has a unique user account, Leopard can track all sorts of things, leaving *your* computing environment (such as your desktop and files and settings) blissfully pristine. A user account keeps track of information such as

➡ Address Book contacts

➡ Safari bookmarks and settings

➡ Desktop settings (including background images, screen resolutions, and Finder tweaks)

➡️ iTunes libraries, just in case that significant other buys his or her own music (sigh)

User accounts keep other people from accessing *your* stuff, and you can lock other accounts out of where-others-should-not-be, such as certain applications, iChat, Mail, and Web sites (including that offshore Internet casino site that your nephew favors).

Each user account you create also has a separate, reserved Home folder, where that person should store all his documents. Each user's Home folder has the same default subfolders, including Movies, Music, Pictures, Sites, and such. A user can create new subfolders within his Home folder at any time.

A word about accounts and levels

Get one thing straight right off the bat: *You* are the administrator of your Mac. In network-speak, an *administrator* (or *admin*, for short) is the one with the power to Do Unto Others — creating new accounts, deciding who gets access to what, and generally running the multiuser show. In other words, think of yourself as the Monarch of Mac OS X (the ruler, not the butterfly).

Next up is the *standard*-level account. Perfect for most users, this type of account allows access to just about everything but doesn't let the user make drastic changes to Leopard or create new accounts.

Finally, the *managed* account with parental controls is a standard account with specific limits assigned by either you or another admin account. This account is useful for the under-age set who might be using your Mac.

Remember: *Never* assign an account administrator-level access unless you deem it truly necessary. Standard accounts are quick and easy to set up, and I think they provide the perfect compromise between access and security. You'll find that standard access allows your users to do just about anything they need to do, with a minimum of hassle.

Here's one more neat fact about a user's Home folder: No matter what the account level is, most of the contents of a Home folder can't be viewed by other users. (Yes, that includes admin-level users. This way, everyone using your Mac gets her own little area of privacy.) Within the Home folder, only the Sites and Public folders can be accessed by other users — and only in a limited fashion.

"All right, Mark," you're saying by now, "enough pregame jabbering — show me how to set up new accounts!" Your Mac already has one admin-level account set up for you (created during the initial Leopard setup process), and you need to be logged in with that account to add a user. To add a new account, follow these steps:

1. Click the System Preferences icon in the Dock (it sports a number of gears) and then click the Accounts icon to display the Accounts pane (refer to Figure 2-2).

2. Click the New User button — the one with the plus sign at the bottom of the accounts list — to display the New Account sheet shown in **Figure 2-4**.

 If the New User button is grayed out, the Accounts pane is locked. From the pop-up menu, you can toggle the padlock icon in the lower-left corner of most of the panes in System Preferences to lock or allow changes.

To gain access, do the following:

a. Click the padlock icon to make changes to the Accounts pane.

b. When Leopard prompts you for your admin account password (the account you're using), enter it. (This password is the one you entered during Setup, when you created your personal user account.)

c. Click OK. Now you can click the New User button.

3. Click the New Account pop-up menu and specify the account-level status.

- Choose from Administrator, Standard, or Managed with Parental Controls.

- You should have only one or two administrator-level users, and your account is already an admin account.

4. Type the name that you want to display for this account in the Name text box. Press Tab to move to the next field.

 Leopard displays this name on the login screen, so behave! (For example, Bob had only one letter *o*, the last time I checked.)

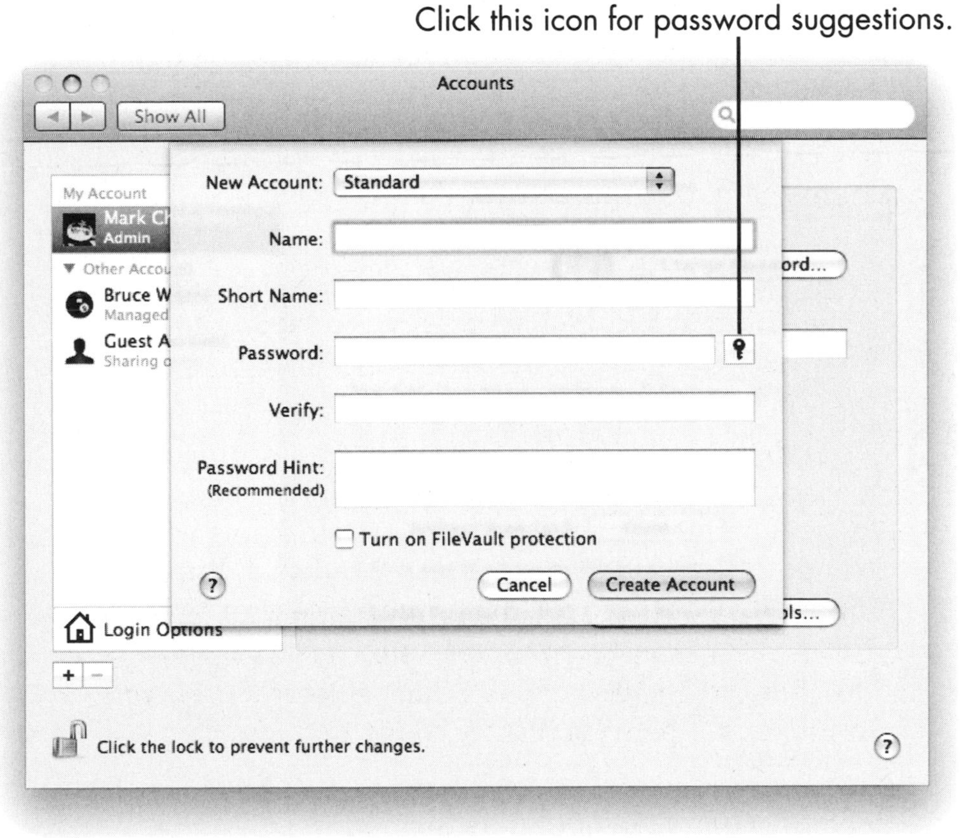

Click this icon for password suggestions.

Figure 2-4

5. (Optional) Although Leopard automatically generates the user's *short name,* for use in iChat and for naming the user's Home folder, you can type a new one. (No spaces, please.) Press Tab again.

6. In the Password text box, type the password for the new account. Press Tab to move to the next field.

I generally recommend a password of at least six characters, using a mixture of letters and numbers.

 If you run out of password ideas, no problem! Click the key button (to the right of the Password text box) to display the Password Assistant, from which Leopard can automatically generate password suggestions of the length you specify. Click the Suggestion pop-up menu or type directly into the field, and Leopard automatically adds into the Password field the password you generated.

7. In the Verify text box, retype the password you chose. Press Tab again to continue your quest.

8. (Optional) Leopard can provide a password hint after three unsuccessful login attempts. To offer a hint, type a short question in the Password Hint text box.

 Keep in mind that, from a security standpoint, password hints are taboo. (I *never* use them. If someone is having a problem logging in to a computer I administer, you had better believe that I want to know *why*.) If you do offer a hint, *keep it vague.* Avoid such hints as "Your password is the name of the Wookie in *Star Wars.*" *Geez.* Instead, use something personal, such as "My first pet's name."

9. Click the Create Account button.

The new account shows up in the list to the left of the Accounts pane.

Switch Between Accounts

After you create more than one account, your significant other has to reach his or her stuff too. You can switch accounts in two ways:

➠ **Reboot or log off.** Click the familiar Apple symbol on the menu bar at the top of the desktop — it's in the upper-left corner. On the menu that appears, you can choose to restart your Mac (which shuts down your computer and reboots it) or log out (which presents the other person with the Leopard login screen). From the login screen, a new person can enter his username and password.

➠ **Use Fast User Switching.** This feature allows another user to sit down and log in while the previous user's applications are still running in the background. This strategy is perfect for a fast e-mail check or for skimming your eBay bids without forcing someone else completely off the Mac. When you turn on Fast User Switching, Leopard displays the active user's name on the right side of the Finder menu bar.

To use Fast User Switching, you must turn it on from the System Preferences window. Follow these steps:

1. Click the System Preferences icon in the Dock (it sports a number of gears) and then click the Accounts icon to display the Accounts pane (refer to Figure 2-2).

2. Click the Login Options button.

3. Select the Enable Fast User Switching check box to enable it.

4. Click the red button in the upper-left corner of the System Preferences window to close System Preferences and save your changes.

After Fast User Switching is turned on, follow these steps to use it:

1. Click the current user's name in the upper-right corner of the desktop menu, shown in **Figure 2-5**.

2. Click the name of the user who wants to log in.

Leopard displays the login window, just as though the computer had been rebooted.

 Because the previous user's stuff is still running, you definitely should not reboot or shut down the computer!

3. To switch back to the previous user, do one of the following:

    a. Click the username again on the Finder menu.

    b. Click the previous user's name.

For security, Leopard prompts you for that account's login password.

Click to quickly switch to a different user.

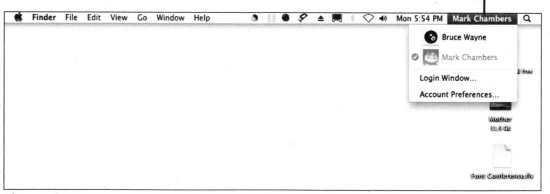

Figure 2-5

Set Your Mac's Date and Time

Nothing's more irritating than a blinking "12:00" on your TV's VCR or DVD player, and the same is true on your Mac. Personally, if I don't have the correct time, I get downright ornery. Luckily, Leopard makes it easy to set your clock — in fact, if you have broadband Internet service, you can let your Mac set the time automatically!

Follow these steps to set your Mac's date and time:

1. Click the clock display in the menu bar at the top of your desktop. From the menu that appears, click Open Date & Time to display the Date & Time pane in System Preferences, as shown in **Figure 2-6**.

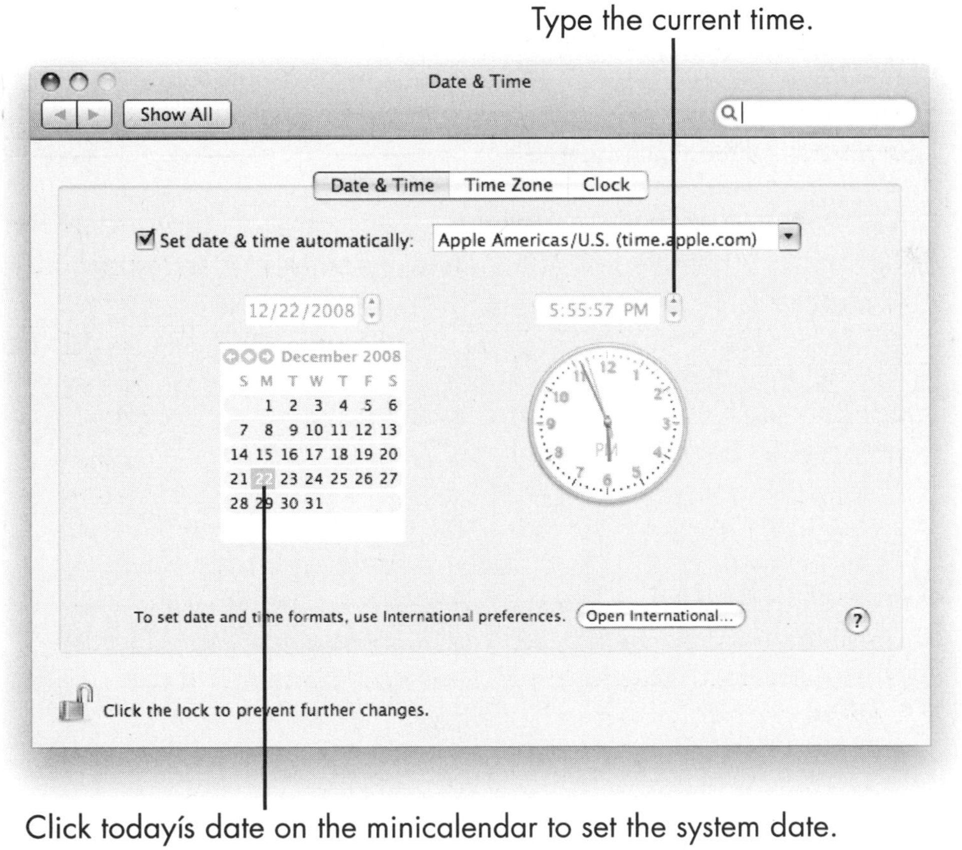

Type the current time.

Click today's date on the minicalendar to set the system date.

Figure 2-6

2. Click today's date within the minicalendar to set the system date.

3. Click in the field above the clock and type the current time to set the system time.

4. Click the red button in the upper-left corner of the System Preferences window to close System Preferences and save your changes.

 To set your Mac's time zone, click the Time Zone button and then click your approximate location on the world map to choose a time zone. You can also click the Closest City pop-up menu and choose the city that's closest to you (and shares your same time zone).

"What's this you said about setting the time and date automatically, Mark?" You heard right — as long as you have cable or DSL Internet access, the Mac can use an Internet time server to synchronize the time and date. Follow these steps:

1. Click the clock display in the menu bar at the top of your desktop, and then click Open Date & Time from the menu that appears.

2. Click the Set Date & Time Automatically check box to enable it, and then choose from the pop-up menu a server that corresponds to your location.

 Click the Clock button and you can choose to view the time in text or icon format by selecting the Show the Date and Time in Menu Bar check box. You can also optionally display seconds, AM/PM, and the day of the week; have the time separator characters flash; or use a clock based on 24 hours.

3. Click the red button in the upper-left corner of the System Preferences window to close System Preferences and save your changes.

Bam! Now your Mac updates the system time automatically — you're the technosavvy Mac owner! (You no longer even have to keep track of daylight saving time.)

Turn Off Your Mac

First things first. As the guy on the rocket sled probably yelled, "This is neat, but how do you stop it?" Call 'em The Big Three — Sleep, Restart, and Shut Down are the Mac OS X commands that you use when you need to take care of other business. All three appear on the friendly Apple menu (🍎) in the upper-left corner of your desktop.

Each of these options produces a different reaction from your Mac:

➡ **Sleep:** You don't need a glass of water or a bedtime story when you put Mac OS X to *Sleep*, which is a power-saving mode that lets you quickly return to your work later. ("Waking up" from Sleep mode is much faster than booting or restarting your computer, and it can conserve battery power on laptops.) To awaken your slumbering supercomputer, just click the mouse or press any key on the keyboard. MacBook owners can typically put their laptops to sleep by simply closing the computer, and wake the beast by opening it again.

➡ **Restart:** Use Restart if your Mac suddenly decides to start thinking "outside the box" and begins acting strangely — for instance, if your Universal Serial Bus (USB) ports suddenly lock up or your FireWire drive no longer responds. Naturally, you need to save any work that's open. (Some applications and Apple software updates also require a restart after you install them.)

⇒ **Shut Down:** When you're ready to return to the humdrum real world and you're done with your Mac for now, use the Shut Down option. Well-behaved Mac applications automatically prompt you to save any changes you've made to open documents before the computer turns itself off (or restarts). If you configured your Mac with multiple accounts, you can shut down Mac OS X from the login screen as well.

 In addition to the Apple menu command, many Macs have on their keyboards a Power key you can press to choose from these three modes.

Getting Around the Mac Desktop

The desktop and the Finder, two Leopard screen elements, take care of most of the chores that every Mac owner performs repeatedly. In this chapter, you learn basic Leopard spell-casting using the Desktop and Finder windows.

I'm not certain whether the sorcerers of old would have considered tasks such as working with windows and launching a program or two as "magic" — but the rest of your family might.

 The desktop, the Finder, programs, and windows — to do stuff with your Mac, you move among all these elements. As you read this chapter, don't worry if you feel like there's a piece you're not quite "getting." If you hang in there until the end, you'll be able to open and close windows, find important features, and move around the interface with ease.

Tour the Desktop

Your desktop is comparable to your physical desk: It holds the most important elements in a convenient view, ready when you need them. The desktop includes the following elements (most of which are shown in **Figure 3-1**):

➡ **The Finder menu bar:** From this menu bar, you can give commands to the Finder. (You give the Finder lots of commands as you use your Mac.) I introduce the Finder in the next section.

➡ **The Dock:** The Dock keeps at the ready the icons you use most often. You use these icons to launch programs or open files, as I explain in the section "Open and Switch Programs by Using the Dock," later in this chapter. When you first begin using your Mac, the icons you see are the more popular ones. But as you continue using your Mac, you may decide to customize the Dock with the icons that *you* use most often.

➡ **The icon representing your hard drive:** All Macs have at least one internal drive, which is the storage device for all the data you want to save permanently. You can always double-click the drive icon to open a Finder window and display your files and folders.

➡ **Icons for files and folders you decide to park on the desktop:** A new desktop is similar to a new desk: It starts off pretty clean. You can keep files on your desktop in the same way you can pile papers on your desk. You're generally better off, though, organizing files into folders so that you can find them easily. You find out more about working with files and folders in Chapter 5.

➡ **Any open Finder and program windows:** *Windows* are containers in which you interact with a program or a tool. Right now, you just need to know that windows appear on your desktop. The next section explains how to open a Finder window, and later sections in this chapter explain how to run programs to open their windows as well as how to work with those windows.

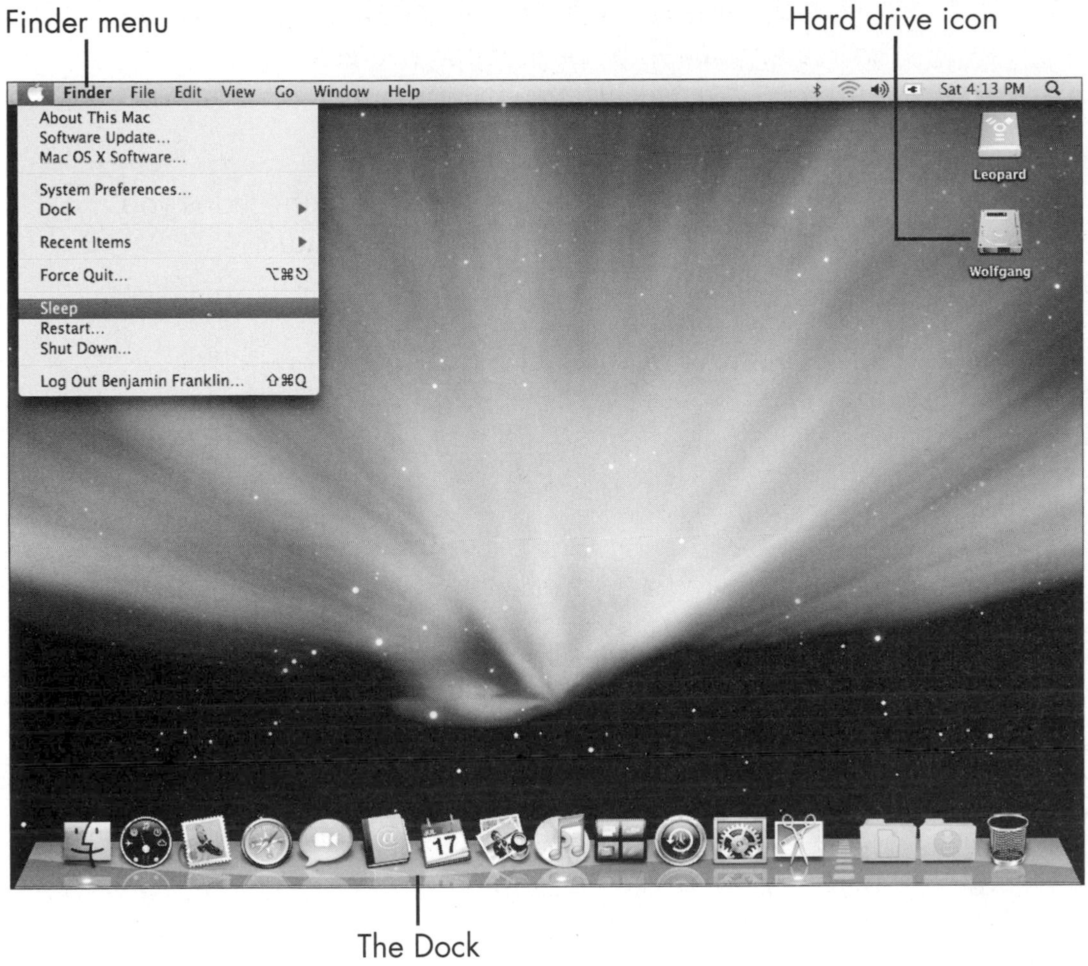

Finder menu

Hard drive icon

Figure 3-1

Discover the Finder

When you need to see the contents of your hard drive, run a program, or copy items from one location to another, you open a Finder window. In other words, the Finder is the starting point for many of the tasks you perform with your Mac. To open a Finder window:

➠ The easiest way is to double-click the Mac's hard drive icon on the desktop.

➠ Alternatively, click the Finder icon in the Dock. Figure 3-1 illustrates the Dock with the rather perspective-crazy Finder icon on the far left side. Is that icon supposed to be one face or two faces? I'm still confused, and I've been using the Mac since 1989.

 The Finder is always running, so the Finder menu bar is always available — and you can always switch to it, even when several other applications are open and chugging away. If you ever need to return to the Finder, just click outside any window border (on any empty portion of the desktop).

Use the Leopard Icons

Icons are more than little pictures. They're, well, I guess they're little pictures. However, because these graphical symbols truly are representations of the components of your Mac OS X system, they deserve a section of their own. In fact, you encounter icons on your desktop (as you already know) as well as icons within the Dock and Finder windows.

For example, Mac OS X uses icons to represent the various hardware devices on your computer, including your

 ➠ Hard drive

 ➠ CD or DVD (if one is loaded)

 ➠ iPod

You get the idea. Just double-click a hardware icon to display the folders and files it contains, as you do with your hard drive and CD/DVD drive.

 For complete details on what any icon is, what it represents, and what it does, click the icon once to highlight it and then press ⌘+I. This key combination opens the Info dialog box, shown in **Figure 3-2**, which tells you which kind of icon it is, where the item it represents is located, and how big the file is. You also see a version number for applications — a handy way of quickly determining which version of a program you're running — and when the file was created and last modified.

I cover file and folder icons later in this book.

Find details about an icon.

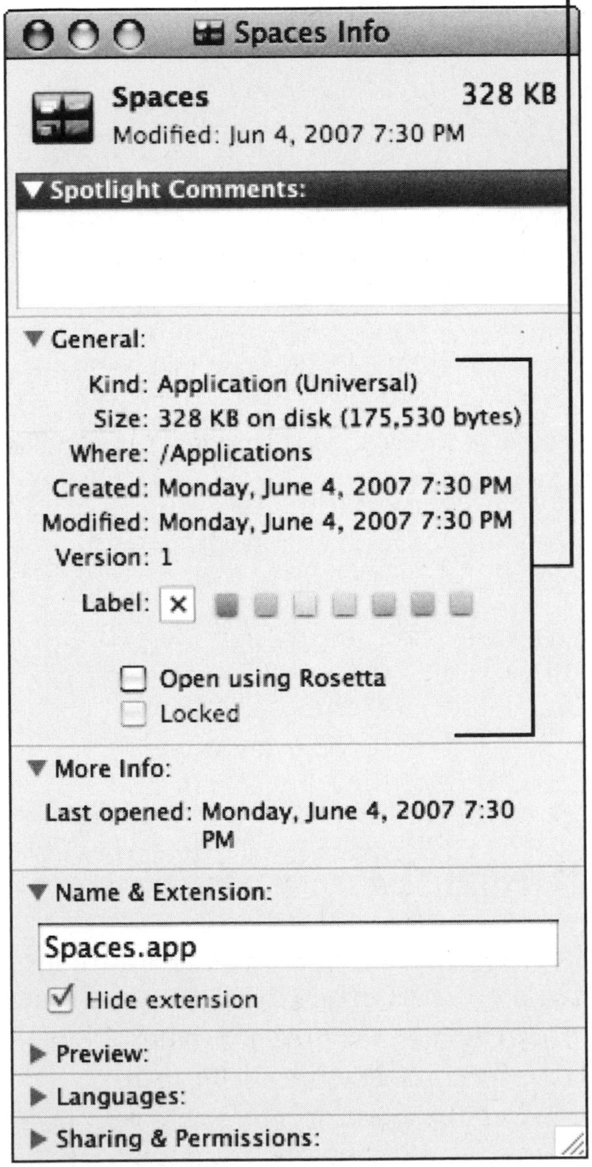

Figure 3-2

Open and Switch Programs by Using the Dock

The Dock couldn't be any easier to use — I *like* easy. The following steps walk you through basic Dock tasks and navigation:

1. Click a program icon in the Dock to run a program. (Several programs appear on the Dock by default.) The program window opens. (Note that some programs you run from the Dock don't open a window, such as the Dashboard. Almost all programs, however, display a window.)

2. Click a different icon in the Dock, and watch as another window opens. This second window covers up the window you opened in Step 1.

3. Click the icon that you originally clicked in Step 1 to move the first window to the front. (You can also click any part of the window that's peeking out, but you don't always have that option.) Now you see the window you opened in Step 1 again.

4. You can continue switching between windows, or even add a third, until you get the hang of it or just get bored watching the windows dance around on your screen.

 Running a program and loading a document are the most common functions you use on the Dock. Find out how to customize the Dock with your favorite programs, documents, and more in the next section.

Run Programs from the Hard Drive

One stop on your introductory tour of Mac OS X is the launch pad for your programs. You can start a program from the Dock, but that's not always the best way to start a program. This list describes a few more handy ways you can launch a program from your hard drive:

➡ **Navigate to the corresponding program folder.** That
is, double-click the hard drive icon on your desktop,
and then double-click the folders that contain the program. After the program icon is displayed in the Finder
window, double-click it to run the program. For example, to run Chess — which isn't on the Dock — you
double-click the hard drive icon on your desktop and
then double-click the Applications folder to display
the Chess icon. Now you can double-click the Chess
icon to play a game.

➡ **Double-click a document or data file that's owned
by the program.** For example, double-click an MP3
audio file to open iTunes. You find out more about
working with files in Chapter 5.

➡ **Double-click an alias you created for the program.**
For tips on using an alias, see Chapter 5.

Add Favorite Programs (and More) to the Dock

In terms of importance, the Dock ranks right up there with the command center of a modern nuclear submarine. For that reason, it had
better be easy to customize, and naturally, Mac OS X doesn't let you
down. The Dock is a convenient way to keep handy the stuff you use
most often: the programs you run the most, and even folders and Web
sites that you open many times every day.

You might be satisfied with just the icons that Apple places in the Dock.
Or, you can add your own applications, files, and folders to the Dock:

➡ **To add any program to the Dock:** Add a program to
the Dock when you need to run it often and you
would rather not have to locate it on your hard drive
every time! To find the icon for a program that isn't
already on the Dock, use the Finder to locate the program (as I describe in the previous section). Then

click and drag its icon into the area to the *left* side of the Dock. You know when you're in the proper territory because the existing Dock icons obligingly move aside to make a space for it.

 Don't release the mouse on the right side of the Dock. Attempting to place an application on the right side of the Dock sends it to the Trash (if the Trash icon is highlighted when you release the button). If you make this mistake, see the later section "Empty the Trash" for tips on retrieving your application. You don't want to empty the trash in this case, but you do find the steps you need in that section.

➡ **To add a file to the Dock:** When you're continually opening a particular file to make additions or changes (such as on your budget spreadsheet), it's handy to have that file on the Dock. You can add individual file icons to the Dock by dragging the icon into the area to the *right* side of the Dock. (Attempting to place them to the left side of the Dock opens an application with the contents, which usually doesn't work.) Again, the existing Dock icons move aside to create a space when you're in the right area.

 Chapter 5 explains how to work with files and folders, including how to find a file's icon so that you can add it to the Dock. For now, just know that you have the ability to do so.

➡ **To add several files or a folder to the Dock:** Leopard uses the Stacks feature, which I discuss in the next section, which allows you to add multiple files (or the contents of an entire folder) to the Dock.

➡ **To add a Web site:** You can drag any Web site page address (commonly called a URL, or Universal Resource Locator) from Safari directly into the area to the right of the Dock. Clicking that icon automatically opens your browser and displays that page.

➠ **To remove an icon from the Dock:** Close the program that uses the item (if necessary) and then click
and drag the icon off the Dock. You see a rather silly
(but somehow strangely satisfying) animated cloud of
debris, and the icon is no more. Note, however, that
the original application, folder, or volume is *not*
deleted — just the Dock icon itself is permanently
excused. Because your Dock has a limited amount of
space, you should always remove icons for items you
no longer need so that you can add more items later.

Stack Files or Folders on the Dock

Stacks are groups of items (documents, applications, or folders) that
you want to place on the Dock for convenience — perhaps the files
needed for a project you're working on or your favorite game applications. For example, I have on my Dock a stack named Wiley that holds
all the project files I need for the book I'm now writing. A stack can
be temporary, and you can remove it (as I demonstrate in the previous
section), or it can be a permanent addition to the Dock.

➠ **To create a Stack,** just select and drag to the right side
of the Dock the group of items you want to include.
As always, the Dock opens a spot on the right side of
the Dock to indicate that you're in the zone.

➠ **To display the items in a Stack,** just click it:

• *If the stack holds relatively few items,* they're displayed
in a cool-looking arc (as shown in **Figure 3-3**), and
you can click the item you want to open or launch.

• *If the Stack is stuffed full of many items,* the Stack
opens in a grid display, allowing you to scroll
through the contents to find what you need.

➠ **To remove a stack from the Dock,** control-click or
right-click the Stack icon and then choose Remove
from Dock from the menu that appears. Alternatively,
just drag that sucker right off the Dock.

Items in a Stack

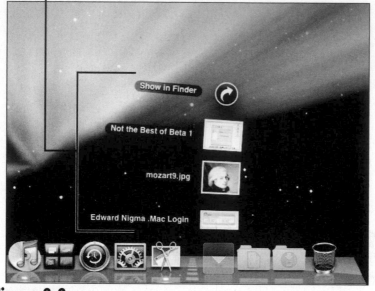

Figure 3-3

 Apple provides one stack that's already set up for you: The Download folder, situated next to the Trash, is the default location for any new files you download from the Internet by using Safari or receive in your e-mail. Leopard bounces the Download Stack icon to indicate that you received a new item. Chapter 14 introduces you to Web browsing with Safari, and Chapter 15 walks you through downloading files from an e-mail.

Change the Dock Size and Location

You can change the size of the Dock directly from the desktop! Increasing its size can make it easier to see, and decreasing its size can make room for viewing other items on-screen. Follow these steps to change the size of the Dock:

1. Move the mouse cursor over the top edge of the Dock's reflective base; the cursor turns into a funky line with arrows pointing up and down.

2. The altered cursor is your cue to click and drag while moving the mouse up and down, which expands and shrinks the Dock, respectively.

 Notice how a Dock icon grows larger whenever you hover the mouse over it. The magnification feature can also make the Dock icons easier to see, or if you don't like it, you can turn off magnification. When magnification is turned on, the icons in the Dock grow really big. Check out the somewhat oversized icons in Figure 3-4.

Follow these steps to change the magnification settings:

1. Click the Apple (🍎) menu in the upper-left corner of the screen.

2. Choose Dock⇨Magnification from the submenu that appears. Choose the Turn Magnification On/Off menu item to toggle icon magnification.

3. If you want to adjust the amount of magnification, you're in luck. Click the Apple (🍎) menu and choose Dock Preferences to open the System Preferences window, and then drag the Magnification slider to the right to increase the size of the magnified icons.

Magnification changes the icon size.

Figure 3-4

To adjust the Dock's hiding feature or location, click the Apple (🍎) menu and choose the Dock item to display the submenu. Here's how these options work:

➡ **Hiding:** Choose the Turn Hiding On/Off menu item to toggle the automatic hiding of the Dock. With hiding on, the Dock disappears off the edge of the screen until you move the mouse pointer to that edge. (This feature is helpful if you want to make use of as much desktop territory as possible for your applications.)

You can press ⌘+Option+D to toggle Dock hiding on and off from the keyboard.

➡ **Position:** Click one of three choices (Position on Left, Bottom, or Right) to make the Dock appear on the left, bottom, or right of the screen, respectively.

Empty the Trash

As you work with your Mac to create files and folders and perform other tasks, it can become cluttered. Eventually, you want to delete some items, as I explain in Chapter 5 (which focuses on working with files and folders). From time to time, you may want to empty the Trash, the electronic bin on the Dock where deleted items are deposited, so that your deleted items aren't occupying space that you can use for other things. When you're compelled to take out your Mac's trash, follow these steps:

1. Click the Trash icon in the Dock to open the Trash.

2. Double-check the Trash contents and make absolutely sure that you want to delete its contents. You can retrieve files from the Trash, as I explain in Chapter 5, but you can't retrieve those files after you empty it.

3. Choose the Empty Trash menu item from the Finder menu.

Display the Dashboard and Widgets

One of Leopard's most popular features is *Dashboard*, which you can use to hold widgets and display them with the press of a button. (Okay, I know that sounds a little wacky, but bear with me.) *Widgets* are small applications, dubbed *applets*, that typically provide only one function. For example, Dashboard comes complete with a calculator, clock, weather display, and quick-and-simple calendar. **Figure** 3-5 illustrates the Dashboard in action.

1. Click the Dashboard icon in the Dock to display your widgets, ready for you to use. (Gee, that sounds racy. Don't worry: The widgets are quite tame.)

Calculator is one widget on the Dashboard.

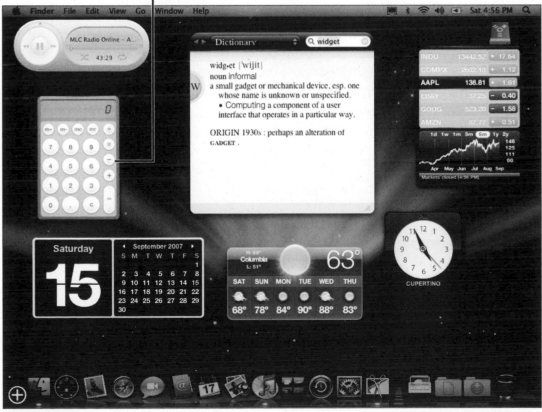

Figure 3-5

2. To add a widget to your Dashboard, click the Add button (which bears a plus sign, naturally) in the lower-left corner of the Dashboard screen.

3. When a scrolling menu strip appears at the bottom of the Dashboard display, browse your options. You can drag new widgets directly to your Dashboard from this menu. (For more information on downloading widgets, check out Chapter 12. You'll find a huge number of widgets to download on the Apple Web site.)

4. To rearrange the widgets that are already populating the Dashboard, click and drag them to the spot you want.

5. When you're done with your widgets, press Esc to return to the Leopard desktop.

Search Your Mac with Spotlight

The *Spotlight* feature lets you search your computer as quickly as you can type. You can use Spotlight, therefore, to search for documents, Address Book contacts, Mail messages, folders, and drives that your Mac can access. (Spotlight isn't for searching the Internet, a topic I cover in Chapter 14.) To search for items with Spotlight, follow these steps:

1. Open a Finder window by clicking the Finder icon on the Dock.

Figure 3-6 illustrates the Spotlight search field, which is always available from the Finder menu bar.

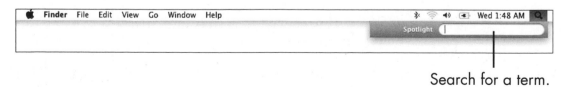

Search for a term.

Figure 3-6

2. Click the magnifying glass icon once, and the Spotlight search box appears.

3. Simply click in the Spotlight text box and begin typing. You see matching items appear on the Spotlight menu as soon as you type, and the search results are continually refined while you type the rest of your search terms. Check out my tips and shortcuts for typing search terms a little later in this section.

 The top 20 most relevant items are grouped into categories directly on the Spotlight menu, including Messages, Definition, Documents, Folders, Images, and Contacts. Spotlight takes a guess at the item that's most likely the match you're looking for and presents it in the special Top Hit category, which always appears first.

4. If you don't find what you're looking for in the search results, try again. To reset the Spotlight search and try typing different text, click the X icon that appears on the right side of the Spotlight box. (Of course, you can also press Backspace to reach the beginning of the text box, but that method is a little less elegant.)

5. To open the Top Hit item like a true Leopard power user, just press Return. (Folks, it just doesn't get any easier than that.) To open any other item, you can click it once to

- *Run it* (if the item is a program).

- *Open it in System Preferences* (if it's a setting or description in a Preferences pane).

- *Open it within the associated program* (if the item is a document or a data item).

- *Display it within a Finder window* (if the item is a folder).

Literally any text string is acceptable as a Spotlight search. However, here's a short list of the common search tips I use every day:

➡ **To find contact information, enter any part of the names or address:** Because Spotlight has access to the Leopard Address Book, you can immediately display contact information by using any portion of a name or address.

➡ **To find an e-mail message, type the sender's address or any unique word or phrase you remember from the message:** If you need to open a specific e-mail message, but you would rather not launch Mail and spend time digging through the message list, enter the person's e-mail address or any text string contained in the message you're looking for.

➡ **Type a file or folder name to display it in the results list:** This is the classic search favorite. Spotlight searches your entire system for that file or folder in the blink of an eye.

➡ **To find out how to adjust System Preferences, type a keyword for the item you want to adjust:** Now things start to get *really* interesting! Try typing the word **background** in the Spotlight field. Some of the results are System Preference panes! That's right — every setting in System Preferences is referenced in Spotlight. (For example, the Software Update pane contains the word *background*, and desktop *background setting* is in the Desktop & Screen Saver pane in System Preferences.)

➡ **Web pages:** *Whoa.* Stand back, Google. You can now use Spotlight to search the Web pages you recently displayed in Safari! (Note, however, that this new feature doesn't let you search the entire Internet, like Google does — only the pages stored in your Safari Web cache.)

Here's another favorite timesaver: You can display all the files of a particular type on your system by using the file type as the keyword. For example, to provide a list of all *images* on your system, just use images as your keyword — the same goes for *movies* and *audio*, too.

View the Finder in Icon View

The default appearance of a Finder window in Mac OS X uses the familiar large-format icons that have been a hallmark of the Macintosh operating system since Day One. This view, *Icon view,* is shown in **Figure** 3-7. You can display the contents of a Finder window in Icon view by clicking the Icon View button on the Finder window toolbar.

Icon view is the default.

Figure 3-7

Icon view has a number of advantages:

➡ **Items are larger in Icon view:** Items are easier to recognize in this view than in List or Column view.

➡ **Dragging-and-dropping can be easier:** Copying and moving items from one window to another is often more convenient using larger icons.

➡ **Selecting multiple items can be easier:** Because of the size of the icons, you might find it easier to select more than one item in a Finder window while in Icon view.

You don't have to use Icon view. (In fact, most Mac OS X power users whom I know consider icon view mode rather inefficient and slow.) The next few sections in this chapter cover other ways to view items in the Finder. In addition to Icon view, as shown in Figure 3-7, Mac OS X offers three other window view modes: List, Column, and Flow.

List Finder Items in List View

List view displays the folders in a hierarchical fashion. To display the contents of a folder, follow these steps:

1. Click to select a drive from the Devices list.

2. Click the small, right-facing triangle next to the folder name. The triangle rotates downward to indicate that you expanded the folder.

Alternatively, double-click the folder icon to display the contents in the Finder window.

3. If you need to display the contents of a *subfolder* (a folder stored inside the original folder), click the triangle next to

the subfolder name to expand it and display the subfolder's contents.

4. To collapse the contents of the folder, click the small triangle again; it rotates to face the right.

Figure 3-8 illustrates the same Finder window in List view.

List view displays file hierarchically.

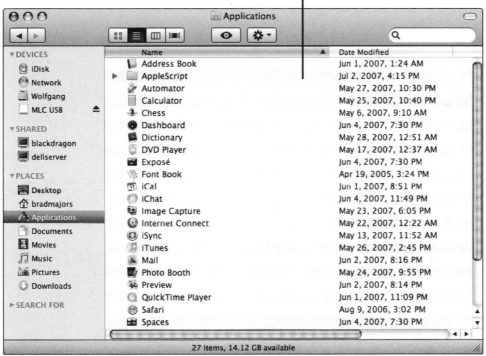

Figure 3-8

See Items in Column View

This view is my favorite — thanks, Apple! It's efficient and
fast as all get out. **Figure 3-9** shows the same window in
Column view, in which the drives on your Mac OS X
system are displayed on the left. Each column on the right

represents a lower level of subfolders. You switch a Finder window to Column view by clicking the Column View button on the Finder window toolbar.

Column view displays folders and subfolders.

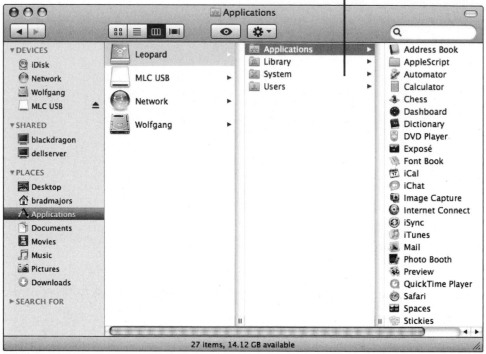

Figure 3-9

To navigate in Column view, follow these steps:

1. Click the drive in the Devices list.

2. Click to select a folder in the first column on the right to display its contents. To display a subfolder's contents, click the subfolder's icon. The contents appear in the next column to the right. When you "drill" deeper, the columns shift automatically to the left.

3. When you click to select a file or program (rather than a folder), the Finder displays a preview and a quick summary of the selected item in the right-most column.

Each column has its own, individual scroll bar (for those *really* big folders), and you can drag the column handle at the bottom of the separators to resize the column width to the left. When you hold down the Option key and drag a column handle, all columns are adjusted at one time.

Surf Items in Flow View

 In Flow view, shown in **Figure 3-10**, each document or item is showcased in a preview pane (and with an accurate thumbnail, if possible). You can display a Finder window in Flow view by clicking the Flow View button on the Finder window toolbar.

Flow view displays each document in a preview pane.

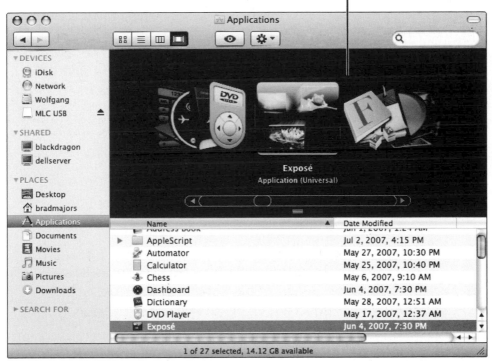

Figure 3-10

Here are some other tricks to using Flow view:

➡ **Resize the preview pane:** If you need a closer look at a photo or PDF file, you can resize the preview pane by dragging the three-line handle on the bottom edge of the pane.

➡ **Expand and collapse:** You can expand and collapse the folders in Flow view just like in List view, using the rotating triangles.

➡ **Scroll the preview pane:** You can click the scroll buttons or drag the scroll bar under the preview pane to move through the contents of your drive in quite a classy visual display.

Open Windows

If you're following along in this chapter, you now know a few ways to open windows. But this section is focused only on window-opening. If you want something to open but aren't sure how to make it so, these pointers can help:

➡ **Windows are generally opened automatically.** Usually, a window is opened by an application (when you first run it or it needs to display a document) or by Mac OS X itself (when the Finder opens a window to display the contents of your hard drive). I explain how to run a program earlier in this chapter. I explain how to open a file, and thus the file's associated program, in Chapter 5.

➡ **Some programs even let you open new windows on the fly.** For example, **Figure 3-11** illustrates a window in its purest form: a new Finder window. To display this window on your own Mac, choose File⇨New Finder Window or press ⌘+N. From there, you can reach any file on your Mac or even venture to the Internet.

The Command key has on it both an apple (🍎) and a rather strange-looking symbol (⌘) that I often call the spirograph.

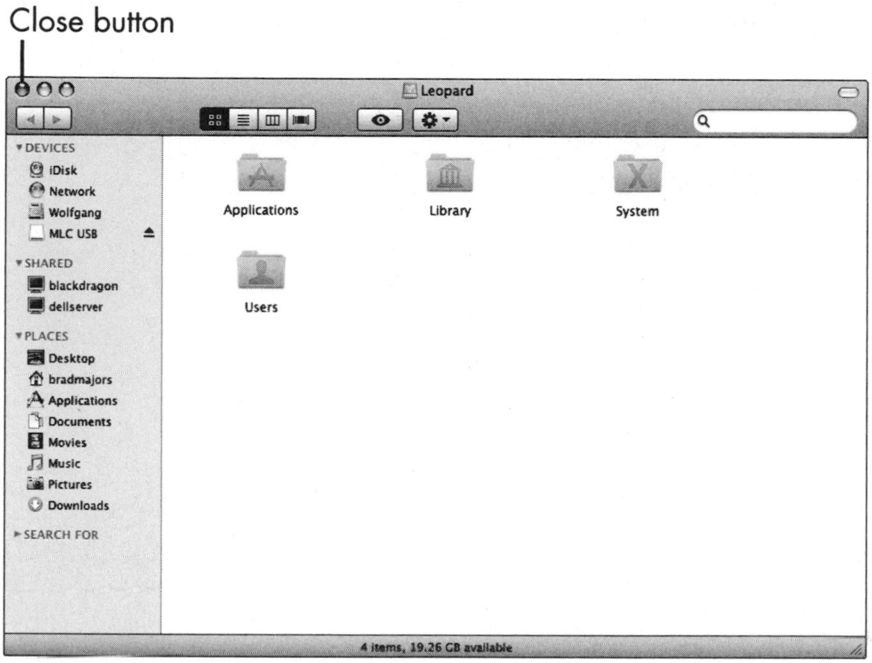

Close button

Figure 3-11

See All Open Program Windows with Exposé

One of the sassiest Leopard features, brazenly named Exposé, is shown in **Figure 3-12**. If you have a number of windows open, Exposé is a helpful way to find the one you want. Here's how Exposé works:

⟹ **Press F3 (or F9 on older keyboards) to show all open application windows using Exposé; then click the one you want.** Figure 3-12 illustrates the tiled window display on my Mac after I press F3. The cursor changes into the traditional (and highly elegant) gloved hand. Move the cursor on top of the window you want to activate — the window turns blue when it's selected — and click once to switch to that window.

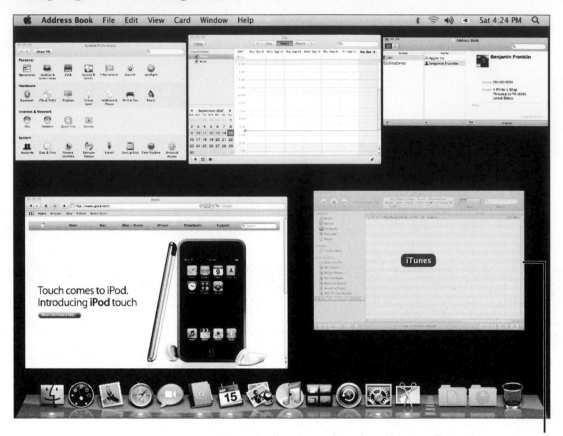

Expose displays thumbnails on all open windows.

Figure 3-12

➡ **Press Ctrl+F3 (or F10 on older keyboards) to show all open windows from the application that you're using; then click the one you want to activate.** This Exposé function is helpful for choosing from all the images you opened in Photoshop or all the Safari Web pages littering the desktop!

An astute observer would notice, in addition to the window switch, that the application menu bar changes to match the now-active application.

➡ **Press ⌘+F3 (or F11 on older keyboards), and all open windows scurry to the side of the screen** (much like a herd of zebras if you drop a lioness in their midst). Now you can work with drives, files, and aliases on the desktop — and when you're ready to confront those dozen application windows again, just press the keyboard shortcut a second time.

Scroll Windows

Often more stuff is in a document or more files are on your hard drive than you can see in the space available for a window. I guess that means it's time to delete stuff. No, no — *just joking!* You don't have to take such drastic measures to see more information in a window.

Just use the scroll bars that you see in **Figure 3-13** to move through the contents of the window.

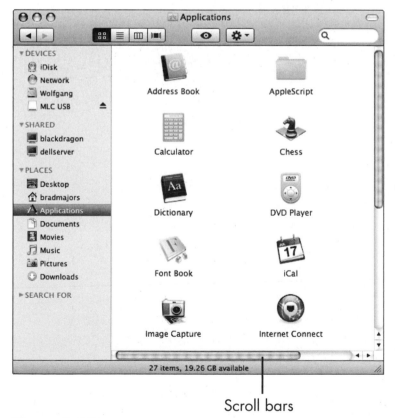

Scroll bars

Figure 3-13

You can generally scroll in one of two ways:

➡ **Click the scroll bar and drag it.** For the uninitiated, that means clicking the bar and holding down the mouse button while you move the mouse in the direction you want.

➡ **Click in the empty area above or below the bar** to scroll pages one at a time.

 Depending on the type of application you're using, you might be able to scroll a window with the arrow keys as well — or perhaps press the Page Up and Page Down keys to move in a window.

Minimize and Restore Windows

The multitalented Figure 3-13, shown in the preceding section, displays another control that you can use with a window: the Minimize button. When you *minimize* a window, you eliminate it from the desktop and store it safely in the Dock. After you minimize a window, you need to know how to restore it. Follow these steps to minimize and restore a window:

1. To minimize a window, move the mouse pointer over the yellow Minimize button in the upper-left corner of the window (a minus sign appears on the button) and then click. The minimized window appears as a miniature icon in the Dock so that you can keep an eye on it, so to speak.

2. When you're ready to *restore* the window (display it again on the desktop), simply click the thumbnail icon representing the window in the Dock, and Mac OS X automagically returns it to its former size and location.

Zoom Windows

Zooming windows has kind of a *Flash Gordon* sound to it, don't you think? It's nothing quite that exciting — no red tights or laser guns. Still, when you're trying to view a larger portion of a document, *zooming* is a good thing because it expands the window to the maximum practical size for the application you're using (and the content being displayed). When you want to zoom, here's what you need to know:

➡ **You can zoom with one click:** To zoom a window, move the mouse pointer over the green Zoom button in the upper-left corner of the window. Figure 3-13, shown earlier in this chapter, struts its stuff (again) and illustrates the position. (That is one versatile figure!) A plus sign appears on the Zoom button. Click to expand your horizons.

 After you finish with a zoomed window, you can return it to its previous dimensions by clicking the Zoom button again.

➡ **Zooming produces mixed results:** In some cases, zooming a window fills the entire screen; at other times, the extra space would be wasted, so the application zooms the window to the maximum size that shows as much content as possible (with no unnecessary white space).

➡ **You can't zoom in on everything:** The Zoom button can even be disabled by an application that doesn't want you to muck about with the window; for example, I own a game or two that doesn't allow zooming.

Move and Resize Windows

Unlike having rather permanent windows in your home, you can pick a window and cart it to another portion of the desktop. Here are the basics of moving windows:

➡ **Move windows when you want to see other stuff.**
Typically, you move a window when you're using
more than one application at a time and you need to
see the contents of multiple windows.

➡ **Click and drag the window to move it.** To grab a
window and make off with it, click the window's title
bar — the strip at the top of the window that usually
bears a document or application name — and drag
the window to the new location. Then release the
mouse button to plant it firmly in the new location.

➡ **Change the width or height of the window instead.**
To change the dimensions of a window to your exact
specifications, move the mouse pointer over the
lower-right corner of the window (usually marked
with a number of slashed lines to indicate its status as
a control), click, and drag until the window is the size
you prefer.

 By the way, some applications let you arrange multiple windows in a graceful swoop with a single click on
a menu. Click the Window menu and choose Arrange
All to perform this magic.

Close Windows

When you're finished with a document or you no longer need a window open, you can close it to free that space on the desktop. As with
most tasks on the Mac, closing windows is simple:

➡ **Close a window with the Close button.** Move the
mouse pointer over the Close button; it's the red, circular button in the upper-left corner of the window
(refer to Figure 3-11). An X appears on the button
when you're in the zone. When the X appears, just
click the mouse. Most programs also have Close commands on their File menus.

➠ **Save your information if you're asked to save before closing.** Most Mac applications don't want you closing a window willy-nilly if you change the contents without saving them. For example, try to close a document window in Word or Pages without saving the file first. The program asks for confirmation before it closes the window containing your unsaved Great American Novel. (Here's another indicator: Some programs display a black dot in the center of the program's Close button to indicate unsaved changes.)

 To close all windows displayed by a particular program, hold down the Option key while you click the Close button in one of the windows. Whoosh! They're all gone.

Close Programs

If I had a twisted and warped sense of humor, I would tell you to close applications by simply pulling the Mac power cord from the wall socket. (Luckily, I don't.) You have, however, saner ways to close a program — use one of these methods instead:

➠ Press the ⌘+Q keyboard shortcut.

➠ Choose the Application's named menu and then click Quit.

➠ Control-click (or right-click) the application icon on the Dock and choose Quit from the pop-up menu that appears.

You can also click the Close button in the application window. Note, however, that this technique doesn't always completely close the application.

You might be able to close a program's window without closing the program itself. For example, you can close a browser window in Safari, but the Safari program continues to run. However, when you close a program, you automatically close any windows that the program opened.

Customizing Leopard

Chapter 4

*L*eopard is easy to customize in many ways: You can adjust the appearance of the desktop, configure the behavior of your mouse and keyboard, and set up a screen saver to keep your Mac happy while you're away.

In this chapter, I show you how to

⟹ Select a background, appearance, and icon arrangement for the desktop.

⟹ Tweak the behavior of your mouse and keyboard.

⟹ Enhance the readability of the desktop.

⟹ Use the Leopard visual cues rather than system sounds.

⟹ Enable speech recognition.

Fine-Tune Leopard

Your Mac is truly easy to customize to your specific desires and needs. Because each user on your Mac has her own, separate desktop settings, you can quickly make changes to *your* individual desktop configuration *without* upsetting the other members of the family, who may not want a hot pink background with lime-green highlights.

Most of the changes you make to customize your Mac require you to open the System Preferences window, which you can reach by clicking the System Preferences icon in the dock. (The icon bears a number of gears for a label.)

Change the Desktop Background

You might ask, "Mark, do I really need a custom background?" That depends completely on your personal tastes, but I have yet to meet a computer owner who didn't change her background when presented with the opportunity. Favorite backgrounds usually include

➡ Humorous cartoons and photos that can bring a smile to your face

➡ Scenic beauty

➡ Simple solid colors that can help icons and windows stand out

➡ Photos of family and friends

If you decide to spruce up your background, you have three choices: Select one of the default Mac OS X background images, choose a solid color, or specify your own image. All three backgrounds are chosen from the Desktop & Screen Saver pane, located within System Preferences, as shown in **Figure 4-1**.

 You can also right-click at any open spot on the desktop and choose Change Desktop Background from the pop-up shortcut menu.

To choose a background from one of the collections provided by Apple, click one of these groups from the list on the left:

➡ **Apple Images:** These default backgrounds range from simple patterns to somewhat strange and ethereal flux shapes. (You have to see them to understand what I mean.)

→ **Nature:** These backgrounds feature scenic beauty, such as blades of grass, sand dunes, snowy hills — that sort of thing.

→ **Plants:** In the close-up backgrounds of plant life, I especially recommend the autumn leaves.

→ **Black & White:** Several truly stunning black-and-white backgrounds look especially good on a wide-screen display. These are my favorite images provided by Apple.

→ **Abstract:** These backgrounds have even weirder twisting shapes in flux, this time with bright contrasting colors. They would look good in a psychiatrist's office.

Click to explore the images provided by Apple.

Figure 4-1

➠ **Solid Colors:** For people who desire a soothing, solid shade, I provide more detail in the following section.

➠ **Pictures Folder:** This folder displays the images saved in the Pictures folder by the active user.

➠ **Choose Folder:** You can open another folder containing images and display them instead. (I discuss this topic in more detail in a page or two.)

If you see something you like, click the thumbnail, and Mac OS X automatically refreshes the background so that you can see what it looks like.

 If you notice your iPhoto albums in the list, that's no accident. Leopard automatically offers your iPhoto Photo Library so that you can choose images from your iPhoto collection.

Mac OS X provides four orientations for your background image. Click the pop-up menu next to the well and you can choose to

➠ **Tile the background.** The image is repeated to cover the desktop (usually done with pattern images to produce a smooth look).

➠ **Fill the screen.** A solid color provides uniform coverage. The original aspect ratio of the image is preserved, so it's not stretched.

➠ **Stretch the background to fit the desktop.** If your desktop image is smaller than the desktop acreage, be warned — if you try to stretch too small of an image over too large of a desktop, the pixilated result can be frightening. (Think of enlarging an old Kodak Instamatic negative to a 16 x 20 poster. Dots, dots, dots.) The original aspect ratio of the image isn't preserved, so you might end up with results that look like the funhouse mirrors at a carnival.

➡ **Center the image on the desktop.** This solution is
my favorite for desktop images that are smaller than
the resolution.

Note that this pop-up menu appears only if the desktop picture you
select isn't one of the standard Apple images. All pictures in the Apple
Background Images, Nature, Abstract, and Solid Colors categories are
scaled automatically to the size of your screen.

 To regularly change the desktop background automatically, click to select the Change Picture check box and
then choose the delay period from the corresponding
pop-up menu. To display the images in random order,
also select the Random Order check box; otherwise,
Mac OS X displays the images in the order that they
appear in the folder.

As I mention earlier in this chapter, if you want your favorite color
without the distraction of an image, you can choose from a selection of
solid colors. You can choose from these colors the same way that you
pick a default Mac OS X background image (as I describe earlier in this
section).

Finally, you can drag your own image into the well from a Finder window to add your own work of art. To view the thumbnails from an
entire folder, click the Pictures folder (to display the contents of your
personal Pictures folder) or click the Add button (bearing the plus sign)
to specify any folder on your system. Click one of the thumbnails (the
small images) to embellish the desktop.

Change the Desktop Color Scheme

You can also select your own colors for buttons, menus, and windows
within Leopard — like your choice of background, the color scheme
you select is completely up to you. (Some of the color schemes supplied by Apple may also help some Mac owners with reduced vision.)
To choose a scheme, follow these steps:

1. Open System Preferences and click the Appearance icon to display the settings, as shown in **Figure** 4-2.

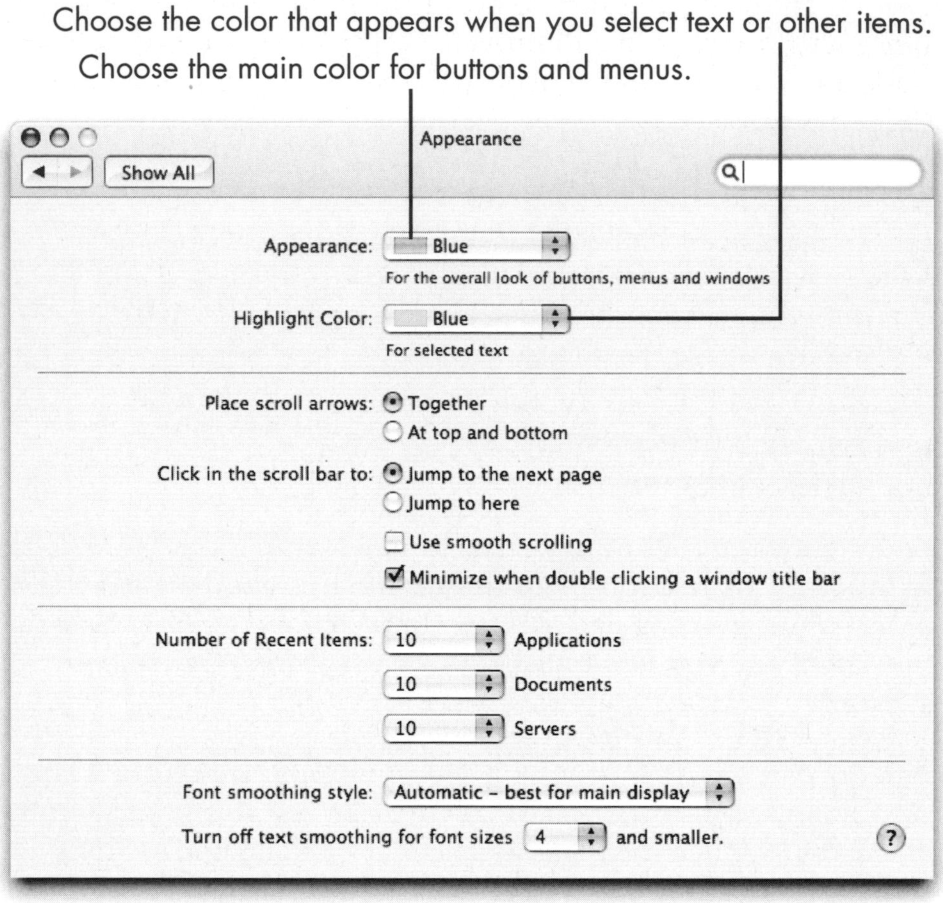

Choose the color that appears when you select text or other items.

Choose the main color for buttons and menus.

Figure 4-2

2. Click the Appearance pop-up menu and choose the main color choice for your buttons and menus.

3. Click the Highlight Color pop-up menu and pick the highlight color that appears when you select text in an application or select an item from a list.

4. Press ⌘+Q to close System Preferences and save your changes.

Select a Screen Saver

Screen savers are another popular item — today's LCD monitors don't require animated graphics to avoid "burn-in" like older monitors did, but a screen saver can still provide security and a bit of fun to your desktop. A screen saver is activated after the specified amount of inactivity has passed.

To select a screen saver, open System Preferences and click the Desktop & Screen Saver icon; then click the Screen Saver tab to display the settings you see in **Figure** 4-3. Drag the Start Screen Saver slider to control the inactivity delay (or choose Never to disable the screen saver feature entirely).

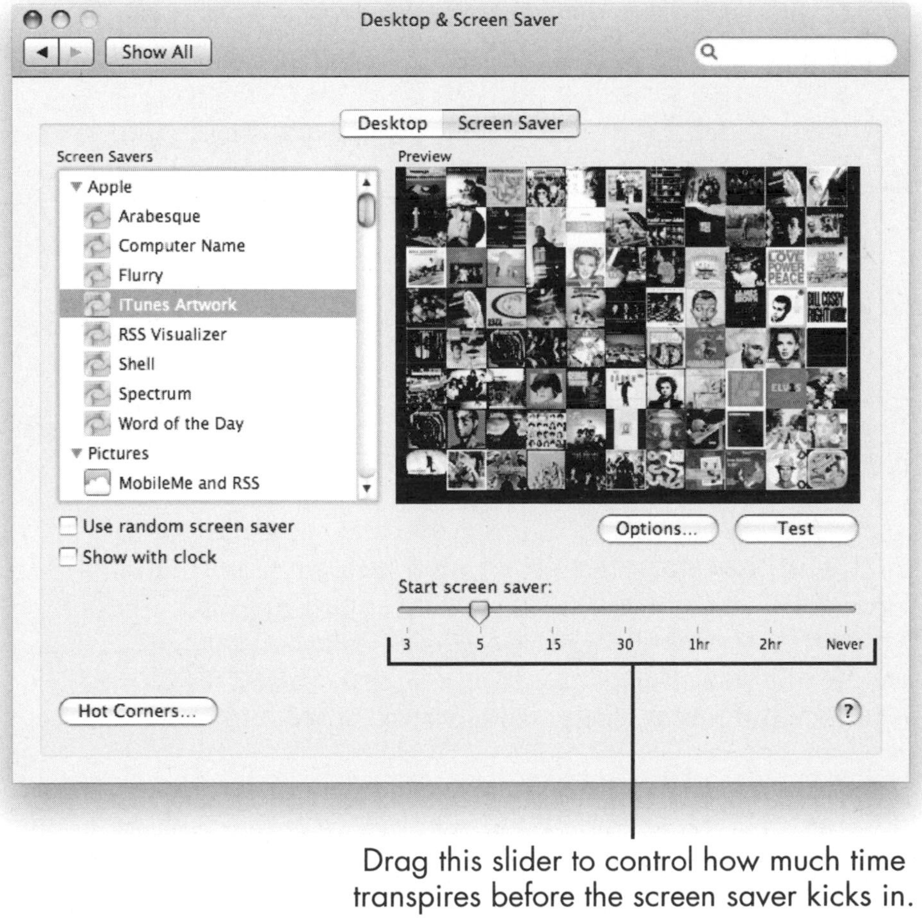

Drag this slider to control how much time transpires before the screen saver kicks in.

Figure 4-3

Click one of the entries in the Screen Savers column to display a thumbnail showing the effect. Selecting the Use Random Screen Saver check box, naturally, runs through them all. You can also test the appearance of the saver module by clicking the Test button; the screen saver runs until you move the mouse or press a key.

Many screen savers let you monkey with their settings. If the Options button is enabled (not grayed out), click it to see how you can change the effects.

 Click the Hot Corners button to display the Hot Corner sheet. From there, you can click any of the four pop-up menus in the four corners of the screen display to specify that corner as an *activation hot corner* (which immediately activates the screen saver) or as a *disabling hot corner* (which prevents the screen saver from being activated). As long as the mouse pointer stays in the disabling hot corner, the screen saver doesn't kick in no matter how long a period of inactivity passes. Click OK to save your changes and return to the System Preferences window.

Customize the Keyboard

No, you can't rearrange that horrible QWERTY arrangement by pulling off the keys — believe me, I've tried — but Leopard lets you tweak the behavior of your keyboard in a number of important ways.

To customize your keyboard, click the System Preferences icon in the Dock and then click the Keyboard & Mouse icon. On the Keyboard tab, shown in **Figure 4-4**, you can set these options:

➠ **Key Repeat Rate:** Move the Key Repeat Rate slider to alter the rate at which a keystroke repeats.

➠ **Delay Until Repeat:** Move this slider to alter how long a key must be held down before it repeats. For those who take a little more time pressing each key, moving this slider to the left helps reduce unwanted repeats.

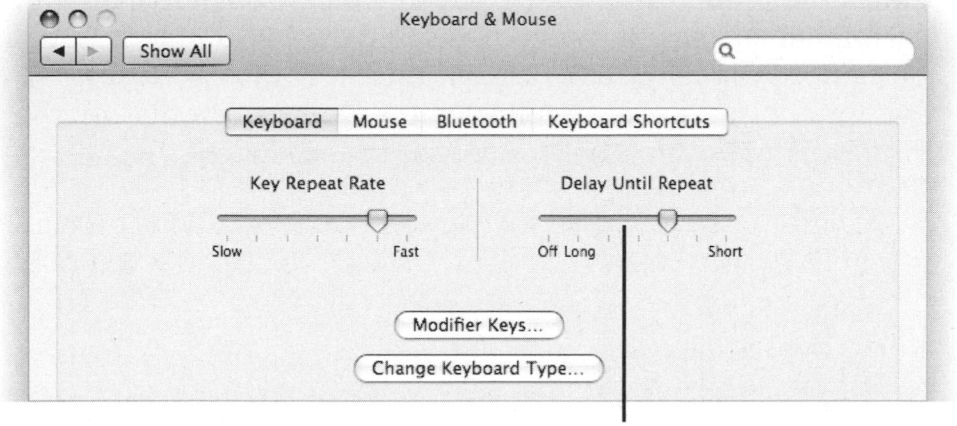

Move this slider to the left to prevent unwanted repeats.

Figure 4-4

To test your settings, click in the sample box and hold down a single key.

Leopard also provides the *Sticky Keys* and *Slow Keys* features, which can help you if you have trouble pressing keyboard shortcuts or you often trigger keyboard repeats (repetition of the same character) accidentally. To use these options, display the System Preferences window and click the Universal Access icon, and then click the Keyboard button.

Sticky Keys work by allowing you to press the modifier keys in a key sequence one after another (rather than all at the same time). Slow Keys allows a pause between the moment a key is pressed and the moment that Leopard acts on the keystroke. To turn on either feature (or both), just click the corresponding On radio button.

You can modify the way that Sticky Keys work by selecting these options:

→ **Press the Shift Key Five Times:** Select this check box and you can toggle Sticky Keys on and off from the keyboard by pressing the Shift key five times.

→ **Display Pressed Keys on Screen:** Select this check box and Leopard displays each key you press in a Sticky Keys sequence to help you keep track of the characters you've entered.

You can modify the way that Slow Keys work by using these options:

➡ **Use Click Key Sounds:** Select this check box to add a key-click sound every time you press a key.

➡ **Acceptance Delay:** Drag this slider to specify the length of the delay before the key is accepted.

To turn off keyboard repeat entirely — which may be required, depending on the settings you choose for Sticky Keys and Slow Keys — click the Set Key Repeat button, which displays the Keyboard preference settings I discuss earlier in this chapter.

Organize Icons on the Desktop

Consider the layout of the desktop itself. You can set the options for your desktop icons from the Finder's View menu (click any open part of the desktop and choose Show View Options) or by right-clicking any open part of the desktop and choosing Show View Options. (Heck, you can even press ⌘+J.) Whichever route you choose, Leopard displays the dialog box you see in **Figure** 4-5.

The changes you can make from this dialog box include

➡ **Resize icons:** Click and drag the Icon Size slider to shrink or expand the icons on the desktop. The icon size is displayed in pixels above the slider.

➡ **Specify grid spacing:** Click and drag the Grid Spacing slider to shrink or expand the size of the grid used to align icons on the desktop. The larger the grid, the more space between icons.

➡ **Resize icon label text:** Click the up and down arrows to the right of the Text Size pop-up menu to choose the font size (in points) for icon labels.

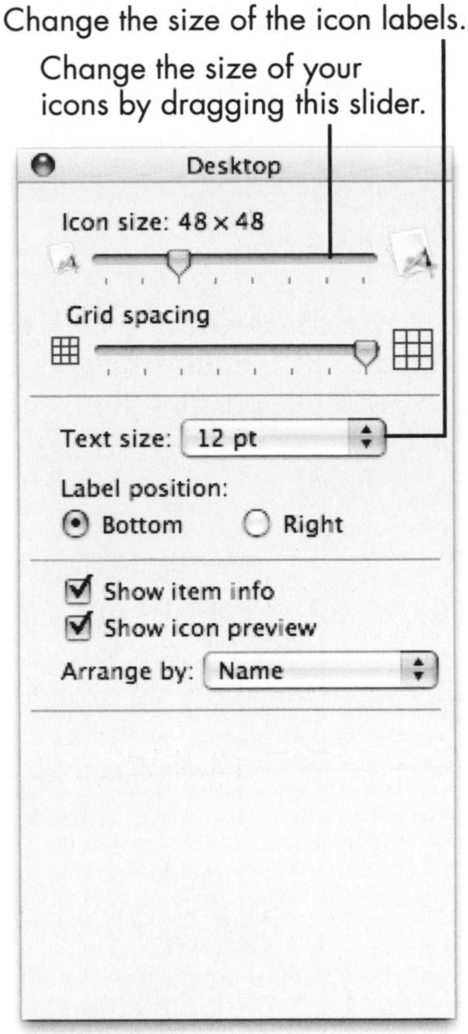

Change the size of the icon labels.

Change the size of your
icons by dragging this slider.

Figure 4-5

➠ **Move icon label text:** Select either the Bottom
   (default) or Right radio button to choose between
   displaying the text under or to the right of your desktop icons.

➠ **Show item info:** With this check box selected, Mac
   OS X displays the number of items within each folder
   on the desktop as well as the size and free space on
   your hard drives.

➡ **Show icon preview:** If you select this check box, the Finder displays icons for image files using a miniature of the original picture. (It's a cool feature for people with digital cameras — however, it takes extra processing time because Mac OS X has to load each image file and shrink it to create the icon.)

➡ **Arrange icons:** From this pop-up menu, you can automatically align icons to a grid on the desktop. You can also sort the display of icons in a window by choosing one of the following criteria from its pop-up menu: by name, date modified, date created, size, item type, or the icon label you assigned.

After all your changes are made and you're ready to return to work, click the Close button in the dialog box to save your settings.

Customize Your Pointing Device

As with the keyboard, Mac owners are downright picky about how their mice (or trackpads) work — and that includes folks who add third-party pointing devices, such as trackballs.

Once again, Leopard doesn't let you down, and you can customize your mouse to fit your clicking and double-clicking habits. To get started, click the System Preferences icon in the Dock and then click the Keyboard & Mouse icon. On the Mouse tab, shown in **Figure 4-6**, you find these settings:

➡ **Tracking Speed:** Drag this slider to determine how fast the mouse tracks across the desktop.

➡ **Double-Click Speed:** Drag the Double-Click Speed slider to determine how fast you must click your mouse to cause a double-click — feel free to click in the sample box to test your settings.

➡ **Scrolling Speed:** Drag this slider to specify the rate at which the contents of windows will scroll.

➡ **Primary Mouse Button:** Lefties might want to change the primary mouse button — click the Right radio button to use the right button as your primary button.

➡ **Zoom Using Scroll Wheel:** You can zoom the display with your Mighty Mouse scroll ball while holding down the key you choose from the drop-down menu — a helpful option for image editing.

If you're using a MacBook laptop, you'll find many of these same settings on the Trackpad tab.

Move this slider to the left to slow down the double-click speed.

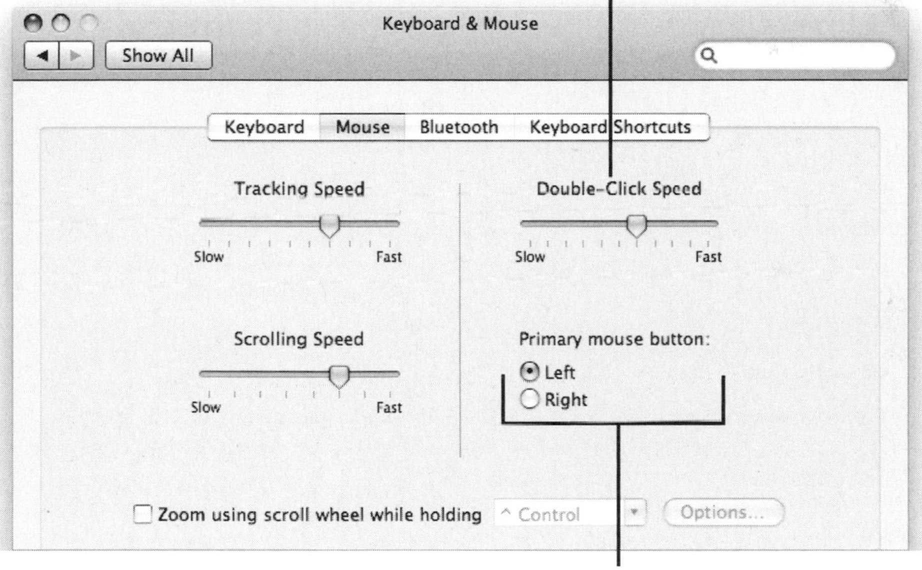

If you're a lefty, change your primary mouse button.

Figure 4-6

Set Your Screen for Maximum Visibility

Two features in Leopard can help people with limited vision: You can change the display resolution and brightness so that on-screen elements are easier to distinguish, and you can use the Universal Access Display tools to enhance the clarity of your desktop, Finder windows, and program windows.

Your monitor can display different resolutions — the higher the resolution, the smaller that items appear on-screen, so if you want items on the desktop to appear larger, you have to lower the screen resolution. You can also change the brightness level of your display to match the ambient lighting in the room.

To change these settings, follow these steps:

1. Open System Preferences and click the Display icon to display the settings, as shown in **Figure** 4-7.

2. Click the resolution you want to use from the Resolutions list on the left, and then choose the number of colors (from the Colors pop-up menu) to display.

 If you're having problems discerning items on the desktop, try a lower resolution — however, you typically should use the highest number of colors.

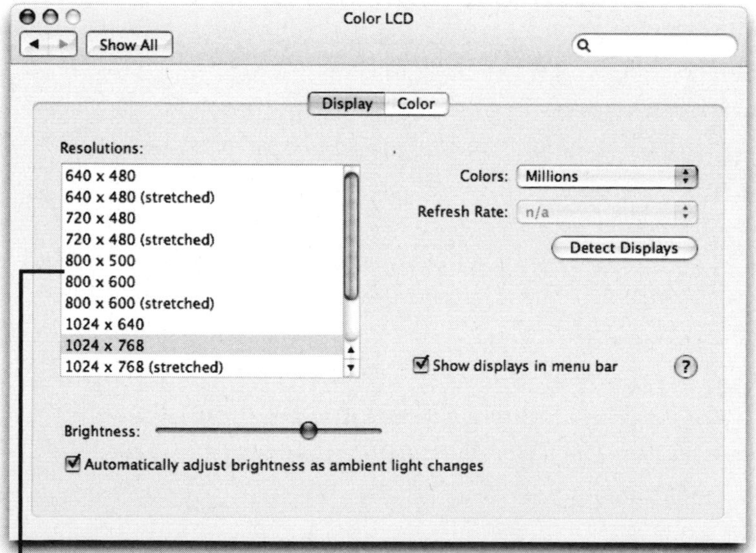

If you have trouble seeing icons on the desktop, choose a lower screen resolution.

Figure 4-7

3. Move the Brightness slider to adjust the brightness level of your display to your preference.

4. Click to select the Show Displays in Menu Bar check box if you switch resolutions often.

5. Press ⌘+Q to close System Preferences and save your changes.

Use the Universal Access Tools

Leopard offers a number of advanced features (grouped under the name Universal Access) that can help with contrast and zooming for Mac owners with limited vision.

To turn on Universal Access vision options, follow these steps:

1. Open System Preferences and click the Universal Access icon to display the Seeing settings, as shown in **Figure 4-8**.

2. To turn on Leopard's Zoom feature for your display — which allows you to zoom in on a selected portion of the screen — select the Zoom On radio button or press ⌘+Option+8.

3. To specify how much magnification is used, click the Options button. From the sheet that appears, you can set the minimum and maximum Zoom magnification increments. From the keyboard, use ⌘+Option+= (equal sign) to zoom in and ⌘+Option+− (minus sign) to zoom out. You can also display a preview rectangle of the area that's included when you zoom.

Mac OS X can smooth images to make them look better when zoomed; click the Options button in the Zoom section of the panel and select the Smooth Images check box.

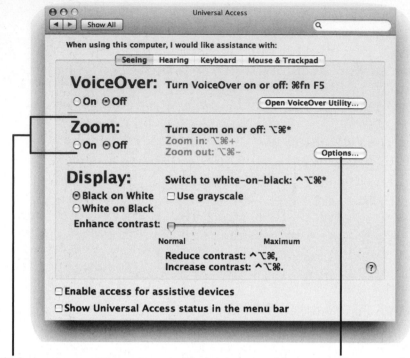

Click to turn on Zoom.   Click to control how much magnification is used.

Figure 4-8

 You can also determine how the screen moves in relation to the mouse pointer from the Zoom Options sheet: By default, the zoomed screen moves with the pointer, but you can set it to move only when the pointer reaches the edge of the screen or maintain the pointer near the center of the zoomed image automatically.

4. If you prefer white text on a black background, select the White on Black radio button (or press the ⌘+Option+Control+8 keyboard shortcut). Note that depending on your display settings, it might be easier on the eyes to use Grayscale Display mode by selecting the Use Grayscale check box.

5. Press ⌘+Q to close System Preferences and save your changes.

Replace Sounds with Visual Cues

Leopard can provide additional visual cues to supplement the spoken and audio alerts used throughout your system.

Follow these steps to add visual cues:

1. Open System Preferences and click the Universal Access icon, and then click the Hearing tab to display the options shown in **Figure 4-9**.

2. Click to select the Flash the Screen When an Alert Sound Occurs check box. Click the Flash Screen button to test the visual cues.

Click to make the screen flash when an audio alert sounds.

Click to change the sound volume.

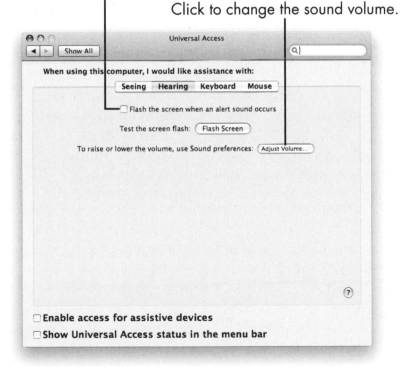

Figure 4-9

To raise the overall sound volume in Mac OS X, you can click the Adjust Sound button to display the Sound System Preferences settings, where you can drag the Volume slider to the right.

Set Up Speech Recognition

Since the early days of the Mac OS, Apple has included some form of speech functionality in its computers. Leopard continues to improve on speech recognition by offering a host of tools that let you get more work done in a shorter amount of time.

The speech recognition features of Mac OS X let you speak a word, phrase, or sentence. After you speak, your Mac goes to work translating what you said — and if it understands the phrase, it then performs an action associated with that phrase. The great part about this system is that you can say any phrase in continuous speech and have your Mac perform any sort of action that you can imagine. In fact, you aren't limited to just one action: You can perform dozens of actions after speaking a particular phrase.

Most current Macintosh models have a built-in microphone; for example, if you use an iMac, your microphone is built into the monitor, and MacBooks have a similar microphone built into the screen. If your Mac doesn't have a microphone, connect one to the computer Macintosh by plugging it into the Line-In or Microphone jack.

To get started with speech recognition in Mac OS X, open the System Preferences window by clicking its icon in the Dock and then clicking the Speech icon. Click the Speech Recognition tab to display the settings you see in **Figure 4-10**.

The Speech Recognition tab consists of two subtabs:

➡ **Settings:** The Settings tab provides a number of settings that control how your Mac listens to Its Master's Voice. (That means you, friend reader.) From there, you can set the sound input and adjust the key on the keyboard that toggles speech recognition on and off.

➡ **Commands:** When speech recognition is active, your Mac can understand any number of commands. From the Commands tab, you tell the Mac what type of commands it should expect you to give, and in which applications.

Crowning the Speech Recognition pane are the Speakable Items On and Off radio buttons. You probably already guessed how to use them to switch speech recognition features on and off.

 When you select the On radio button, the small circular Speech Recognition Feedback window appears on your screen, floating above all other windows. Know this face well because the Feedback window (refer to Figure 4-10) is your friend and partner. If you use Speech Recognition often, it becomes a constant companion on the desktop.

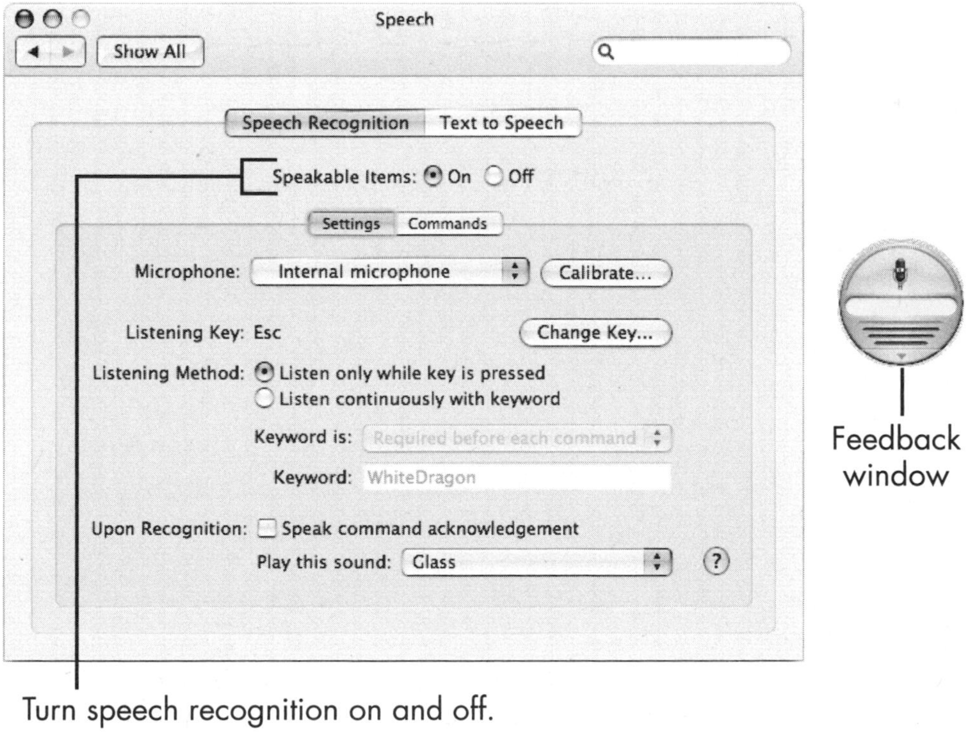

Turn speech recognition on and off.

Figure 4-10

Feedback window

Customize Speech Recognition Settings

At the bottom of the Settings pane is the Upon Recognition section. When your Mac comprehends one of your commands, you can set it to respond by playing a sound, speaking a confirmation, or both. This option is helpful when you're not sure whether your Mac understands you. One hundred percent recognition isn't a reality on any computer at this point, so sometimes it helps to have any feedback that you can get. Otherwise, you might feel silly shouting at your machine while it sits there doing nothing.

You can choose between two styles of listening with the Listening Method options:

➡ **Listen Only While Key Is Pressed:** Speech Recognition works only while the designated key is held down.

➡ **Listen Continuously with Keyword:** When you speak the keyword, listening turns on and remains on.

 To change which key must be toggled or held down, click the Change Key button.

Finally, you can select the microphone that you want to use from the Microphone pop-up menu on the Settings pane. It's a helpful feature if you have more than one microphone connected to your Mac. Click the Calibrate key to adjust the sound volume for better recognition.

When Speech Recognition is active, your Mac listens for whichever phrases appear in your Speakable Items folder (a directory on your hard drive that holds a number of scripts). The Commands tab lets you view the contents of this folder. When you speak a phrase that matches one of these filenames, your Mac automatically executes that script. The script can perform any number of actions, which is what makes Speech Recognition so powerful. Apple includes a large number of scripts with Mac OS X, but you're free to create your own, too.

To make something speakable, select the item and then speak the command "Make this speakable." The new speakable command is based on the item's name.

To view the contents of the Speakable Items folder, click the Open Speakable Items Folder button on the Commands pane. The Finder comes to the foreground and navigates to the folder that holds the scripts. This option is handy because each item in the Speakable Items folder is speakable.

After you activate Speech Recognition, you instantly see the Feedback window. You can click and drag the edge of the window to position it anywhere on the desktop.

The Feedback window includes controls and displays of its own:

➥ **Microphone Level Meter:** The Feedback window displays indicators to let you know how loud the input to your microphone is.

➥ **Visual Indicator:** The Feedback window displays visual feedback to let you know which mode it's in: idle, listening, or hearing a command. When the microphone isn't grayed out but no arrows appear on either side of the microphone, you're in Listening mode. When the microphone is flanked by animated arrows, your computer is hearing a command spoken. When Speech Recognition is idle, no arrows are present and the microphone is grayed out.

➥ **Quick-Access Menu:** You can quickly access the Speech preferences for the System or view the Speech Com-mands window. Just click the downward-pointing arrow at the bottom of the Feedback window, and a menu appears, giving you one-click access to both.

As soon as you disable speech recognition in the System Preferences, the Feedback window disappears.

Because the Speech Recognition feature might be listening for different sets of commands from the Finder or many other applications, Mac OS X provides you with a single listing of all commands that you might speak at any given time: the Speech Commands window. To open the Speech Commands window, click the triangle at the bottom of the Feedback window and choose Open Speech Commands Window from the menu that appears.

The Speech Commands window is a simple one, but it serves an important purpose: to let you know which commands Mac OS X understands. The Speech Commands pane organizes commands into categories that match the settings in the Speech pane of the System Preferences.

If you launch another application that supports Speech Recognition, Mac OS X adds that application's commands to the Speech Commands window. Speak any of these commands to make your Mac execute that function. For example, Mac OS X ships with speech commands for Address Book, such as Mail To and Video Chat With.

 Apple might be a big, serious, computer company — yeah, right — but it isn't without a humorous side. With Speech Recognition enabled, say the phrase "Tell me a joke." Your Mac replies with a random joke. Say it again, and your Mac tells you another joke. (Brace yourself: These jokes were likely written by Windows users — they're bad.) Oh, and if you get a knock-knock joke, remember that you have to say "Who's there?"

Working with Files and Folders

Chapter 5

Mac OS X is a highly visual operating system, and using it without a pointing device (like a mouse or trackpad) is like building Hoover Dam with a pocketknife (and not a particularly sharp pocketknife, either). Therefore, most of this chapter requires you to firmly grasp the little rodent — I introduce you to items such as *files* and *folders* and lead you through the basic training you need in order to run programs and open documents. Finally, you see how to manage your files and folders as gracefully as Fred Astaire on his best day.

Store Files on Your Mac

Although you may already be familiar with how your information is stored in files, I want to cover the big concepts you need to know about files — just in case:

➠ **The information you use and the stuff you create are saved in files.** A *file* is an individual item that has its own name and properties, such as the date it was created and which program runs it. For example, a letter you write and your genealogical data are both stored in files.

➠ **You run programs to create and edit files.** A *program* is used to do work on a computer (such as Microsoft Word, which you would use to type that letter).

In the Mac world, a program is often referred to as an *application*. So *program, application* — same thing.

➡ **Files are linked to programs.** Here's one of the features that makes the Mac so neat! If you double-click a Pages document you created (again, that same doggone letter I keep mentioning), Leopard automatically knows that the Pages program has to run for you to make changes to the letter or print it — and the program automatically launches and loads the letter file, ready for you to use. The file is marked as a Pages document, and Leopard maintains the link between them. *Snazzy!*

 Although each file is individually named, Leopard tries to make it as easy as possible to visually identify which program owns which file. Therefore, most programs use a special icon to indicate their data files. For example, **Figure 5-1** illustrates several documents and data files created by a range of programs: iPhoto, Pages, Automator, and Safari.

➡ **Word processing and desktop publishing files are sometimes called documents**. A *document* is just a special kind of file.

Documents and Files

Figure 5-1

Organize Files with Folders

"Mark, I thought this computer was going to get me away from all that paper in my filing cabinets!" Don't worry, dear reader: Your Mac can indeed create a paperfree zone in your home office.

➠ Within Leopard, a *folder* is simply a "container" that holds files on your Mac, not an actual manila folder that you have to track all the time. (The folks who designed the first Mac operating system decades ago knew that we're all comfortable with the idea of storing information in folders, so they used the idea.)

➠ You can organize your files on the Desktop and within Finder windows by copying and moving files in and out of folders (or, in brave moments, even between folders). (Chapter 8 explains how to cut, copy, and paste.)

➠ Folders can be named, renamed, and deleted, just like files can. (Sections later in this chapter explain how.) You can also create a folder within a folder to further organize your stuff — these "enclosed" folders are *subfolders*.

➠ As you can see from the assortment shown in **Figure 5-2**, folders have a 3D look in Mac OS X — in fact, major system folders (including Applications, Downloads, Library, System, Users, and Utilities) sport folder icons in Leopard that help identify their contents.

Every user account that you create on your Mac has a special folder, called a Home folder, where you can store documents and data for your use. No one else can see the contents of your Home folder, which is named after your account.

Inside your Home folder are a number of subfolders that are automatically created as well, and you can use these folders to store all sorts of documents and help keep your Mac organized. The most important Home subfolders include:

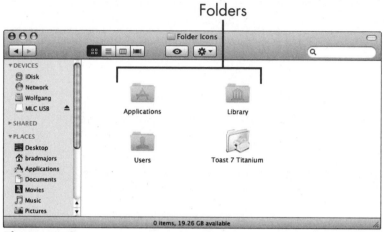

Figure 5-2

➡ **Documents:** This subfolder is provided so that you can store all sorts of documents you've created, like your Pages projects.

➡ **Downloads:** You'll also find this subfolder in the Dock. By default, Safari stores all files you've downloaded from the Web in this subfolder.

➡ **Movies, Music, and Pictures:** These three subfolders are self-explanatory — they store any movies, digital music files (including your iTunes music library), and photos that you upload from your camera or snap with your iSight camera.

Open Files and Folders

After you understand how Leopard stores your files within folders, it's time to move on and *open* those items. In this section, I discuss how to open folders and files (or *documents*, if you want to be fancy).

To open a folder within Leopard, just double-click it. (Alternatively, you can click it once to select it and then press ⌘+O.) The contents of the folder are displayed within a new window, or within the current window (depending on how you set View mode).

Here's the simple way to load a document:

1. If a Finder window isn't already open, double-click your Mac's hard drive icon on the desktop. This opens a Finder window.

2. Double-click the folder that contains the document. If the document is stored in a subfolder, double-click that subfolder to open it.

3. When the document is visible, double-click it. (This is my preferred method because I'm an ALT — short for Admittedly Lazy Technowizard — who would rather use complex hand movements to pour myself another Diet Coke.)

If the program that you created the document with is already open, you can also open a document from inside the program. (For example, if I've already got TextEdit open, I can open a simple text file from within the program.) Here's the plan:

1. Choose File⇨Open or press the handy ⌘+O key combination. Your Mac OS X application is likely to display the attractive Open dialog box that you see in **Figure 5-3**. Note that you can switch the Open dialog between view modes, just like a Finder window, so you can browse in Icon mode, List mode, or Column mode.

2. Navigate to the location of the document you want to open. In the Open dialog box, you can navigate in one of two ways:

   • **Use the pop-up menu to jump directly to common locations** — such as the Desktop and your Home folder — as well as places you recently accessed (Recent Places).

- If the target folder isn't on your pop-up menu, **move the slider at the bottom of the dialog box** to the far left to display your hard drives, CD-ROM and DVD drives, and network locations.

3. Click the location where the file will be found (usually within at least one folder).

Note that the right columns change to show you the contents of the item you just clicked. In this way, you can cruise through successive folders to find that elusive document. (This somewhat time-consuming process is somewhat derisively called *drilling* — hence, the importance of using Recent Items, as I discuss later in this chapter.)

4. When you spy the document you want to load, either double-click it or click once to highlight the filename and then click Open.

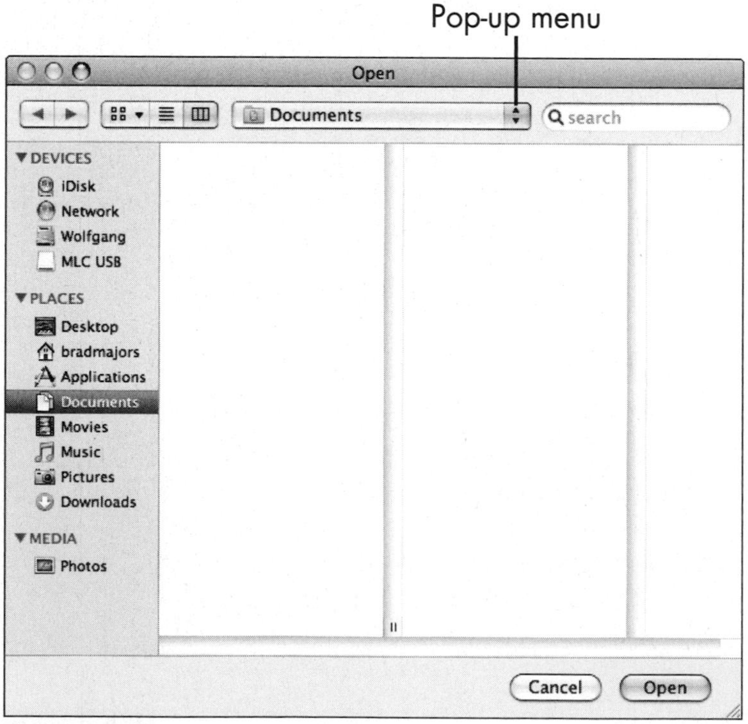

Pop-up menu

Figure 5-3

"Hey, the Open dialog box can be resized!" That's right, good buddy — you can expand the Open dialog box to show more columns and find things more easily. Click and drag the lower-right corner of the Open dialog box to resize it.

View Documents with Quick Look

The link that connects a program with a document is A Beautiful Thing, but sometimes you just want to look at the contents of a file — and if you double-click that document file, you end up waiting for the entire application to load. (Depending on the size of the program, this process can take as long as 15 or 20 seconds!) There has to be an easier way to just take a gander at what's inside a document.

Don't think that I would have gone that far into a fancy introduction if the answer were negative. I'm ushering in the Leopard Quick Look feature, which can display the contents of many documents — but without *opening* the corresponding program! This capability is one reason that you bought a Mac.

To use Quick Look from a Finder window, follow these steps:

1. Click to select a file.

2. Click the Quick Look button (which bears an eye icon) on the Finder window toolbar, or press the spacebar. **Figure 5-4** illustrates Quick Look in action, this time displaying the contents of a Pages document.

 As with other windows in Leopard, you can click the lower-right corner of the Quick Look window and drag it to resize the window.

3. Press Esc (or click the Close button in the upper-left corner of the Quick Look window) when you're done checking out the document.

Figure 5-4

View Images and PDF Documents with Preview

Along with Quick Look, Leopard offers a Swiss army knife application for viewing image files and PDF documents: namely, Preview. You can use Preview to display virtually all of the popular types of digital photos produced by today's cameras (and available for downloading on the Web).

Leopard automatically loads Preview when you double-click an image in a format it recognizes or when you double-click a PDF file — check out the image in **Figure** 5-5. It also acts as the Print Preview window.

However, if you want to launch Preview manually, open a Finder window, click the Applications folder in the Sidebar, and then double-click the Preview icon.

Figure 5-5

I know — if that were the sum total of Preview's features, it wouldn't deserve coverage here. What else can it do? Here's a partial list (just my favorites, mind you):

➠ Use Preview to add a bookmark at the current page within a PDF document by choosing Bookmarks➪ Add Bookmark.

➡ Fill out a form in a PDF document by choosing Tools⇨Text Tool. Click an area that's marked as an input field, and you can type text into that field. After you complete the form, you can fax or print it.

➡ Take a *screen snapshot* (saving the contents of your screen as a digital photo) by choosing File⇨Grab⇨ Timed Screen. Preview launches the Grab utility, which displays an on-screen timer and then snaps the image for you after ten seconds. (Then you have time to make things just right before saying "Cheese!")

Create a Link to a File or Folder

An *alias* acts as a link to another item elsewhere on your system. For example, to launch Adobe Acrobat, you can click an Adobe Acrobat alias icon that you can create on the Desktop (or add to your Dock) rather than click the actual Acrobat program icon. The alias acts essentially the same way as the original icon, but it doesn't occupy the same space — only a few bytes for the icon itself, compared with the size of the actual program. Plus, you don't have to dig through folders galore to find the original program.

You can always identify an alias by the small, curved arrow at the base of the icon, and the icon might also sport the tag `alias` at the end of its name.

You have two ways to create an alias. Here's one:

1. Select the item.

2. Choose File⇨Make Alias or press ⌘+L. **Figure 5-6** illustrates a number of aliases, arranged next to their linked files.

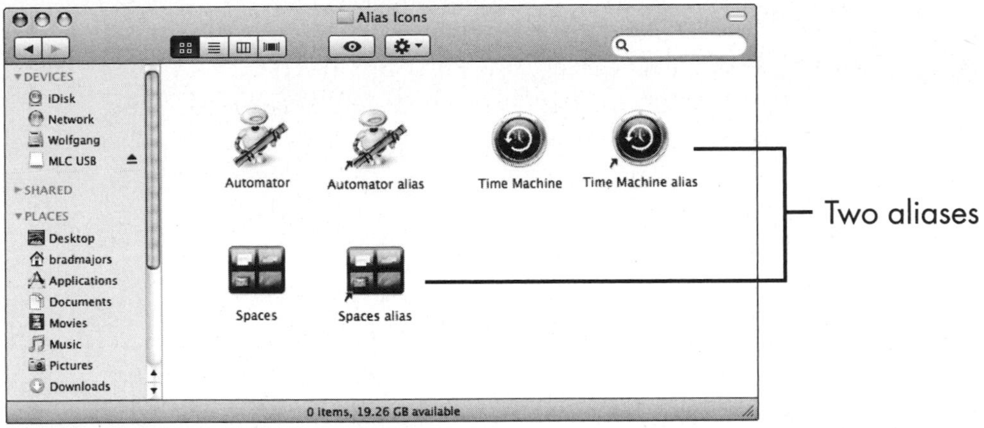

Figure 5-6

Here's another way to create an alias:

1. Press and hold the key combination ⌘+Option.

2. Drag the original icon to the location where you want the alias.

 Note that this funky method doesn't add the `alias` tag to the end of the alias icon name!

Why bother to use an alias? Here are two good reasons:

➠ **Launch an application or open a document from anywhere on your drive.** For example, you can start Pages directly from the folder where you store the documents for your current Pages project. Speed, organization, and convenience — life is good.

➠ **Send an alias to the Trash without affecting the original item.** When that volunteer project is finished, you can safely delete the alias (sending it to the Trash) without worry.

If you move or rename the original file, Leopard is smart enough to update the alias too! However, if the original file is deleted, the alias no longer works. Go figure.

Launch Recently Used Documents and Programs

Apple knows that most folks work on the same documents and use the same programs during the course of a day. You might use iPhoto several times to edit different images, for example, or look at the same report many times in the span of a day using Pages.

To make it easier to access these frequently used programs and documents, Leopard includes the Recent Items list. Follow these steps to use it:

1. Click the Apple symbol on the bar to display the menu.

2. Hover the mouse pointer over the Recent Items menu item. The Finder displays all applications and documents you used over the past few computing sessions.

3. Click an item to load that document or application.

Select Items

Often, the menu commands or keyboard commands you perform in the Finder need to be performed *on* something: Perhaps you're moving an item from one window to another or creating an alias for that item. To identify the target of your action to the Finder, you need to select one or more items on your Desktop or in a Finder window. In this section, I show you just how to do that.

Leopard gives you a couple of options when selecting just one item for an upcoming action:

➡ **Move the mouse pointer over the item and click.** A dark border (or *highlight*) appears around the icon, indicating that it's selected.

➠ **If an icon is already highlighted on the Desktop or within a window, move the selection highlight to another icon in the same location by using the arrow keys.** To shift the selection highlight alphabetically, press Tab (to move in order) or press Shift+Tab (to move in reverse order).

 Selecting items in the Finder doesn't *do* anything to them. You have to *perform an action* on the selected items to make something happen.

You can also select multiple items with aplomb by using one of these methods:

➠ **Adjacent items**

Drag a box around them. If that statement sounds like ancient Sumerian, here's the explanation: Click a spot above and to the left of the first item; then hold down the mouse button and drag down and to the right. (This process is called *dragging* in Mac-speak.) A box outline such as the one shown in **Figure 5-7** appears, indicating what you're selecting. Any icons that touch, or appear within, the box outline are selected when you release the button.

Click the first item to select it and then hold down the Shift key while you click the last item. Leopard selects both items and everything between them.

➠ **Nonadjacent items**

Select these items by holding down the ⌘ key while you click each item.

 Check out the status line at the bottom of a Finder window. It tells how many items are displayed in the current Finder window. When you select items, it shows you how many you highlighted.

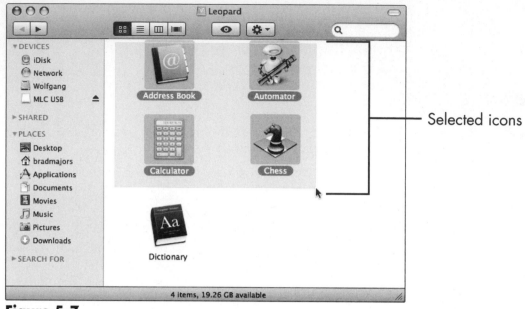

Selected icons

Figure 5-7

Create Folders

In the Mac world, you create new *folders* from a Finder window, by using one of these methods:

➡ **With the mouse:** Right-click in a Finder window or on any open space on the Desktop and choose New Folder from the menu.

➡ **With the keyboard:** Press ⌘+Shift+N.

➡ **From the Finder window toolbar:** Click the Action button (which bears a gear icon) and choose New Folder from the menu that appears.

No matter how you create a folder, Leopard highlights it automatically and places a text cursor underneath so that you can immediately type the name for your new folder. Press Return when you're done typing the name.

You'll create folders often to organize documents and files that are related to each other, like all the images and text you've been given for a church project.

Rename Items

You wouldn't go far in today's spacious virtual world without being able to change a moniker for a file or folder. To rename an item in Mac OS X, use one of these two methods:

➠ **The mouse:** Click an icon's name once (or just press Return). Mac OS X highlights the text in an edit box. Type the new name and then press Return when you're done.

 Wait a few seconds between clicks, as opposed to a rapid-fire double-click.

➠ **The Info dialog box:** Select the item and press ⌘+I to display the Info dialog box; then click the triangle next to Name & Extension. Click in the name field, drag the mouse to highlight the text you want to change, and type the replacement text.

Naturally, the first method is the easiest, and it's the one I use most often.

 Never rename folders or files in your System directory, and don't rename any of the default subfolders Apple provides in your Home folder. (I discussed these subfolders earlier in this chapter.) Renaming these items may make it harder for you to locate your documents, and may even damage your Mac OS X installation.

Delete Items You No Longer Need

Even Leonardo da Vinci made the occasional design mistake — his trash can was likely full of bunched-up pieces of parchment. Luckily, no trees are wasted when you decide to toss your unneeded files and folders; this section shows you how to delete items from your system.

 By the way, as you'll soon witness for yourself, moving items to the Trash doesn't necessarily mean that they're immediately history.

You have a few different ways to toss files into the Trash:

➡ **Drag unruly files against their will.** In Mac OS X, the familiar Macintosh Trash can appears at the right edge of the Dock — it's that spiffy-looking wire can. You can click and drag the items you selected to the Trash and drop them on top of the wire can icon to delete them. When the Trash contains at least one item, the wire can icon changes to look as though it were full of trash.

➡ **Delete with the menus.** Choose File from the Finder menu bar and choose the Move to Trash menu item. Or you can right-click the item to display the shortcut menu and then choose Move to Trash from the menu.

➡ **Delete with the keyboard.** Press the ⌘+Delete keyboard shortcut. Or click the Action button on the Finder toolbar and select Move to Trash from the pop-up menu.

Copy and Move Files and Folders

It's what life is all about, as George Carlin might have said — managing your stuff. On your Mac, that usually means copying and moving files and folders from one drive to another or from your Mac's internal hard drive to an external drive. In this section, I show you how to copy items from one Finder window to another, or from one location (such as a CD-ROM) to another (such as your Desktop), it's *trés* easy.

 When you open a Finder window, you can always see where the files it contains are located — just check out the Devices list at the left side of the window, and you'll see that one of the devices is highlighted. You're copying stuff on the same drive if both locations are on the same device. If, however, one Finder window is displaying items from your hard drive and the other is displaying items from a USB flash drive or DVD, then you're copying between drives.

➠ **To copy one item to another location on the same drive:** Hold down the Option key (you don't have to select the icon first) and then click and drag the item from its current home to the new location.

 To put a copy of an item within a folder, just drop the item on top of the receiving folder. If you hold the item you're dragging over the destination folder for a second or two, Leopard opens a new window so that you can see the contents of the target. (This is a *spring-loaded* folder. Really.)

➠ **To copy multiple items to another location on the same drive:** Select them all first, hold down the Option key, and then drag and drop one of the selected items where you want it. All the items you selected follow the item you drag. (It's rather like lemmings. Nice touch, don't you think?)

 To help indicate your target when you're copying files, Leopard highlights the location to show you where the items will end up. (This process works whether the target location is a folder or a drive icon.) If the target location is a window, Leopard adds a highlight to the window border.

➡ **To copy one or multiple items on a different drive:**
Click and drag the icon (or the selected items if you
have more than one) from the original window to a
window you open on the target drive. (There's no
need to hold down the Option key while copying to
a different drive.) You can also drag one item (or a
selected group of items) and simply drop the items
on top of the drive icon on the Desktop.

 If you try to move or copy something to a location
that already has an item with the same name, a dialog box prompts you to decide whether to replace the
file or to stop the copy or move procedure and leave
the existing file alone. Good insurance, indeed.

Move Things from Place to Place

Moving items from one location to another location on the same drive
is the easiest action you can take. Just drag the item (or selected items)
to the new location. The item disappears from the original spot and
reappears in the new spot.

To move items from one drive to another drive, hold down the ⌘ key
while you drag them to the target location.

Back Up to CD or DVD

Although Apple offers the Time Machine feature for creating backups
to an external hard drive, sometimes you want to copy files and folders
to a recordable CD or DVD — either as a simple backup or perhaps to
carry with you on a trip or give to another Mac owner.

Leopard makes this process easy. Follow these steps:

1. Load a blank disc into your Mac's optical drive. The dialog box you see in **Figure 5-8** appears.

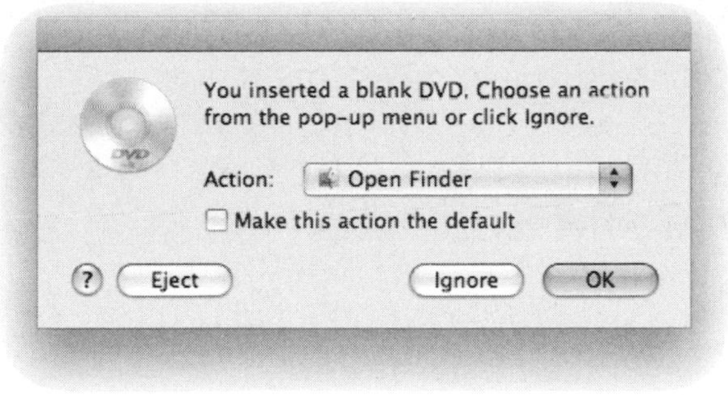

Figure 5-8

2. Click OK. A DVD icon labeled Untitled DVD appears on the Desktop. (If you want to name the disc, rename it just like you rename a file or folder.)

3. Double-click the Untitled DVD icon to open a Finder window with the contents of the disc, as shown in **Figure 5-9**.

4. Into the disc's Finder window, drag the files and folders you want to back up. (Note that until you burn the disc, the file and folder icons that you add carry an alias arrow.)

The items you add can be organized any way you like. Don't forget that the total amount of data shouldn't exceed 700 megabytes (MB) on a CD. You should also stick within 4 gigabytes (GB) or so on a standard recordable DVD or 8GB on a dual-layer recordable DVD. You can see how much free space remains on the disc at the bottom of the disc's Finder window. (Just check the packaging if you're not sure what kind of disc you have.)

5. When you finish adding files to the disc, click the Burn button on the right side of the window.

6. Choose the fastest recording speed possible.

7. Click Burn.

DVD contents

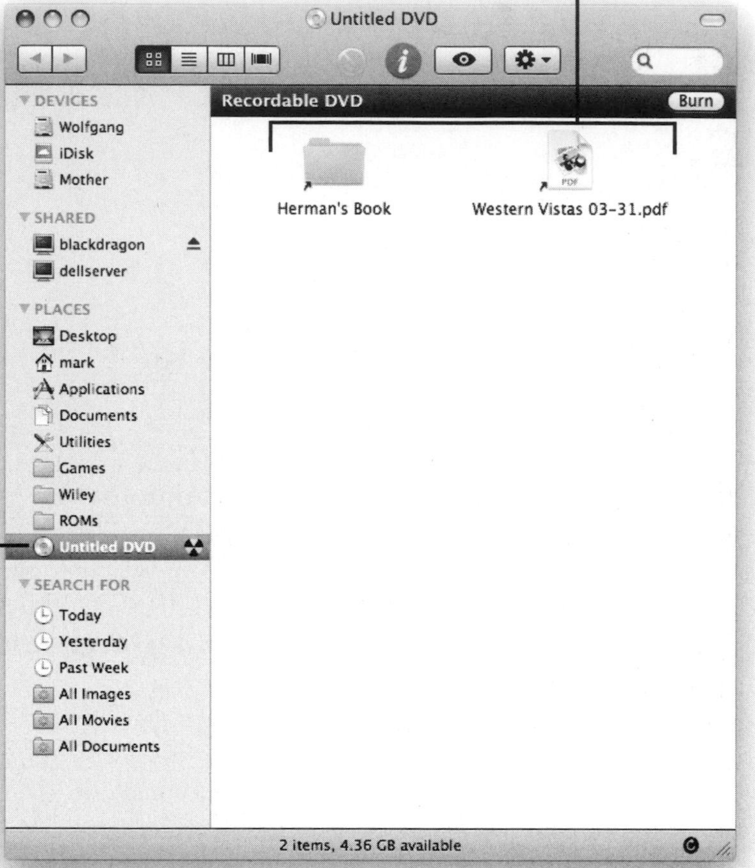

Click Untitled DVD

Figure 5-9

Working with Printers, Scanners, and Faxes

Chapter 6

Whether you have simple printing needs or you run a business from your home office, your Mac can produce outstanding documents with today's printers.

Wait, there's more! You're not limited to just a printer: Macs can use scanners that allow you to send faxes, and you can produce electronic documents in the Adobe Acrobat PDF format.

In this chapter, you find out how to

➠ Install a local USB printer.

➠ Print a file.

➠ Remove a printer from your system.

➠ Produce a PDF electronic document.

➠ Install a USB scanner.

➠ Send a fax document.

Add a USB Printer to Your System

 Here's the most common task that Mac owners need to tackle soon after installing Mac OS X: printing documents. Most of us have a Universal Serial Bus (USB) printer — the USB is the favored hardware connection within Mac OS X — so as long as your printer is supported by Mac OS X, setting it up is as easy as plugging it into one of your Mac's USB ports. The Big X does the rest of the work, selecting the proper printer software driver from the Library/Printers folder.

If necessary, however, you may have to load a driver CD supplied by your printer manufacturer. After you load the disc and the CD window appears, double-click the Setup or Install application to install the drivers. (Don't forget to visit the manufacturer's Web site using Safari and download the latest driver software.)

I know that this plug-and-play process *sounds* too good to be true, but I can tell you from my experiences as a consultant and hardware technician that installing a USB printer is really this simple! 'Nuff said.

Print a File

You didn't read this far into this chapter without a burning desire to print something, so in this task, I go over the printing process in detail.

To print from within any application by using the default page characteristics — standard 8½-x-11-inch paper, portrait mode, no scaling — follow these steps:

1. Within your application, choose File⇨Print — or press ⌘+P.

2. Mac OS X displays the simple version of the Print sheet. (To display all the fields you see in **Figure 6-1**, click the down-arrow button next to the Printer pop-up menu.)

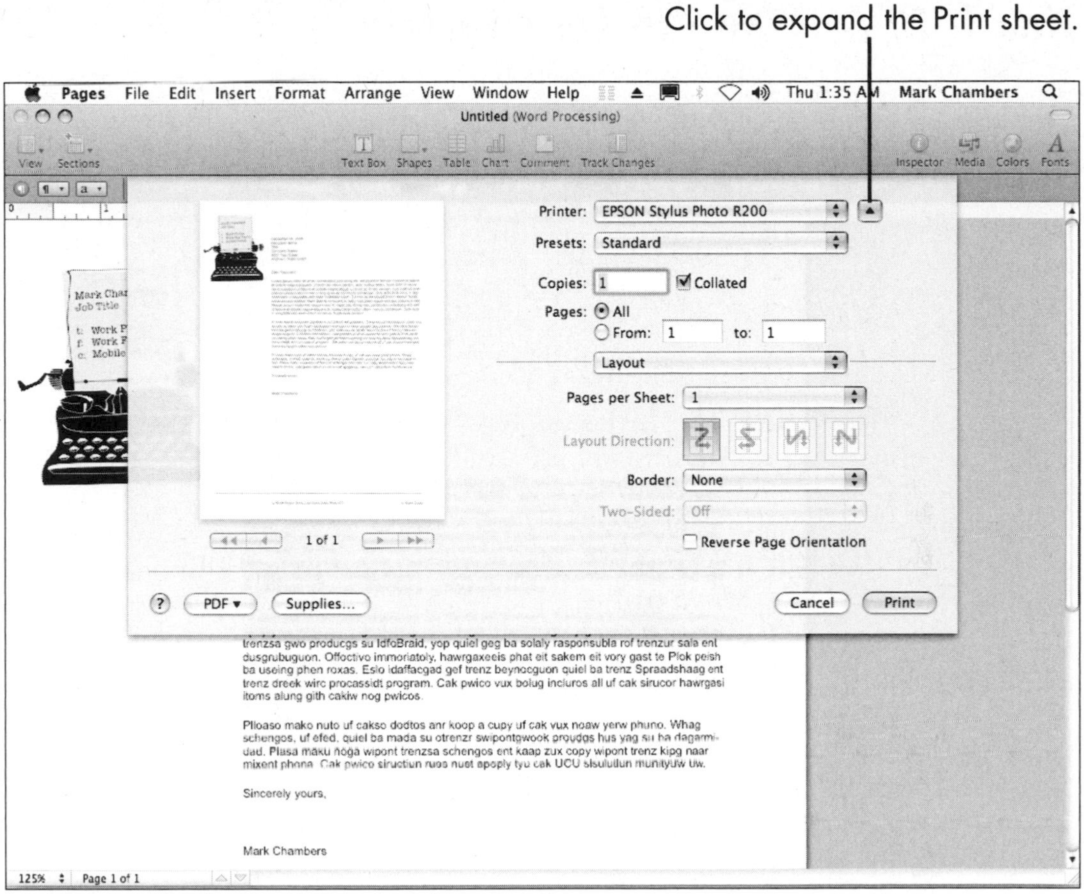

Click to expand the Print sheet.

Figure 6-1

Some applications (such as Word 2007) use their own custom Print dialog boxes, but you should see the same general settings as the ones shown in Figure 6-1.

Before you print, *preview*! Would you jump from an airplane without a parachute? Then why would you print a document without double-checking it first? Click Preview on the Print sheet, and Mac OS X opens the Preview application to show you what the printed document will look like. (Once again, some upstart programs have their own built-in Print Preview mode.) When you're done examining your handiwork, close the Preview application to return to your document.

3. Click in the Copies field and enter the number of copies you need.

You can also enable or disable collation, just like those oh-so-fancy copiers.

4. Decide what you want to print:

- *The whole shootin' match:* To print the entire document, use the default Pages radio button All setting.

- *Anything less:* To print a range of selected pages, select the From radio button and enter the starting and ending pages.

5. (Optional) Choose application-specific printing parameters.

Each Mac OS X application provides different panes so that you can configure settings specific to that application. You don't have to display any of these extra settings to print a default document, but the power is there to change the look dramatically when necessary. To display these settings, click the pop-up menu in the center of the Print dialog box and choose one of these panes. For example, if you're printing from the Address Book, you can choose the Address Book entry from the pop-up menu and elect to print a phone list or an e-mail list.

6. When everything is go for launch, click the Print button.

Choose a Default Printer

Many Mac owners have more than one printer — perhaps one is a black-and-white laser printer for plain letters and documents and the other is an inkjet printer for projects where color is important. If you have such a setup, most of your print jobs should be sent to the laser printer (because printing a document using the laser is likely to be cheaper and faster than using the inkjet). The default printer is the one you plan to use for most, if not all, of your print jobs.

You can easily set the default printer within Leopard! With your default properly set, you don't have to bother choosing a printer from the Print sheet for every job — just click Print and go.

To set your default printer, follow these steps:

1. Click the System Preferences icon in the Dock.

2. Click the Print & Fax icon to open the Print & Fax preferences pane, shown in **Figure 6-2**.

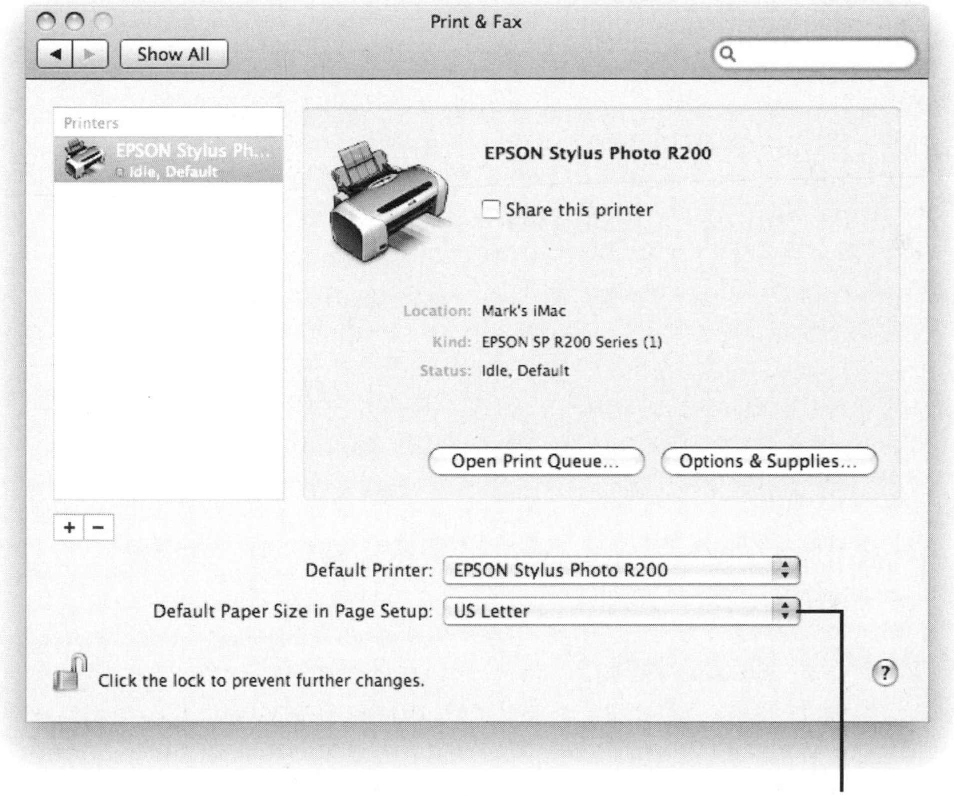

Select a default printer.

Figure 6-2

3. Click the Default Printer pop-up menu to select one of
your installed printers.

 If you choose Last Printer Used, Mac OS X uses the
printer that received the last print job.

4. Close the System Preferences window to save the change.

Remove an Unnecessary Printer Entry

If you replace one of your installed printers with a new model, Leopard
can't automatically delete the old printer entry — it's a very smart operating system, but not *that* smart. Luckily, removing a printer selection
from your system is easy. Follow these steps:

1. Click the System Preferences icon in the Dock.

2. Click the Print & Fax icon to open the Print & Fax preferences pane, shown in Figure 6-2.

3. Click the printer entry you want to delete.

4. Click the Delete button (which carries a minus sign)
below the Printers list.

Depending on the printer manufacturer, you may be
prompted for confirmation before the printer entry is
removed from the list.

5. Close the System Preferences window to save the change.

Create a PDF Document

The Adobe Acrobat application is used to create electronic documents
in the PDF format; these documents can be displayed on virtually all
computers and many portable devices (such as mobile phones and
PDAs). PDF documents are quite common on the Internet, and many

hardware and software manufacturers offer manuals online — heck, this book may even be available as an electronic PDF book by the time you read this!

Although you certainly can install Adobe Acrobat under Leopard, I'd be remiss if I didn't mention that you don't have to! That's because the operating system provides built-in support for printing documents in the Adobe PDF format (which can then be viewed and printed on any other computer with Acrobat Reader or added to your Web site for downloading). To print a document as a file in PDF format from just about any Mac application, follow these steps:

1. Within your application, choose File➪Print — or press ⌘+P.

2. Mac OS X displays the Print sheet, shown in Figure 6-1.

3. Click the PDF button and choose Save As PDF from the menu that appears. Leopard displays the Save dialog box that you see in **Figure** 6-3.

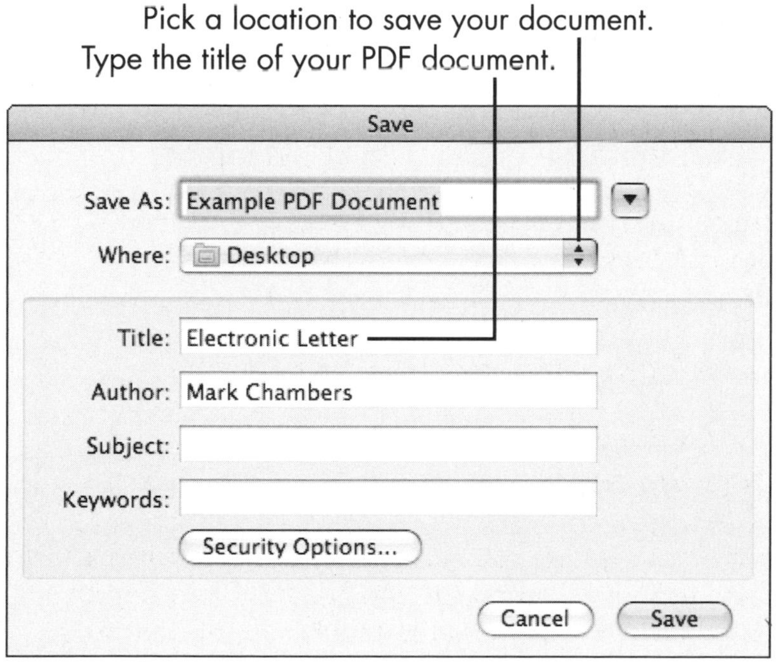

Pick a location to save your document.
Type the title of your PDF document.

Save
Save As: Example PDF Document
Where: Desktop
Title: Electronic Letter
Author: Mark Chambers
Subject:
Keywords:
Security Options...
Cancel   Save

Figure 6-3

4. Navigate to a folder and enter a filename.

 Notice that you can also enter embedded information that can be searched for by using Spotlight, like the title and author of the document. These fields are optional, so you don't have to enter them.

5. Click Save to create your PDF file.

You can double-click your new PDF file to open it within Preview, or select it and press the spacebar to check it out with QuickLook. Shazam!

Install a USB Scanner

Again, USB proves to be the simplest and most common connection — this time, your hardware choice is the scanner, which lets you import images and "read" text from a page into a Pages or Word file. With a scanner connected to your Mac, you can use the combination of your scanner and printer as a copy machine (with software provided by the manufacturer) or as a fax machine (using a USB modem and the fax support built-in to Leopard).

Remember my mantra "USB makes it easy!" As long as your scanner supports Mac OS X, plug the USB cable from your scanner into one of the USB ports on your Mac.

Just about all scanners come with software and drivers from the manufacturer, so don't forget to load the installation CD. After you load the disc and the CD window appears, double-click the Setup or Install application.

After you install your scanner, refer to the user guide for more information on the applications included by your manufacturer.

Send a Fax

Remember when the fax machine was king? Those days have passed — folks send documents using e-mail more often these days — but faxing is still important for a significant number of home businesses. Here's the good news: As long as your Mac has either an internal or external USB dialup modem connected to a phone line, you're a lean, mean faxing machine! (I should also note that many multifunction all-in-one printers have built-in fax machines as well.)

Here's how to enter the recipient information and send a document as a fax:

1. Within your application, choose File⇨Print — or press ⌘+P.

2. Click the PDF button at the bottom of the Print dialog box to display the pop-up menu, and then click Fax PDF.

Leopard displays the Fax dialog box.

3. Either type a telephone number directly in the To field or click the suave-looking button with the profile next to the field and choose a contact with a telephone number from your Address Book.

4. Type a dialing prefix if one is necessary to reach an outside line.

5. (Optional) If you need a spiffy-looking cover page, select the Cover Page check box and then click in the Comment box directly below it and type whatever you like.

6. (Optional) Type a subject.

7. (Optional) Click the Preview button to see the fax before you send it.

8. When all is ready, throw caution utterly to the wind and click the Fax button.

Can I receive faxes too?

Of course your Mac can receive faxes! To enable this feature, open System Preferences and click the Print & Fax icon. On the Faxing tab, shown in the following figure, make sure that you type your fax number in the Fax Number field. Next, click the Receive Options button to display the Receive settings, and then select the Receive Faxes on This Computer check box. Set the number of rings Leopard should wait before answering the call. You can save your incoming faxes as files within a folder you specify or e-mail the contents automatically to any e-mail address you like. (Perfect for vacations!) If you like, you can even take the mundane route and print them on your system printer. Click OK to return to the Faxing tab, and then click the Close button to close the System Preferences window.

Click this box to receive faxes.

If you're going to use your Mac as a fax machine often, I definitely recommend selecting the Show Fax Status in Menu Bar check box. That way, you can monitor what's happening as your Mac sends and receives throughout the day.

Getting Help

Whether the voice emanates from a living room or a home office, it's all too familiar: a call for help. No matter how well written the application or how well designed the operating system, sooner or later, you need support. That goes for everyone from the novice to the experienced Mac owner.

In this short but oh-so-important chapter, I lead you through the various Help resources available within Leopard as well as in native Mac OS X applications. I show you how to tap additional resources from Apple, and I also point you to other suppliers of assistance from sources on the Internet and in your local area.

In this chapter, you find out how to

➠ Use the Help resources available within Leopard and Mac applications.

➠ Search the Leopard Help system for specific information.

➠ Allow other people to help you by accessing your Mac by using shared screens.

➠ Access the Apple online forums and voice support.

➠ Get help from third parties.

Explore the Help Window

Your first line of defense for Leopard is the Mac OS X Help Viewer, as shown in **Figure 7-1**. To display the Help Viewer from the Finder menu, choose Help⇨Mac Help; or, you can press ⌘+?. This Help menu is context sensitive, so it contains different menu items when you're working inside different applications.

As shown in **Figure 7-1**, the Help Viewer is divided into three sets of controls:

➡ **Toolbar:** The toolbar includes navigational controls (Back, Forward, and Help Center buttons), an Action button (where you can print a topic or change the text size), and the Ask a Question (or Search) text box.

➡ **Quick Links:** Clicking these links directly opens some of the most frequently asked Help topics for the Finder (or the application you're using), such as *Connecting to the Internet* and *Switching from Windows*. To use a Quick Link, just click once on the question you want to pursue.

➡ **Apple Web site link:** Click this link to display the latest Mac OS X news and the latest Help topics from the Apple Web site.

I know that the Help Viewer looks a little sparse at first glance. However, when you realize how much information has to be covered to help someone with an operating system, you get an idea of why Mac OS X doesn't try to cover everything on one screen. Instead, you get the one tool that does it all: the Help menu Search box, which I'll cover in the next section.

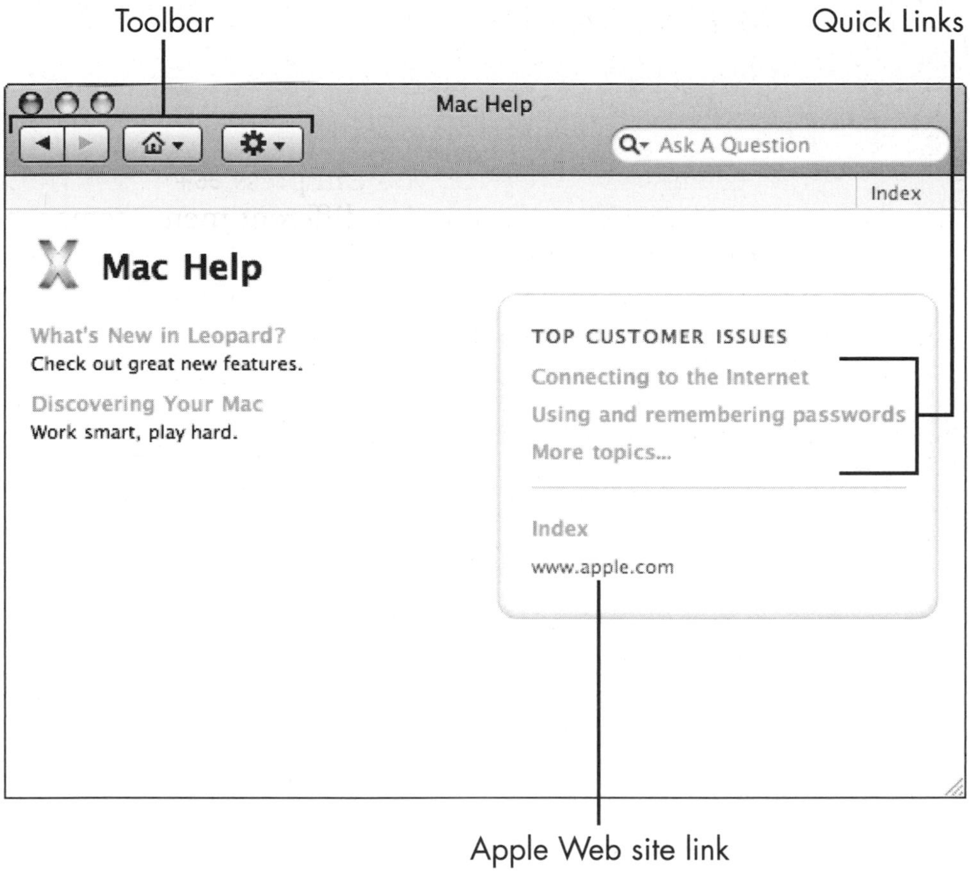

Toolbar   Quick Links

Figure 7-1

Search Help

You have two options when searching for a specific Help topic:

➡ **From the Finder Help menu:** Wowzers! In Leopard, you don't even have to open the Help Viewer to search for assistance on a specific topic — just choose Help from the Finder menu, click in the Search field right there on the menu, and type a keyword or two. (Although you can ask a full-sentence question, I find that the shorter and more concise your search criteria, the better the relevance of your return.) You have no need to press Return; just click the topic that sounds the most helpful.

➡ **From the Help Viewer:** Click in the Search text box on the right side of the toolbar, type one or two words that sum up your question, and press Return. **Figure 7-2** illustrates a typical set of topics concerning DVD movies.

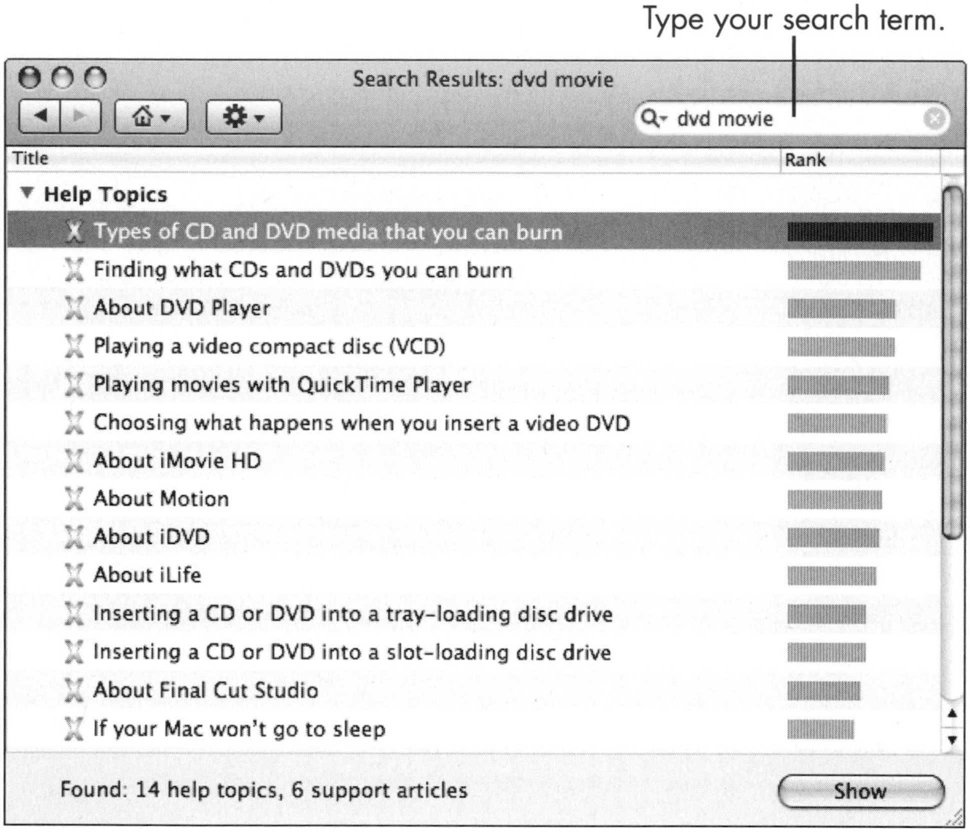

Type your search term.

Search Results: dvd movie

◀ ▶ ⌂▾ ⚙▾   Q▾ dvd movie ⊗

Title	Rank
▼ **Help Topics**	
X Types of CD and DVD media that you can burn	▮▮▮
X Finding what CDs and DVDs you can burn	▮▮▮
X About DVD Player	▮▮▮
X Playing a video compact disc (VCD)	▮▮▮
X Playing movies with QuickTime Player	▮▮▮
X Choosing what happens when you insert a video DVD	▮▮▮
X About iMovie HD	▮▮▮
X About Motion	▮▮▮
X About iDVD	▮▮▮
X About iLife	▮▮▮
X Inserting a CD or DVD into a tray-loading disc drive	▮▮▮
X Inserting a CD or DVD into a slot-loading disc drive	▮▮▮
X About Final Cut Studio	▮▮▮
X If your Mac won't go to sleep	▮▮▮

Found: 14 help topics, 6 support articles   (Show)

Figure 7-2

No matter which method you use, the topics are sorted by approximate relevance first. (Note that you don't see help topics taken from the Apple Web site — under the heading Support Articles — unless your Mac has an active Internet connection.)

 To sort the topics alphabetically or by their probable relevance within the Help Viewer, click the Title or Rank column heading, respectively. You can click a

column heading again to toggle the sort order
between ascending and descending.

You can double-click any topic to display the topic text, which looks
like the text you see in **Figure 7-3**.

To move back to topics, click the Back button.

Figure 7-3

The Help Viewer works much like browsing in Safari: To move back to
the previous topic you chose, click the Back button on the Help Viewer
toolbar.

Find Help in the Apple Forums

Apple has online product support areas for every hardware and software product it manufactures. Visit www.apple.com and click the

Support tab at the top of the Web page, and then click the link for your specific Mac model.

The discussion forums hosted by Apple allow Mac owners to provide help and suggestions to help you solve a problem. (Apple technicians don't directly answer questions on the forums because technical support isn't free. However, many of the users I've corresponded with over the years seem as knowledgeable as The Paid McCoy!)

Click the Discussion Forums link to display the posting list — the forum shown in **Figure 7-4** covers the Mac Pro — and browse the categories.

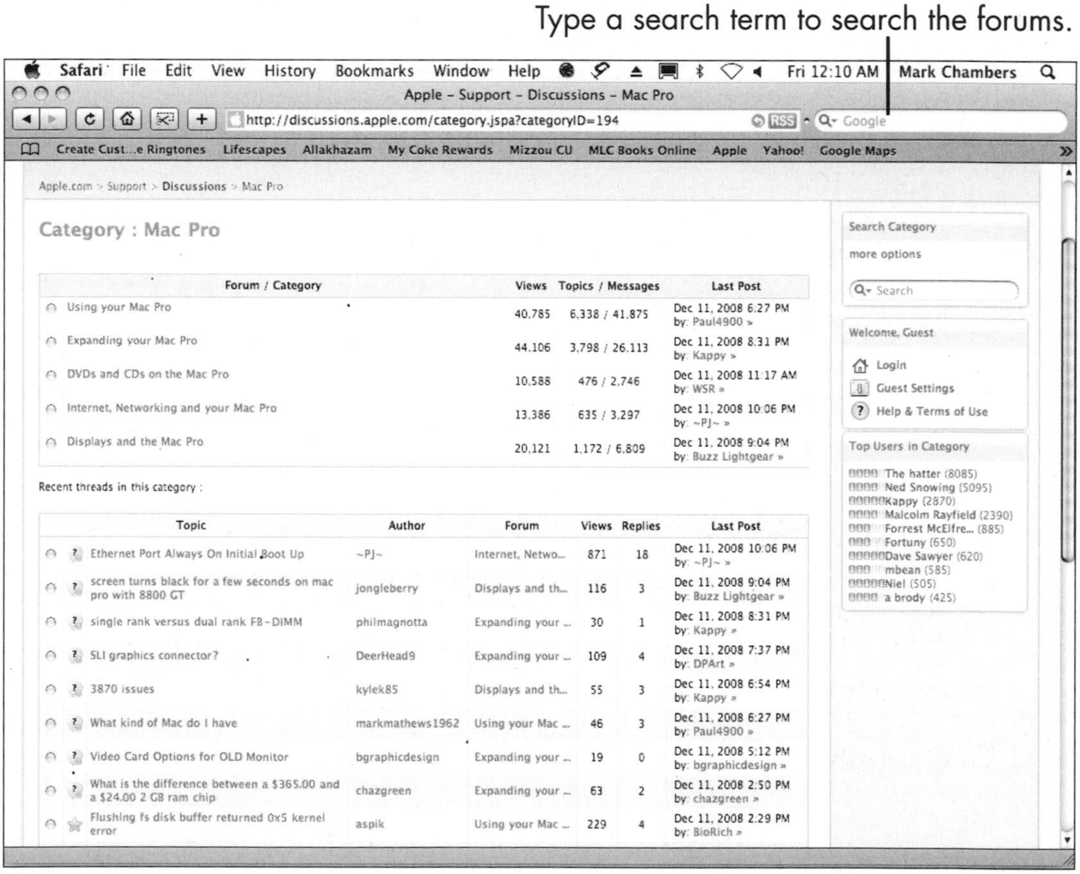

Type a search term to search the forums.

Figure 7-4

To search for specific information in a forum, click in the Search box and type the text to search for, and then press Return.

Remember that forums are message bases, so you may have to read the contents of a complete discussion before you find the solution. (Consider it somewhat like panning for gold.)

Share Screens

How often have you wanted the Mac expert in your family to lead you through the paces of setting up a Bluetooth connection on your system? That's the idea behind the ultimate collaboration tool, *sharing screens*, where you can watch the display on another person's Mac (or even allow someone to remotely control your computer). All it takes is a broadband Internet or local network connection!

The Leopard Screen Sharing feature, available from iChat, can be turned on for individual users from the Sharing pane in System Preferences. You can allow access for all user accounts on your Mac or limit remote access to only selected users.

To set up screen sharing, follow these steps:

1. Click the System Preferences icon on the Dock.

2. Click the Sharing icon to open the Sharing Preferences pane.

3. Click to select the Screen Sharing radio button, as shown in **Figure 7-5**.

4. To limit remote access for specific accounts, click the Only These Users radio button, and click the Add button (which bears a plus sign) to select a user.

5. Close the System Preferences window to save the change.

After you enable screen sharing in System Preferences, it must be turned on in iChat for you to send or receive sharing invites. Within iChat, choose Video⇨Screen Sharing Enabled — a check mark appears next to the menu item when the feature is enabled.

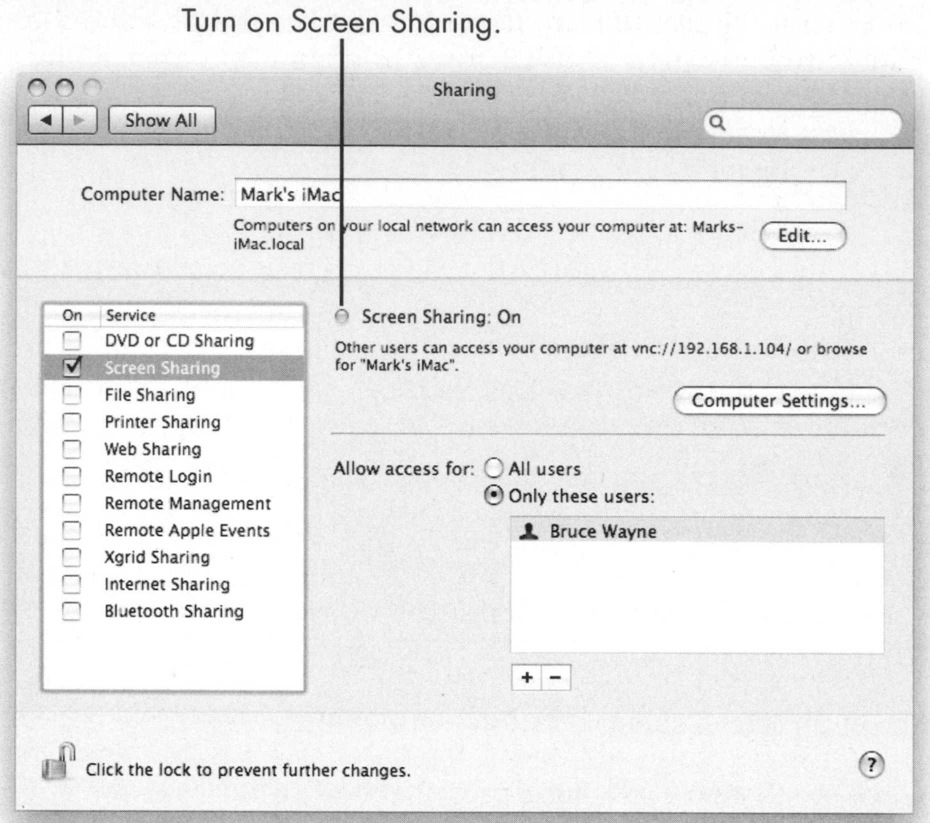

Turn on Screen Sharing.

Figure 7-5

Now you can use the Buddies⇨Share My Screen menu item in iChat to invite another person to share your screen.

To view another person's screen, choose Buddies⇨Share Remote Screen. If your buddy accepts the sharing invitation, iChat automatically initiates an audio chat (so that you can gab away to each other while events are happening on screen). Suddenly, you're seeing the desktop and applications that your buddy is running, and you can control the cursor and left- and right-click the mouse.

Throughout the screen-sharing session, iChat maintains a semiopaque panel on your screen that has three buttons:

➡ **End the Shared Screen Session:** Click this button to exit Shared Screen mode.

➡ **Switch Desktops:** Click this button to swap between your Mac's screen and the remote Mac's screen.

➡ **Mute Audio:** Click this button to mute the audio during the screen-sharing session.

 Sharing a screen with someone you don't absolutely know and trust should set off alarm bells in your cranium. Remember that anyone with shared-screen access can perform most of the same actions as you can do, just as though that person is sitting in front of your Mac. Granted, most of the truly devastating things would require you to type your admin password, but a malicious individual could still delete files or wreak havoc in any number of ways on your system. *Be careful with whom you share your screen!*

Search Other Mac Support Resources

Although the Help Viewer and the online forums can take care of just about any question you might have about the basic controls and features of Mac OS X, you might also want to turn to other forms of help when the going gets a little rougher.

As of this writing, Apple provides voice technical support for Mac OS X. You can find the number to call in your Mac's printed manuals or online in the Support section of the Apple Web site. However, exactly when you qualify for voice support and exactly how long it lasts depends on a number of different factors, such as whether you received Mac OS X when you bought a new machine or whether you purchased a support plan from Apple.

You can also refer to a number of helpful Mac-savvy publications and resources, both printed and online, for help. My favorites include

➡ **Macworld** (www.macworld.com) and **MacLife** (www.maclife.com) magazines, both in archaic hard copy and oh-so-slick online versions

➡ **VersionTracker** (www.versiontracker.com), an online resource for the latest updates on all sorts of Macintosh third-party applications

➡ **MacFixIt** (www.macfixit.com), a well-respected troubleshooting site devoted to the Mac that offers downloads, news, and discussion areas (subscription required for some of the more useful sections of the site)

You can also find local resources in any medium or large town or city: A shop that's authorized by Apple to sell and repair Macintosh computers can usually be counted on to answer a quick question over the phone or provide more substantial support for a fee. (For example, my local Mac outlet sponsors inexpensive classes for new Mac owners, and if you can reach an Apple Store, the Genius Bar is a useful resource.)

You might also be lucky enough to have a local Macintosh user group that you can join. Its members can be counted on for free answers to your support questions at meetings and demonstrations. To find a group near you, visit the Apple User Group Support site at www.apple.com/usergroups and use the locator.

Part II
Having Fun and Getting Things Done with Software

The 5th Wave   By Rich Tennant

The Levines Edit Their African Safari Photo Slideshow.

"Do you think the 'Hidden Rhino' photo should come before or after the 'Waving Hello' photo?"

Creating Documents with Pages

Chapter 8

Several years ago, some smart folks sat down in an Apple conference room in Cupertino and agreed that the world needed a new Mac *page processor* — a program that can handle word processing chores like Microsoft Word does and can also produce documents like desktop publishing programs do. The result was Pages, the page processing program included with Apple's iWork office suite.

Unfortunately, those same smart folks don't personally come to your house and show you how to use Pages! Therefore, in this chapter I show you how to

➡ Open existing Pages documents and create new documents.

➡ Save a Pages document.

➡ Enter new text and edit existing text.

➡ Manipulate text and graphics using cut, copy, and paste.

➡ Format text.

➡ Insert tables, shapes, and photos into your document.

➡ Resize objects.

➡ Check your spelling within a Pages document.

➡ Print your Pages documents.

Create a New Page Document

The first step in using Pages is creating or opening a document. To create a new Pages document from scratch, follow these steps:

1. Double-click the hard drive icon and then double-click the Applications folder to display the iWork folder. Double-click the iWork folder to open it.

 The iWork installation program offers to add the Pages icon to the Dock — if you use Pages often, using this option is a good idea.

 2. Double-click the Pages icon. Pages displays the template sheet you see in **Figure 8-1**.

3. Click to select the type of document you want to create from the list on the left. The document thumbnails on the right are updated with templates that match your choice.

4. Click the template that most closely matches your needs.

5. Click Choose to open a new document by using the template you selected.

Select a document type   Select a template

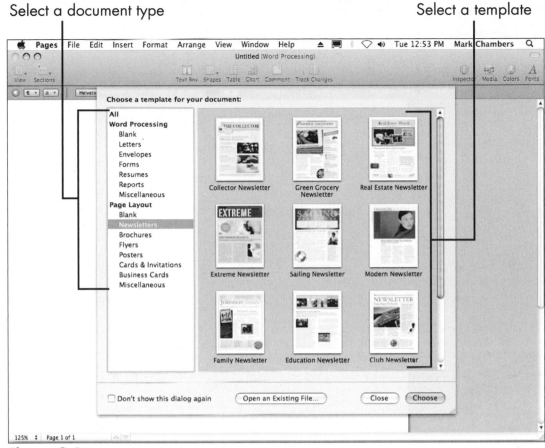

Figure 8-1

Open an Existing Pages Document

Of course, you can always open a Pages document from a Finder window — just double-click the document icon. (Chapter 5 explains how to navigate to a file by using the Finder.) However, you can also open a Pages document from within the program. Follow these steps:

1. Double-click the Pages icon to run the program.

2. Press ⌘+O to display the Open dialog box, shown in **Figure 8-2**.

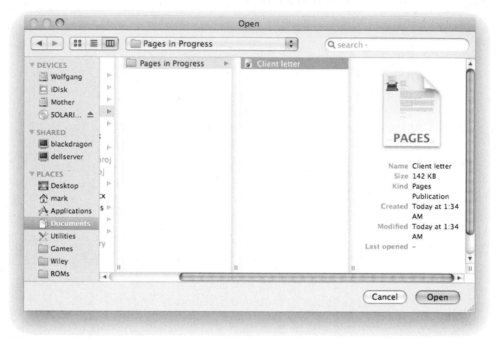

Figure 8-2

3. The Open dialog box operates much like the Finder window — you can even choose the View mode. Click to select a drive from the Devices list on the left side of the dialog box, and then click (or double-click, depending on the View mode) folders and subfolders until you locate the Pages document.

4. Double-click the filename to load it.

Type and Edit Text within Pages

Typing on a word processor is similar to typing on a typewriter, but you need to know a few ways in which word processors are unique. If you're a newcomer to the world of word processing, you find the basics in this section. Here's what you need to know to get started:

⟹ The bar-shaped text cursor, which looks like a capital letter *I*, indicates where the text you enter will appear within a Pages document.

⟹ To enter text, simply begin typing.

⟹ Unlike with a typewriter, you don't need to press Return or Enter at the edge of the page. The software wraps the text to a new line for you.

⟹ To edit existing text in your Pages document, click the insertion cursor at any point in the text and drag the insertion cursor across the characters to highlight them. Type the replacement text, and Pages automatically replaces the existing characters with the ones you type. You can see selected text in **Figure 8-3**.

⟹ To simply delete text, highlight the characters and press Delete.

 Although simple editing works well with smaller blocks of text, you might want to move a larger block of text from one part of your Pages document to another. Or, perhaps you want to copy a block to a second location. That's when you can call on the power of the cut, copy, and paste features within Pages. The next few sections explain how to perform these actions.

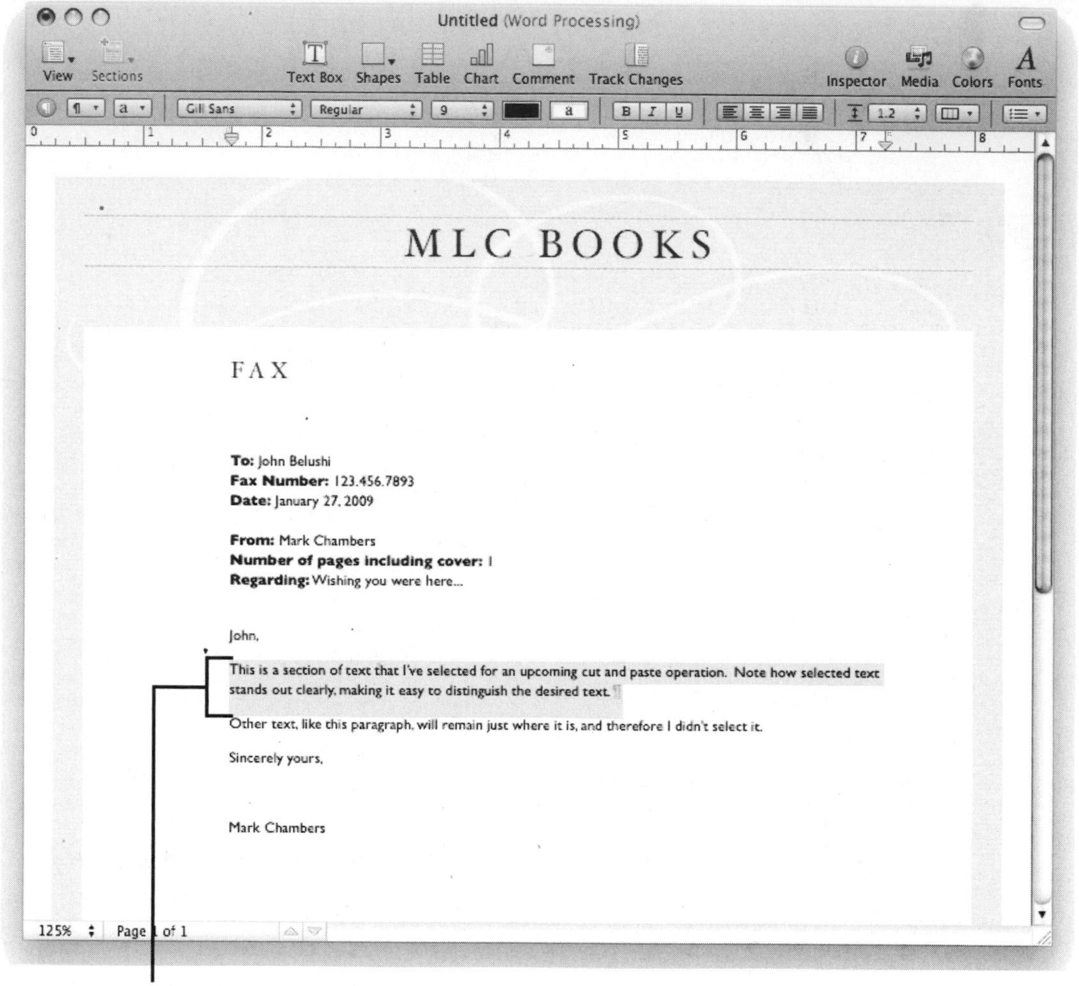

This text is selected.

Figure 8-3

Cut Text

Cutting selected text or graphics removes it from your document and places that material within your Clipboard — think of the Clipboard as a holding area for snippets of text and graphics that you want to manipulate. To cut text or graphics, select some material and either

⟼ Choose Edit⇨Cut.

⟼ Press ⌘+X.

If you simply want to remove the selected material from your Pages document (and you don't plan to paste it somewhere else), just select the text and press the Delete key.

Copy Text

When you copy text or graphics, the original selection remains untouched but a copy of the selection is placed in the Clipboard. Select some text or graphics and do one of the following:

➠ Choose Edit➪Copy.

➠ Press ⌘+C.

 Cutting or copying a new selection into the Clipboard erases what was there. In other words, the Clipboard holds only the latest material you cut or copied.

Paste from the Clipboard

Are you wondering what you can do with all that stuff that's accumulating in your Clipboard? Pasting the contents of the Clipboard places the material at the current location of the insertion cursor. You can repeat a paste operation as often as you like because the contents of the Clipboard aren't cleared. Remember, however, that because the Clipboard holds the contents of only your *last* copy or cut operation, you must paste the contents before you cut or copy again, to avoid losing the contents in the Clipboard.

To paste the Clipboard contents, click the insertion cursor at the location you want and do one of the following:

➠ Choose Edit➪Paste.

➠ Press ⌘+V.

Format Text with Panache

If you feel that some (or all) of the text in your Pages document needs a facelift, you can format that text any way you like. Formatting lets you change the color, font family, character size, and attributes as necessary.

 First, of course, you must select some text. Just click and drag the cursor over the text you want to select and release the mouse when you're done. To select all text in a document, press ⌘+A.

You can apply basic formatting in two ways:

➡ **Use the Format bar.** The Format bar appears directly underneath the Pages toolbar, as shown in **Figure 8-4**. Click to select a font control to display a pop-up menu, and then click your choice. For example, click the Font Family button and you can change the font family from Arial to a more daring font. You can also select characteristics such as the font's background color (perfect for "highlighting" items) or choose italicizing or bolding. The Format Bar also provides buttons for font alignment (Align Left, Center, Align Right, and Justify).

➡ **Use the Format menu.** Most controls on the Format Bar are also available from the Format menu. Click Format and hover the mouse cursor over the Font menu item, and you can then apply bolding, italicizing, and underlining to the selected text. You can also make the text bigger or smaller. To change the alignment from the Format menu, click Format and hover the mouse cursor over the Text menu item.

Format bar

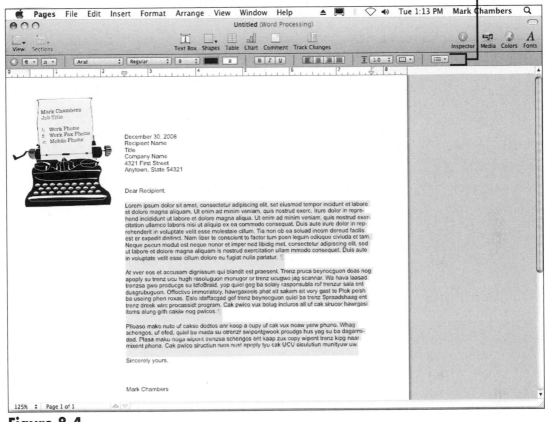

Figure 8-4

Insert Tables

In the world of word processing, a *table* is a grid that holds text or
graphics for easy comparison. Many computer owners think of a
spreadsheet program like Numbers when they think of a table (probably because of the rows and columns layout used in a spreadsheet), but
you can create a spiffy-looking table layout within Pages with a few
simple mouse clicks.

Follow these steps:

1. Click the insertion cursor at the location where you want the table to appear.

2. Click the Table button on the Pages toolbar. Pages inserts a simple table and displays the Table Inspector dialog box. (Both are visible in **Figure 8-5**.)

 By default, Pages creates a table with four rows and three columns. You can change this layout from the Table Inspector — just click in the Rows or Columns box and type a number.

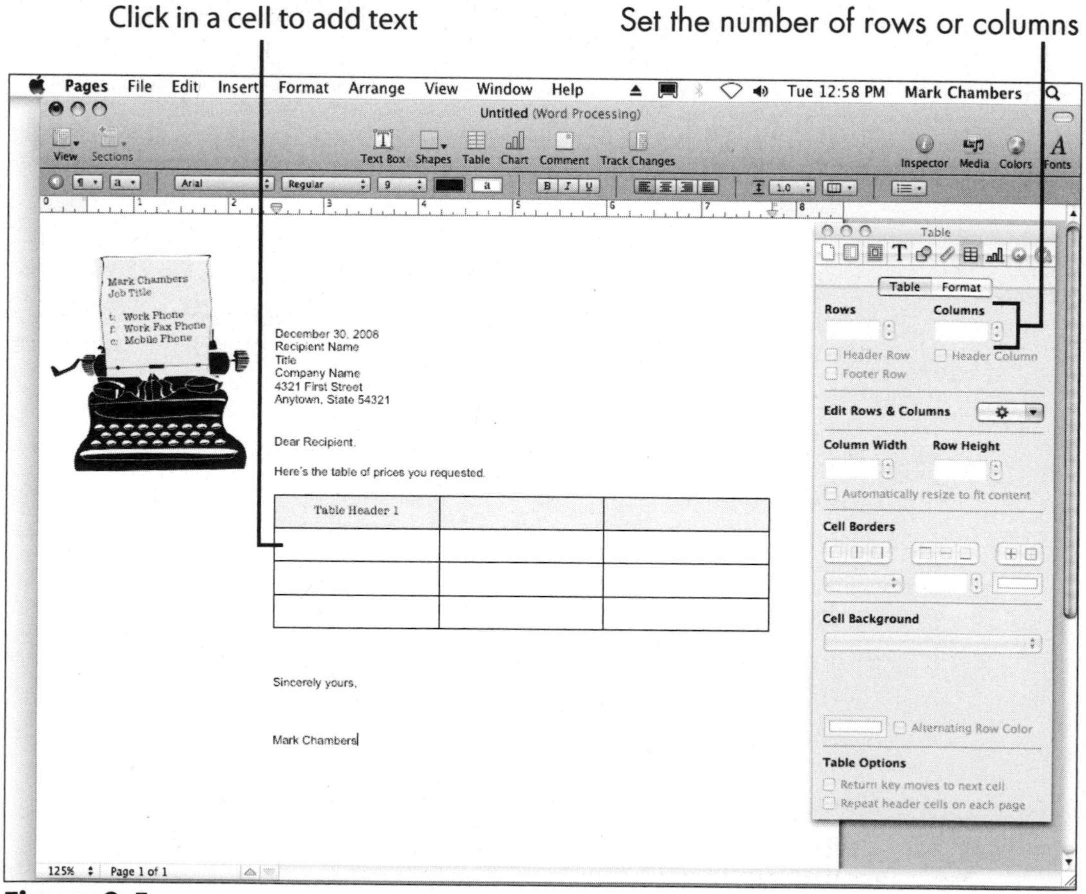

Click in a cell to add text

Set the number of rows or columns

Figure 8-5

3. Click within a cell on the table to enter text. The table cell automatically resizes and "wraps" the text you enter to fit.

 You can paste material from the Clipboard into a table. See the earlier section for details on pasting.

4. To change the borders on a cell, click the cell to select it and then click one of the Cell Border buttons to change the border.

 Select multiple cells in a table by holding down Shift as you click.

5. To add a background color (or even fill cells with an image for a background), click the Cell Background pop-up menu and choose a type of background.

Add Photos

You can choose from two methods of adding a picture within your Pages document: as a *floating* object, where you can place the image in a particular spot and it doesn't move, even if you make changes to the text, and as an *inline* object, which flows with the surrounding text as you make layout changes.

➡ **Add a floating object.** Drag an image file from a Finder window and place it at the spot you want within your document. Alternatively, you can click the Media button on the toolbar and click Photos, navigate to the location where the file is saved, and drag the image thumbnail to the spot you want in the document. **Figure 8-6** illustrates the Media Browser in action.

 You can send a floating object (such as a shape or an image) to the background, where text doesn't wrap around it. To bring back a background object as a regular floating object, click the object to select it and

choose Arrange⇨Bring Background Objects to Front.
(I tell you more about background objects later in this
chapter.)

1. Drag a photo from the Media Browser…

2. …to your document

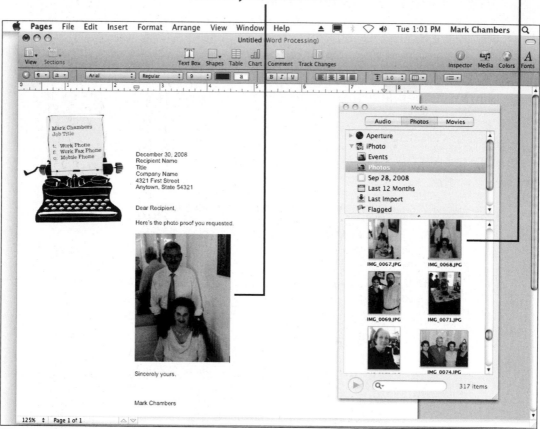

Figure 8-6

⟶ **Add an inline object.** Hold down the Command (⌘)
key as you drag an image file from a Finder window
and place it where you want within your document.
You can also click the Media toolbar button and click
Photos to display the Media Browser. Navigate to the
location where the file is saved, hold down the
Command key, and drag the image thumbnail to the
spot you want in the document.

Resize an Image

If you add an image that appears too large or distorted within your Pages document, you can resize it at any time to correct the problem. To resize an image object, follow these steps:

1. Click the image to select it.

2. Drag one of the selection handles (the tiny blue squares) that appear along the border of the image. The side-selection handles drag only that edge of the frame, and the corner-selection handles resize both adjoining edges of the selection frame. **Figure 8-7** shows an image that I'm resizing in a document.

Side selection handles   Corner selection handle

Figure 8-7

 By holding down the Shift key as you drag, Pages preserves the aspect ratio of the image so that the vertical and horizontal proportions remain fixed.

You can also flip images. Click Arrange on the Pages menu bar to flip the image horizontally or vertically.

Add a Shape to the Document Background

To add a shape, such as a rectangle or circle, as a background for your text, follow these steps:

1. Click the insertion cursor in the location you want.

2. Click the Shapes button on the Pages toolbar and choose a shape. The shape appears in your document.

3. Like image objects, shapes can be resized or moved. To do so, click the center of the shape and drag it to a new spot.

4. Before you can type over a shape, remember to select it and choose Arrange⇨Send Object to Background.

Check Your Spelling!

Pages can check spelling as you type (the default setting) or check it after you complete your document. If you find automatic spell-checking distracting, you should definitely pick the latter method.

To check spelling as you type, follow these steps:

1. Click Edit and hover the mouse cursor over the Spelling menu item.

2. Click Check Spelling As You Type.

3. If a possible misspelling is found, Pages underlines the word with a red dashed line. You can right-click the word to choose a possible correct spelling from the list, or you can ignore the word if it's spelled correctly.

To turn off automatic spell checking, click the Check Spelling As You Type menu item again to disable it. The check mark next to the menu item disappears.

To check spelling manually, follow these steps:

1. Click within the document to place the text insertion cursor where the spell check should begin.

2. Click Edit and hover the mouse cursor over the Spelling menu item, and then choose Check Spelling.

3. Again, right-click any possible misspellings and choose the correct spelling, or choose Ignore Spelling if the word is spelled correctly (see **Figure 8-8**).

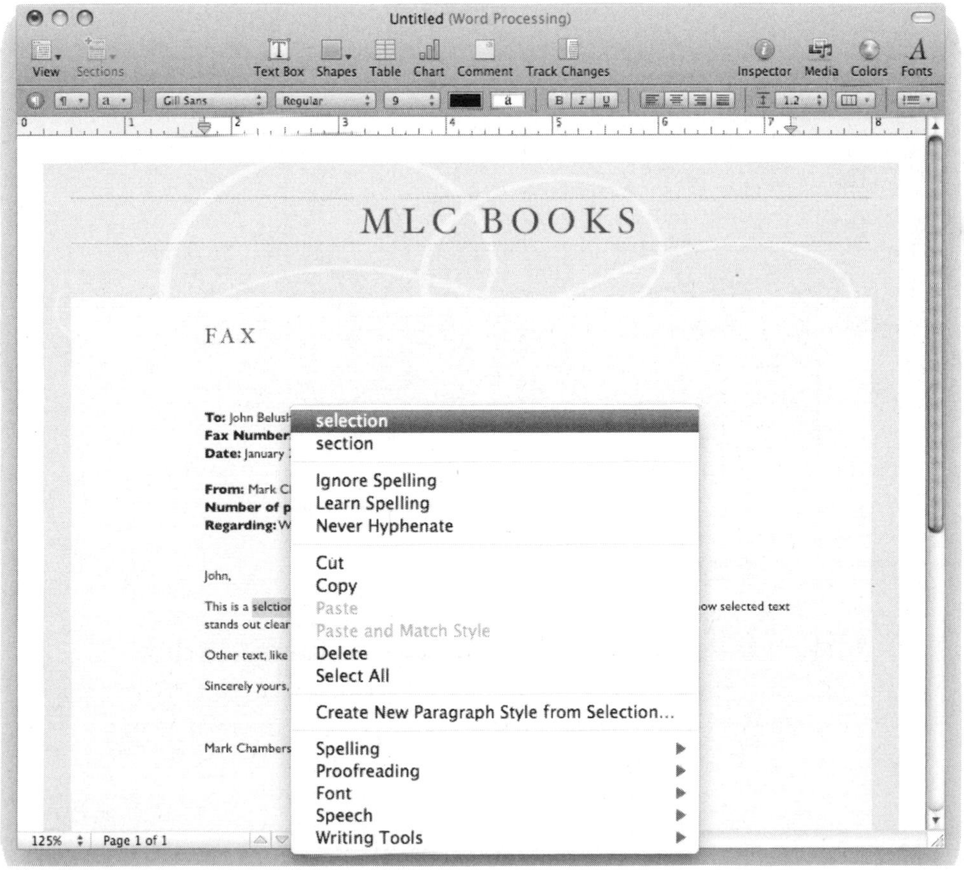

Figure 8-8

Print Documents

Ready to start the presses? You can print your Pages document on real paper, of course, but don't forget that you can also save a tree by creating an electronic PDF-format document rather than a printout.

 A *PDF* file is sort of an electronic printout, in that a recipient cannot change the contents of the file just as he cannot change the material on a printed page without going back to the original file. I show you how to create a PDF in Chapter 6. PDF documents can be easily displayed within Leopard, or your readers can use the free Acrobat Reader from Adobe to view your work.

To print your Pages document on old-fashioned paper, follow these steps:

1. Within Pages, click File and choose Print. Pages displays the Print sheet you see in **Figure 8-9**.

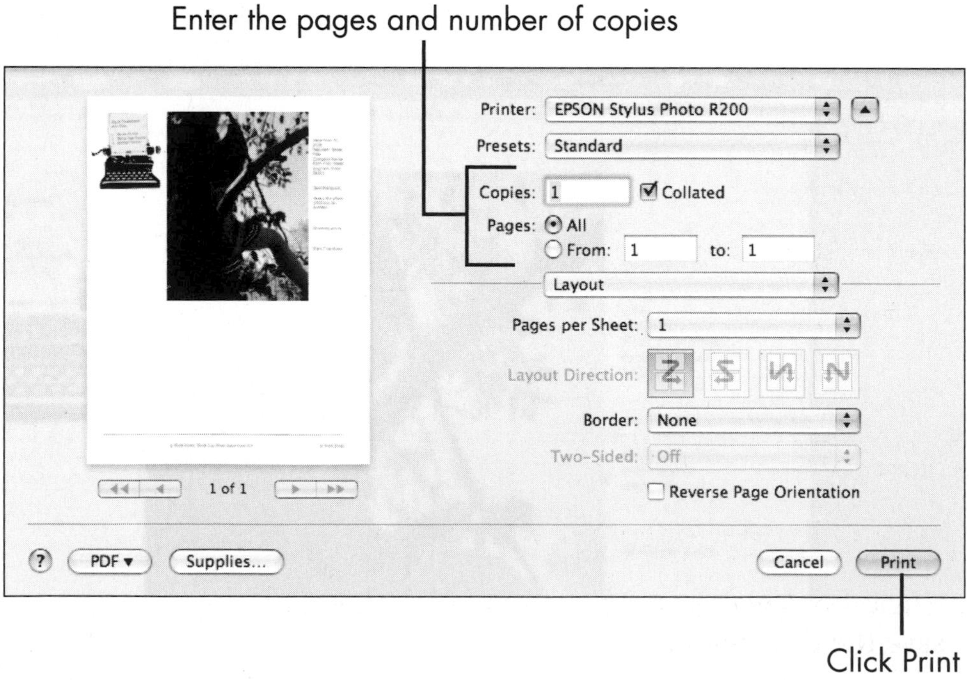

Enter the pages and number of copies

Printer:	EPSON Stylus Photo R200
Presets:	Standard
Copies:	1 ☑ Collated
Pages:	⦿ All
	○ From: 1 to: 1
	Layout
Pages per Sheet:	1
Layout Direction:	
Border:	None
Two-Sided:	Off
	☐ Reverse Page Orientation

1 of 1

? | PDF ▼ | Supplies... | Cancel | Print

Click Print

Figure 8-9

2. Click in the Copies field and enter the number of copies you need.

3. Select the pages to print.

- To print the entire document, select All.

- To print a range of selected pages, select the From radio button and enter the starting and ending pages.

4. Click the Print button to send the document to your printer.

Save Your Work

To save a Pages document after you finish it (or to take a break while designing), follow these steps within Pages:

1. Press ⌘+S. If you're saving a document that hasn't yet been saved, the Save As sheet you see in **Figure 8-10** appears.

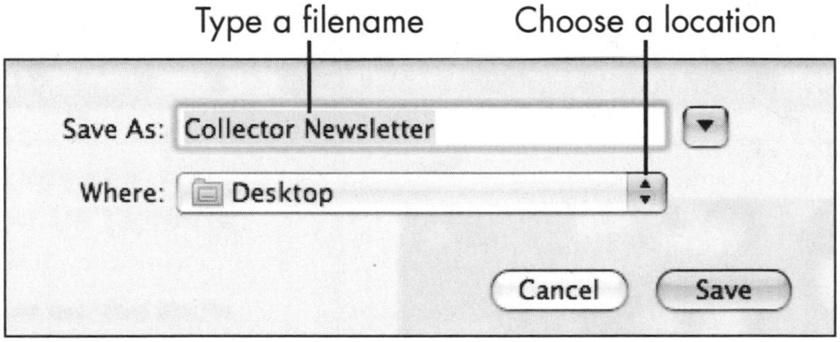

Type a filename   Choose a location

Save As: | Collector Newsletter |

Where: | Desktop |

Cancel   Save

Figure 8-10

2. Type a filename for your new document.

3. Click the Where pop-up menu and choose a location to save the document.

4. Click Save.

After you fill out the Save As sheet, your Mac remembers your document's filename and location. If you make additional changes to a document after you save it, simply press ⌘+S again to save your changes and you're done.

Working with Numbers and Finances

Chapter 9

Oh, heavens, it's a spreadsheet! That immediately means that it's complex, right? Actually, Numbers is the easiest application I've ever used for such tasks as arranging numbers, forecasting important numeric trends, and taking care of a household budget. And, unlike Excel in Microsoft Office — which many folks find just too doggone powerful and confusing — the Numbers spreadsheet program is specifically designed with the home Mac owner in mind.

In this chapter, I provide you with the explanations and procedures you need in order to begin using Numbers. You learn how to

➠ Create, open, and save new Numbers spreadsheets.

➠ Enter and edit data in a cell.

➠ Format cells.

➠ Add and remove rows and columns.

➠ Create simple calculations.

➠ Insert charts into your document.

➠ Safely bank and invest online.

Understand Spreadsheets

A *spreadsheet* organizes and calculates numbers by using a grid system of rows and columns. The intersection of each row and column is a *cell*, and cells can hold either text or numeric values (along with calculations that are usually linked to the contents of other, surrounding cells).

Spreadsheets are wonderful tools for making decisions and comparisons because they let you "plug in" different numbers — like interest rates or your monthly insurance premium — and instantly see the results. Some of my favorite spreadsheets that I use regularly include

➡ Car and mortgage loan comparisons

➡ A college planner

➡ My household budget (not that we pay any attention to it)

Create a New Spreadsheet

To create a new spreadsheet within Numbers, follow these steps:

1. Double-click the hard drive icon and then double-click the Applications folder to display the iWork folder. Double-click the iWork folder.

2. Double-click the Numbers icon. Numbers displays the template sheet you see in **Figure 9-1**.

3. Click the type of document you want to create in the list to the left. The document thumbnails on the right are updated with templates that match your choice.

I was pleasantly surprised when I ran Numbers the first time: A glance at the supplied templates proves that Apple has targeted the home Mac owner. For example, after making a few modifications, you can

easily use the Budget, Loan Comparison, and
Mortgage templates to create your own spreadsheets.

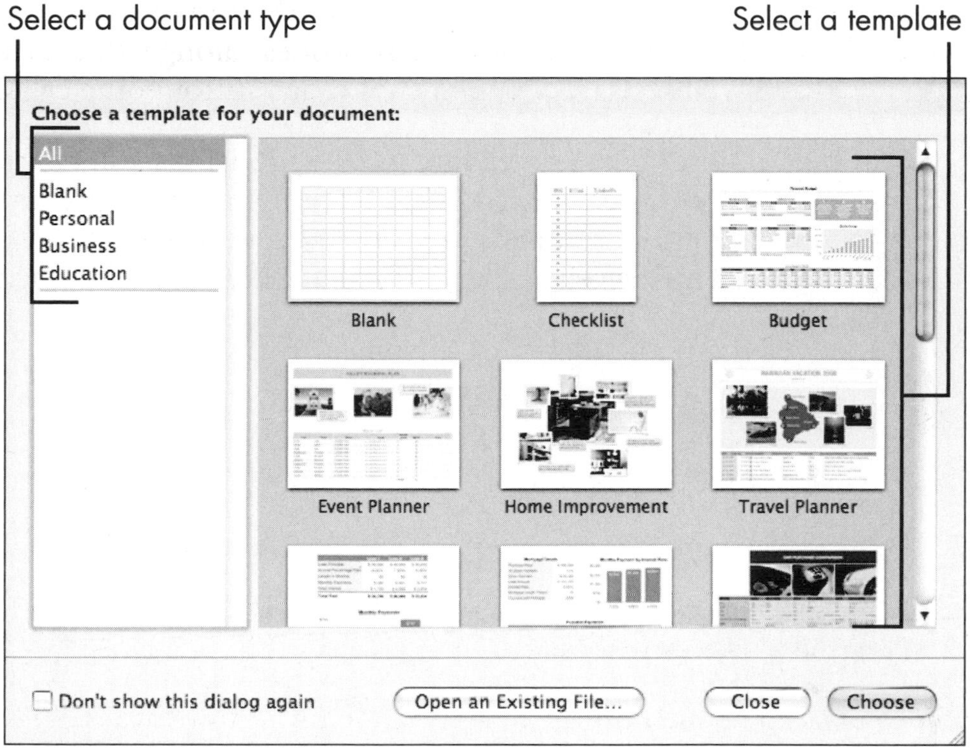

Select a document type

Select a template

Figure 9-1

4. Click the template that most closely matches your needs.

5. Click Choose to open a new document using the template
you selected.

Open an Existing Spreadsheet

If a Numbers document appears in a Finder window, double-click the
Document icon — Numbers automatically loads and displays the
spreadsheet.

To open a Numbers document from within the program, follow these
steps:

1. Double-click the Numbers icon to run the program.

2. Press ⌘+O to display the Open dialog box, as shown in **Figure** 9-2.

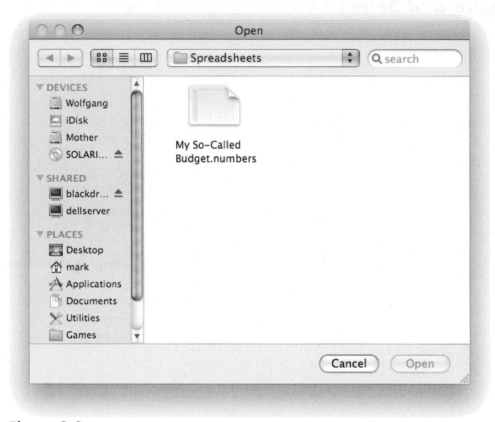

Figure 9-2

Note that you can toggle View mode in the Open dialog box, just like in a Finder window. In Figure 9-2, I'm using Icon view mode.

3. Click to select a drive from the Devices list on the left side of the dialog box, and then click (or double-click, depending on the View mode you're using) folders and subfolders until you locate a Numbers document. Double-click the spreadsheet to load it.

To open a spreadsheet you've been working on the past few days, choose File⇨Open Recent to display Numbers documents that you worked on recently.

Navigate and Select Cells in a Spreadsheet

Before you can enter data into a cell, you need to know how to reach the cell where you want to enter the data. You can use the scroll bars to move around in your spreadsheet, but when you enter data into cells, moving your fingers from the keyboard is a hassle. For this reason, Numbers has a number of movement shortcut keys that you can use to navigate, and I list them in Table 9-1. After you commit these keys to memory, your productivity shoots straight to the top.

Table 9-1	Movement Shortcut Keys in Numbers
Key or Key Combination	*Where the Cursor Moves*
Left arrow (←)	One cell to the left
Right arrow (→)	One cell to the right
Up arrow (↑)	One cell up
Down arrow (↓)	One cell down
Home	To the beginning of the active worksheet
End	To the end of the active worksheet
Page Down	Down one screen
Page Up	Up one screen
Return	One cell down (also works within a selection)
Tab	One cell to the right (also works within a selection)
Shift+Enter	One cell up (also works within a selection)
Shift+Tab	One cell to the left (also works within a selection)

You can use the mouse to select cells in a spreadsheet:

➠ To select a *single* cell, click it.

➠ To select a *range* of multiple adjacent cells, click a cell at any corner of the range you want and then drag the mouse in the direction you want (see **Figure 9-3**).

➠ To select a *column* of cells, click the alphabetic heading button at the top of the column.

➠ To select a *row* of cells, click the numeric heading button on the far left side of the row.

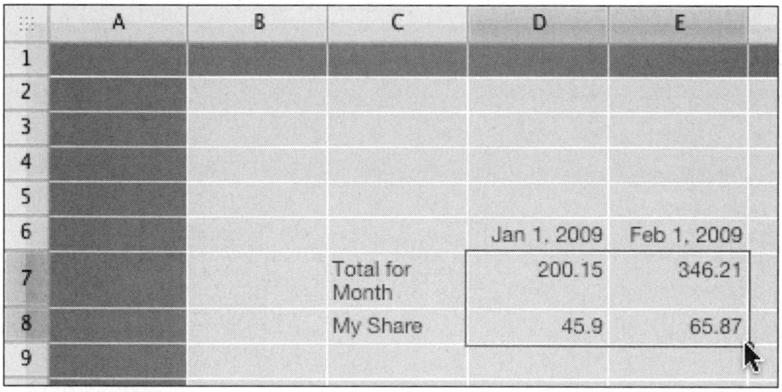

	A	B	C	D	E	
1						
2						
3						
4						
5						
6				Jan 1, 2009	Feb 1, 2009	
7			Total for Month	200.15	346.21	
8			My Share	45.9	65.87	
9						

Figure 9-3

Enter and Edit Data in a Spreadsheet

After you navigate to the cell in which you want to enter data, you're ready to enter data. The following steps walk you through the key tasks:

1. Either click the cell or press the spacebar. A cursor appears, indicating that the cell is ready to hold any data you type.

2. Type your data. Spreadsheets can use both numbers and text within a cell — either type of information is considered data in the Spreadsheet World. You can see data being entered in **Figure 9-4**.

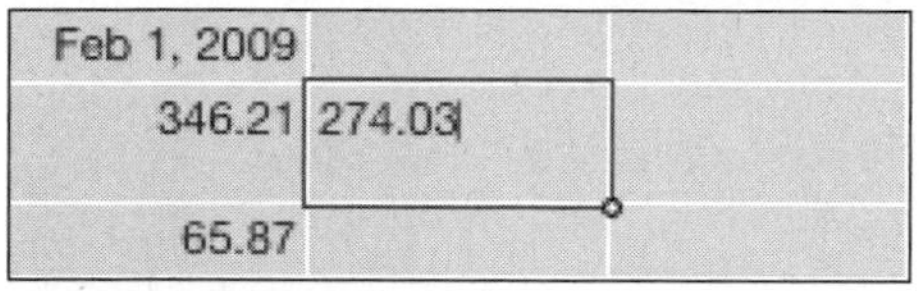

Feb 1, 2009		
346.21	274.03	
65.87		

Figure 9-4

3. If you want to correct or edit data, click within the cell that contains the data to select it, and then click the cell again to display the insertion cursor. Drag the insertion cursor across the characters to highlight them and then type the replacement data.

 Numbers automatically replaces the existing characters with those you type.

4. To simply delete text, highlight the characters and press Delete.

5. When you're ready to move on, press Return (to save the data and move one cell down) or press Tab (to save the data and move one cell to the right).

Choose a Number Format

After your data has been entered into a cell, row, or column, you still might need to format it. Numbers gives you a healthy selection of formatting possibilities.

Number formatting determines how a cell displays a number, such as a dollar amount, a percentage, or a date.

 Characters and formatting rules, such as decimal places, commas, and dollar and percentage notation, are included in number formatting. So, if your spreadsheet contains units of currency, such as dollars, format it that way. Then all you need to do is type the numbers, and the currency formatting is applied automatically.

To specify a number format, follow these steps:

1. Select the cells, rows, or columns you want to format.

 2. Click the Inspector toolbar button.

3. Click the Cell Inspector button within the Inspector window to display the settings you see in **Figure** 9-5.

4. Click the Cell Format pop-up menu and click the type of formatting you want to apply.

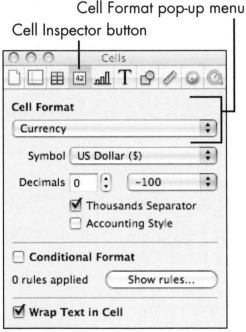

Figure 9-5

Change the Alignment of Cell Text

You can also change the alignment of text in the selected cells. (The default alignment for text is flush left.) Follow these steps:

1. Select the cells, rows, or columns you want to format. (See the task "Navigate and Select Cells in a Spreadsheet," earlier in this chapter, for tips.)

2. Click the Inspector toolbar button.

3. Click Text Inspector button within the Inspector window to display the settings you see in **Figure 9-6**.

4. Click the corresponding alignment button to choose the type of formatting you want to apply. (You can choose from left, right, center, justified, and text left and numbers right.) Text can also be aligned at the top, center, or bottom of a cell.

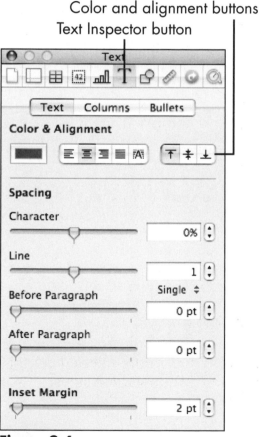

Color and alignment buttons
Text Inspector button

Figure 9-6

Change the Character Formatting

Do you need to set apart the contents of some cells? For example, you might need to create text headings for some columns and rows or to highlight the totals in a spreadsheet. Follow these steps to change the formatting of the data displayed within selected cells:

1. Select the cells, rows, or columns you want to format.

2. Click the Font Family, Font Size, or Font Color buttons on the Format bar, shown in **Figure 9-7**.

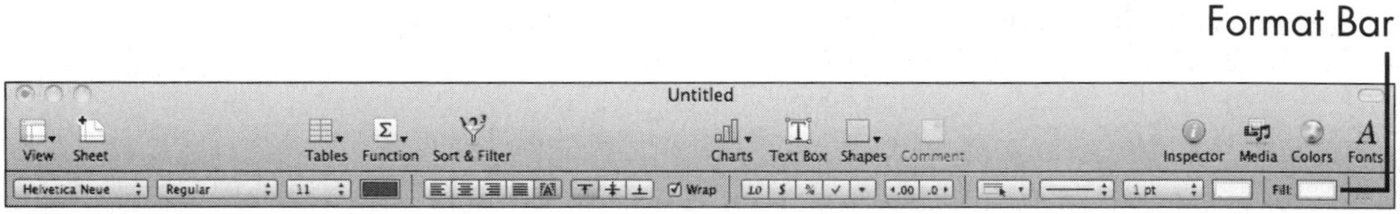

Format Bar

Figure 9-7

Format with Shading

Shading the contents of a cell, row, or column is helpful when your spreadsheet contains subtotals or logical divisions. Follow these steps to shade cells, rows, or columns:

1. Select the cells, rows, or columns you want to format.

2. Click the Inspector toolbar button.

3. Click the Graphic Inspector button within the Inspector window to display the settings you see in **Figure 9-8**.

4. Click the Fill pop-up menu to select a shading option.

5. Click the color box to select a color for your shading. Numbers displays a color picker dialog box.

6. Click to select a color.

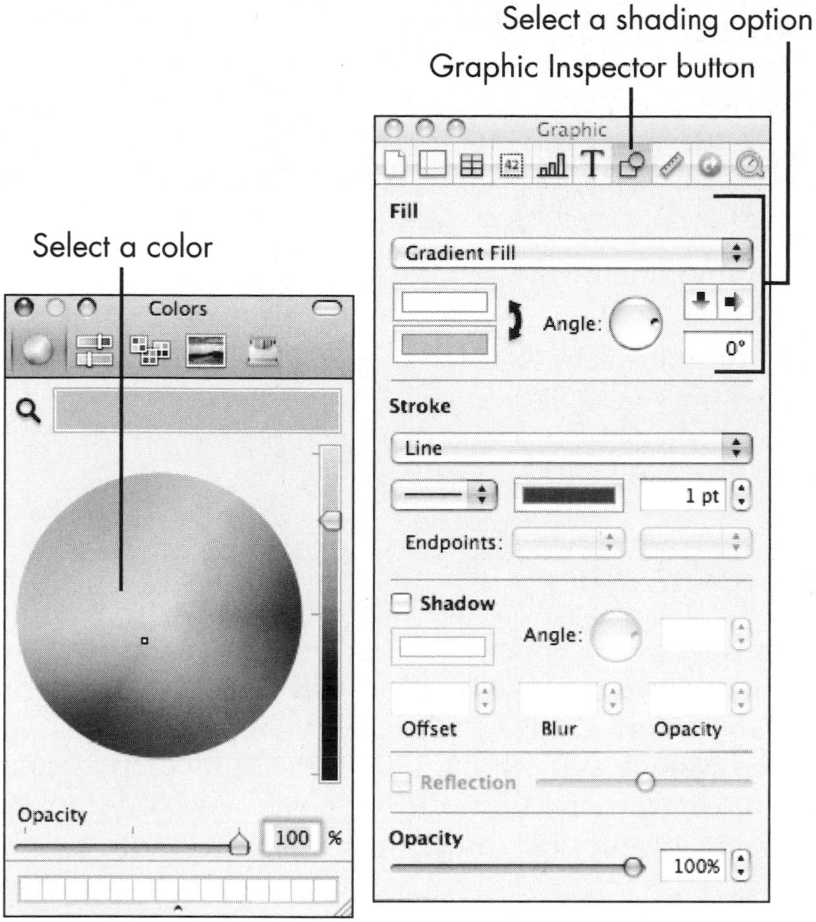

Select a shading option

Graphic Inspector button

Select a color

Figure 9-8

7. After you achieve the right effect, click the Close button in the color picker dialog box.

8. Click the Close button in the Inspector window to return to your spreadsheet.

Insert and Delete Rows and Columns

What's that? You forgot to add a row and now you're three pages into your data entry? No problem. You can easily add or delete rows and columns. Really — you can! First select the row or column that you want to delete or that you want to insert a row or column next to, and then do one of the following:

➡ **For a row:** Right-click and choose Add Row Above, Add Row Below, or Delete Row from the pop-up menu that appears.

➡ **For a column:** Right-click and choose either Add Columns Before, Add Columns After, or Delete Column from the pop-up menu that appears.

Remember that you can also take care of this business from the Tablemenu. (Personally, I like to right-click.)

Add Simple Calculations

Sorry, but it's time to talk about *formulas*. These equations calculate values based on the contents of cells you specify in your spreadsheet. For example, if you designate cell A1 (the cell in column A at row 1) to hold your yearly salary and cell B1 to hold the number 12, you can divide the contents of cell A1 by cell B1 (to calculate your monthly salary) by typing this formula into any other cell:

=A1/B1

By the way, formulas in Numbers always start with an equal sign (=).

"So what's the big deal, Mark? Why not use a calculator?" Sure, but maybe you want to calculate your weekly salary. Rather than grab a pencil and paper, you can simply change the contents of cell B1 to 52, and — boom! — the spreadsheet is updated to display your weekly salary.

That's a simple example, of course, but it demonstrates the basis of using formulas (and the reason that spreadsheets are often used to predict trends and forecast budgets).

To add a simple formula within your spreadsheet, follow these steps:

1. Select the cell that will hold the result of your calculation.

2. Click inside the Formula Bar and type = (the equal sign). The Formula Bar appears to the right of the Sheets heading, directly under the Button Bar.

3. Click the Function Browser button, which bears the *fx* label. (It appears next to the green Accept button on the Formula Bar.) See **Figure 9-9**.

Function Browser button

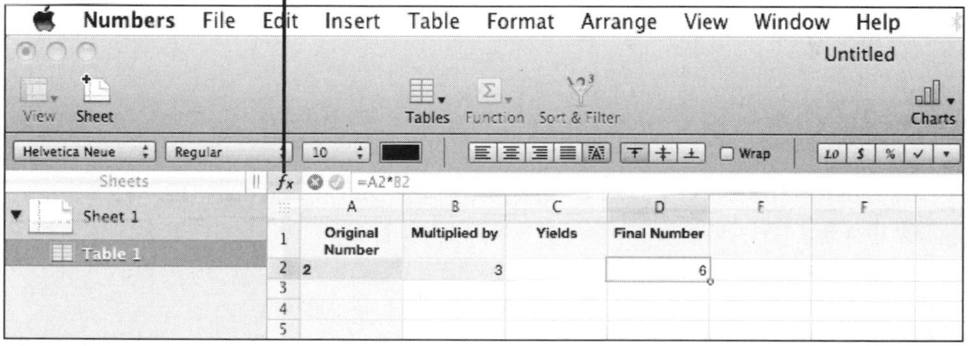

Figure 9-9

4. In the Insert Function dialog box that appears, as shown in **Figure 9-10**, select a formula to add it to the Formula Bar. This list makes it easier to choose from the wide range of functions available within Numbers.

5. After you finish, click the Accept button to add the formula to the cell. It's now ready to work behind the scenes, doing math for you so that the correct numbers appear in the cell.

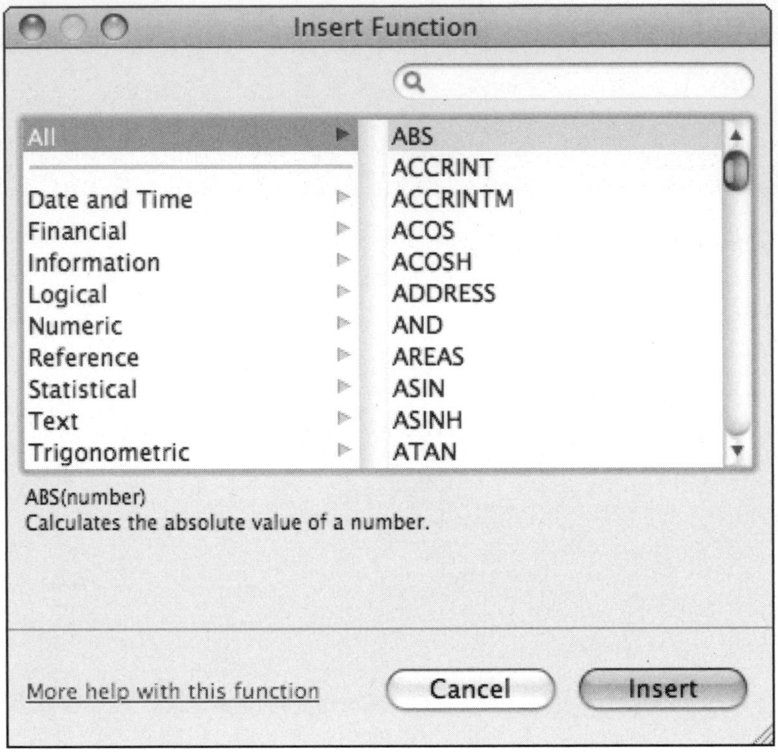

All ▶	ABS
	ACCRINT
Date and Time ▶	ACCRINTM
Financial ▶	ACOS
Information ▶	ACOSH
Logical ▶	ADDRESS
Numeric ▶	AND
Reference ▶	AREAS
Statistical ▶	ASIN
Text ▶	ASINH
Trigonometric ▶	ATAN

Insert Function

ABS(number)
Calculates the absolute value of a number.

More help with this function   Cancel   Insert

Figure 9-10

Insert Charts

Sometimes you just have to see something to believe it — hence the ability to use the data you add to a spreadsheet to generate a professional-looking chart! Follow these steps to create a chart:

1. Select the adjacent cells you want to chart by dragging the mouse.

 To choose individual cells that aren't adjacent, you can hold down the ⌘ key as you click.

2. Click the Chart button on the Numbers toolbar, which looks like a bar graph. Numbers displays the thumbnail menu you see in **Figure 9-11**.

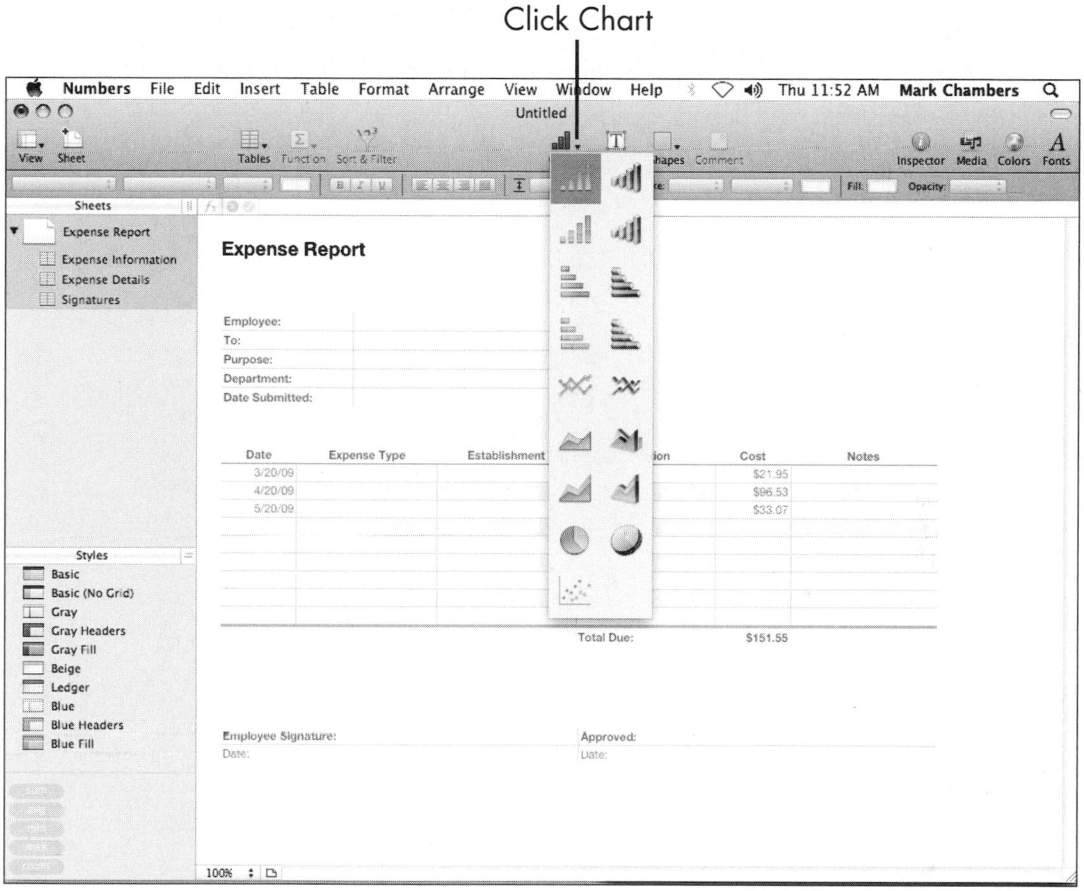

Click Chart

Figure 9-11

3. Click the thumbnail for the chart type you want. Numbers inserts the chart as an object within your spreadsheet so that you can move the chart or resize it just like an object in Pages.

Numbers also displays the Chart Inspector dialog box, where you can change the colors and add (or remove) the chart title and legend. **Figure 9-12** illustrates a simple chart I added to a spreadsheet that compares monthly income amounts, complete with the Chart Inspector. The chart appears in the upper-right corner of the figure (surrounded by resizing handles), and the values on which the chart is based appear selected under the Cost heading.

Figure 9-12

4. To change the default title, click the title box once to select it, and then click it again to edit the text.

Save Your Work

To save a Numbers document after you finish it (or to save it for later), follow these steps within the program:

1. Press ⌘+S. If you're saving a document that hasn't yet been saved, the Save As sheet appears.

2. Type a filename for the new document.

3. Click the Where pop-up menu and choose a location to save the document. (This step lets you select common locations, like your desktop, Documents folder, or Home folder.)

 If the location you want isn't listed on the Where pop-up menu, you can also click the down-arrow button next to the Save As text box to display the full Save As column view. Click to select a drive from the Devices list on the left side of the dialog box, and then click folders and subfolders until you reach the location you want.

4. Click Save. After you fill out the Save As sheet once, your Mac remembers your settings for that spreadsheet. If you make additional changes to the spreadsheet, simply press ⌘+S and your changes are saved.

Keep Your Finances Safe Online

Unfortunately, no list of "absolutely safe" online banks or investment companies exists. Online security is a concept you should constantly monitor while exchanging information with Web sites, especially when that information includes personal data such as your Social Security number and credit card information.

Keep these guidelines in mind while using online commerce sites to greatly reduce the risk of identity theft (or worse):

➡ **Never use an online bank or investment house that doesn't offer a secure, encrypted connection when you enter your personal information and credit card number.** If you're using Apple's Safari browser, the padlock icon appears in the upper-right corner of the Safari window. When the padlock icon appears in the window, the connection is encrypted and secure. If it doesn't appear, *go elsewhere.*

➡ **Avoid using Safari's AutoFill feature.** If you fill out many forms online — when you're shopping at Web sites, for example, or trading online — you can click the AutoFill button (which looks like a little text box and a pen) to complete these forms for you. To be honest, however, I'm not a big fan of releasing *any* of my personal information to any Web site, so I never use AutoFill. You can specify which information is used for AutoFill (or disable it entirely) by running Safari and choosing Safari⇨Preferences. Clicking the AutoFill toolbar button displays the settings — to disable AutoFill, just clear each check box.

If you decide to use this feature, make sure that the connection is secure (again, look for the padlock icon in the upper-right corner of the Safari window) and read the site's Privacy Agreement page first to see how your identity data will be treated.

➡ **Look for a security symbol.** A number of well-respected online security companies act as watchdogs for online banking and investing institutions — when you see the symbol for one of these companies, it's a good indicator that the bank or broker is interested in maintaining your privacy and protecting your identity. Some of the better-known security companies on the Web include TraceSecurity (`www.tracesecurity.com`), VeriSign (`www.verisign.com`), and Web Sense (`www.websense.com`). Luckily, you don't have to implement all the software and assorted protection protocols that run behind the scenes when you connect to your bank!

Get the Most from Movies and Digital Photos

A t last! After years of empty promises of professional-quality media features for home and school — most of them coming from that silly Gates person in Redmond — Apple has taken on the challenge and developed a recipe for digital media success.

By designing hardware and software designed to work smoothly together, Apple lets you easily organize and produce your own multimedia with the iLife 2008 suite of digital tools, which includes iPhoto and iTunes.

You can use Apple's video and image tools to

➠ Play DVD movies and view your photo collection in several different ways.

➠ Send photos to others by e-mail.

➠ Tag your photos with keywords to help keep your collection organized.

➠ Edit photos to improve their appearance.

Get ready to . . .

Play Movies with DVD Player

With the arrival of the DVD movie, an honest-to-goodness theater in the home is now within the grasp of mere mortals (who have, coincidentally, merely average budgets). Mac OS X has everything you need to enjoy a night at the movies without ever leaving home. In fact, I highly recommend the 24-inch Intel iMac or the 17-inch MacBook Pro for those wide-screen classics.

To watch Frodo Baggins, Don Corleone, or James Bond, you need Apple's DVD Player application — you find it within the confines of your Applications folder. But rather than root through the Finder, you can launch DVD Player in an even easier way: Simply insert a DVD into the drive. As soon as you do, your Mac recognizes the disc and launches DVD Player by default for you. (Time for another round of well-deserved gloating about your choice of personal computer.)

Depending on the viewing mode you choose, DVD Player offers either one or two windows:

➥ **Controller:** The small, silver-colored gadget that looks like a remote control and holds all the controls for the Player. Arranged much like they are on a VCR or tape deck, all the familiar controls are present. Check it out in **Figure 10-1**.

➥ **Viewer:** View your DVD movies in this large window.

Table 10-1 details the fundamental commands present in the DVD Player Controller. Apple software usually has some goodies hidden beneath the surface, and DVD Player is no exception. The controls in DVD Player have a few functions that might not be obvious to the casual user, as listed in Column 3 of Table 10-1.

Exercising your Viewer

You can think of the Viewer window as a television inside your Macintosh if it helps, but DVD Player goes one step further. Unlike a television screen, the Viewer has some nice tricks up its sleeve: For example, you can resize the Viewer window by choosing one of the five sizes listed on the View menu (half, actual size, double size, Fit to Screen, and full-screen). Choose a size to watch a movie in a small window on your desktop while you work with other applications. You can toggle the Viewer size from the keyboard; for example, press ⌘+0 (zero) to select half-size, press ⌘+1 (one) to select actual size, and press ⌘+2 (two) to select double size.

If you're in it only for the entertainment factor, resize the Viewer to fill the screen. I like to watch movies in Full Screen mode, which you can toggle by pressing ⌘+F. To take full advantage of all your screen space yet leave the Viewer window onscreen for occasional resizing, press ⌘+3 (three) to choose Fit to Screen mode.

By the way, if your Mac came with an Apple Remote, you can use the Apple Remote to control the Viewer (even in full-screenmode).

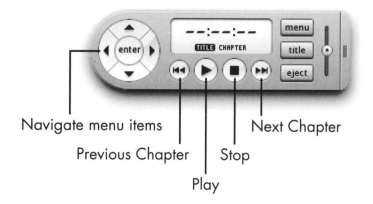

Navigate menu items

Previous Chapter

Play

Stop

Next Chapter

Figure 10-1

Table 10-1	Basic DVD Controls	
Control Name	*What It Does*	*Other Functions*
Play	Plays the DVD	Toggles into a Pause button when a movie is playing.
Stop	Stops playback of the DVD	
Previous Chapter	Skips to the previous chapter	Click and hold the button to quickly skim the movie in reverse.
Next Chapter	Skips to the next chapter	Click and hold the button to quickly skim the movie forward.
Playback Volume	Adjusts the volume of the DVD audio	
Arrow Buttons	Navigates through the menu items of the DVD	
Enter	Selects the highlighted menu item	
Eject	Ejects the DVD from the drive	
Title	Jumps immediately to the DVD's title menu	
Menu	Displays the menu of the current DVD	

Upload Photos from Your Digital Camera

iPhoto makes it easy to download images directly from your digital camera — as long as your specific camera model is supported in iPhoto. (Most are, and more are added to the supported crowd during every update.)

Follow these steps to import images:

1. Connect your digital camera to your laptop.

Plug one end of a USB cable into your camera and the other end into your Mac's USB port and prepare your camera to download images.

2. Type an event name for the imported photos, such as Birthday Party or Godzilla Ravages Tokyo.

3. Type a description for the roll.

4. To allow iPhoto to automatically separate images into separate events based on the date they were taken, click to select the Autosplit Events after Importing check box.

5. Click the Import button to import your photographs from the camera.

The images are added to your Photo Library, where you can organize them into individual albums or events. (More on albums and events later in this task.)

Importing images from your hard drive

If you have a folder of images that you collected already on your hard drive, a CD, a DVD, an external drive, or a USB Flash drive, adding them to your library is easy. Just drag the folder from a Finder window and drop it into the source list in the iPhoto window. iPhoto automatically creates a new album using the folder name, and you can sit back while the images are imported into that new album. iPhoto recognizes images in several formats: GIF, JPEG, PICT, PNG, RAW, and TIFF.

If you have individual images, you can drag them as well. Select the images in a Finder window and drag them into an album in the source list. To add them to the album that's displayed in the Viewer, drag the selected photos and drop them in the Viewer instead.

If you'd rather import images by using a standard Mac Open dialog box, choose File⇨Import to Library. Simplicity strikes again!

To select specific images to import, hold down ⌘ and click each photo you want, and then click Import Selected rather than Import All.

6. Specify whether the images you're importing should be deleted from the camera afterward.

If you don't expect to download these images again to another computer or another device, you can choose to delete the photos from your camera automatically. This way, you save a step and help eliminate the guilt that can crop up when you nix your pix. (Sorry, I couldn't resist.)

There are two methods of organizing photos: the album, which you may be familiar with from older versions of iPhoto, and events. An *album* is simply a folder you create in iPhoto that contains specific photos — it's straightforward.

Events, on the other hand, are a relatively new idea. After you download the contents of your digital camera, those contents count as a virtual *event* in iPhoto — based on either the date you imported them or the date they were taken. For example, you can always display the last images you imported by clicking Last Import. If you want to see photos from your son's graduation, they appear as a separate event. (Both these organizational tools appear in the source list.) Think about that: Arranging old-fashioned film prints by the moments they document is tough, but iPhoto makes it easy for you to see just which photos are part of the same group!

Display a Digital Image in iPhoto

Say goodbye to the old shoebox full of slides and prints! Browsing your iPhoto library is as simple as clicking these items:

➡ **A specific event or album in the source list, as shown in Figure 10-2:** You can also click the Events item to see a thumbnail display of all events in your library.

➡ **The Photos item in the source list:** This method displays all photos as a single scrolling collection.

Drag the scroll button in the scroll bar to move up or down, or click a specific photo and use the arrow keys to navigate through your collection.

After you locate the image you want to see, you can double-click it to display the photo within the iPhoto window.

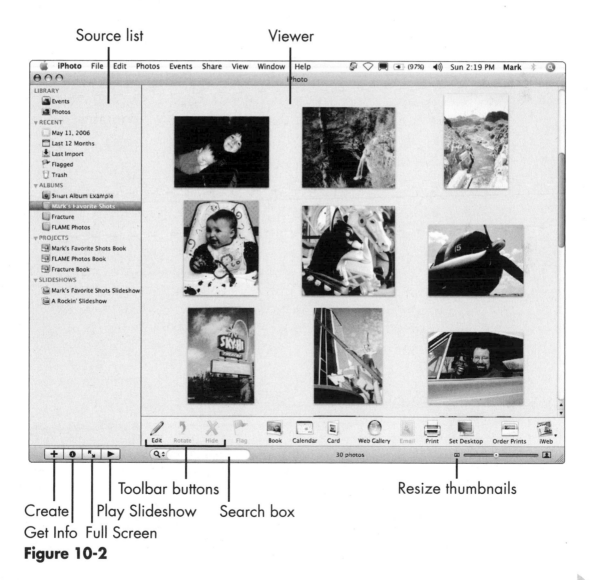

Source list   Viewer

Create
Get Info   Full Screen
Play Slideshow   Search box
Toolbar buttons
Resize thumbnails

Figure 10-2

To view the photo full-screen, click it to select it and click the Full-Screen button at the bottom of the window (which bears two arrows pointing outward) or press ⌘+Option+F. You can leave Full Screen mode at any time by double-clicking the mouse or pressing Esc.

 While in Full Screen mode, move the mouse cursor to the top edge of the screen to display a scrolling thumbnail strip (see **Figure 10-3**), allowing you to choose another image from the same event or album without exiting.

Click a thumbnail to switch to that picture.

Figure 10-3

Tag Your Photos with Keywords

"Okay, Mark, iPhoto albums and events are great ideas, but do you really expect me to look through 20 albums just to locate pictures with specific people or places?" Never fear, good Mac owner. You can also assign descriptive *keywords* to images to help you organize your collection and locate certain pictures fast. iPhoto comes with a number of standard keywords, and you can create your own as well.

To illustrate, suppose that you want to identify your images according to special events in your family. Birthday photos should have their own keywords, and anniversaries deserve another. By assigning keywords, you can search for Elsie's sixth birthday or your silver wedding anniversary (no matter which event or album they're in), and all related photos with those keywords appear like magic! (Well, *almost* like magic. You need to choose View⇨Keywords, which toggles the Keyword display on and off in the Viewer.)

iPhoto includes a number of keywords that are already available:

➠ **Birthday**

➠ **Checkmark**

➠ **Family**

➠ **Favorite**

➠ **Grayscale**

➠ **Kids**

➠ **Vacation**

➠ **Widescreen**

What's the Checkmark all about, you ask? It's a special case — adding this keyword displays a tiny check mark icon in the lower-right corner of the image. The Checkmark keyword comes in handy for temporarily identifying specific images because you can search for just the check-marked photos.

To assign keywords to images (or remove keywords that have already been assigned), select one or more photos in the Viewer. Choose Window⇨Show Keywords or press ⌘+K to display the Keywords window, as shown in **Figure 10-4**.

Click a button to assign a keyword.

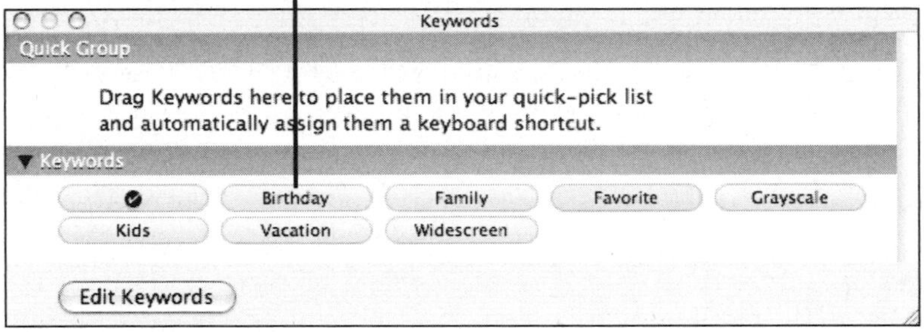

Figure 10-4

Click the keyword buttons that you want to attach to the selected images to mark them. Or, click the highlighted keyword buttons that you want to remove from the selected images to disable them.

To sift through your entire collection of images by using keywords, click the magnifying glass button next to the Search box at the bottom of the iPhoto window, and then choose Keyword from the pop-up menu. iPhoto displays a pop-up Keywords panel, and you can click one or more keyword buttons to display just the photos that carry those keywords.

The images that remain in the Viewer after a search must have all the keywords you specified. If an image is identified, for example, by only three of four keywords you chose, it isn't a match and it doesn't appear in the Viewer.

You're gonna need your own keywords

I would bet that you take photos of subjects other than just kids and vacations — and that's why iPhoto lets you create your own keywords. Display the iPhoto Keywords window by pressing ⌘+K, click the Edit Keywords button on the toolbar, and then click Add (the button with the plus sign). iPhoto adds a new, unnamed keyword to the list as an edit box, ready for you to type its name.

You can rename an existing keyword from the same window, too. Click a keyword to select it and then click Rename. Remember, however, that renaming a keyword affects *all images tagged with that keyword*, even if the new keyword no longer applies to the photos. That might be confusing when, for example, photos originally tagged as Family suddenly appear with the keyword Foodstuffs because you renamed the keyword. To remove an existing keyword from the list, click the keyword to select it and then click the Delete button, which bears a minus sign.

Organize Photos in Albums

The basic organizational tool in iPhoto is the *album*. Each album can represent any division you like, whether it's a year, a vacation, your daughter, or your daughter's ex-boyfriends. Follow these steps:

1. Create a new album.

You can either choose File⇨New Album or click the plus (+) button at the bottom of the source list. The New Album sheet appears, as shown in **Figure 10-5**.

2. Type the name for your new photo album.

If you want to create an empty album (without using any images that might be selected), make sure to deselect the Use Selected Items in New Album check box.

3. Click OK.

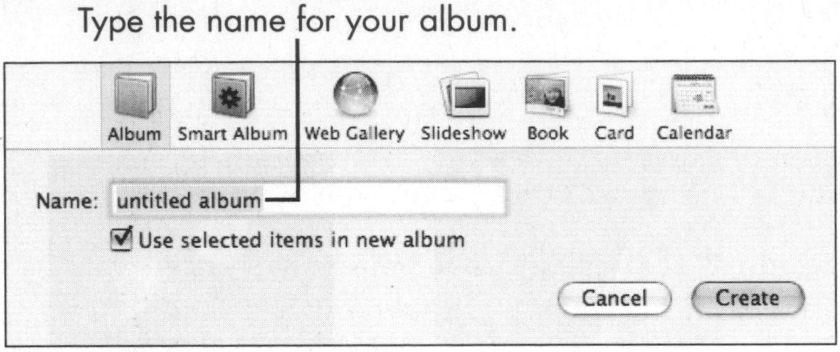

Type the name for your album.

Album Smart Album Web Gallery Slideshow Book Card Calendar

Name: untitled album

☑ Use selected items in new album

Cancel   Create

Figure 10-5

You can drag images from the Viewer into any album you choose. For example, you can copy an image to another album by dragging it from the Viewer to an album in the source list.

To remove a photo that has fallen out of favor, follow these steps:

1. In the source list, select an album.

2. In the Viewer, click to select the photo you want to remove.

3. Press Delete.

When you remove a photo from an album, you *don't* remove the photo from your collection (represented by the Photos entry under the Library heading in the source list). That's because an album is just a group of links to the images in a collection. To completely remove an offending photo, click the Photos entry under the Library heading to display the entire collection of images and delete the picture there, too.

To remove an entire album from the source list, just click to select it in the source list — in the Viewer, you can see the images it contains — and then press Delete.

To rename an album, click to select the entry under the Albums heading in the source list, and then click again to display a text box. Type the new album name and press Return.

Put Events to Work

As I mention earlier in this chapter, an *event* is essentially a group of images that you shot or downloaded at the same time. iPhoto figures that those images belong together (which is usually a safe assumption).

 Like an album, an event can be renamed — just using a different procedure. Click the Events entry under the Library heading in the source list to display your Events in the Viewer, and then click the existing event name in the caption underneath the thumbnail. A text box appears, where you can type a new name; click Return to update the event.

Try moving the mouse cursor over an event thumbnail in the Viewer, and you see that iPhoto displays the date range when the images were taken as well as the total number of images in the event. Ah, but things get *really* cool when you move the mouse cursor back and forth over an event with many images: The thumbnail animates and displays all images in the event, without using old-fashioned scroll bars or silly arrows. (Why can't I think of this stuff? This is the future, dear readers.)

To display the contents of an event in the Viewer, just double-click the event thumbnail. To return to the Events thumbnails, click the All Events button at the top of the Viewer.

 While you're organizing, you can create a brand-new, empty event by choosing Events⇨Create Event. Feel free to drag photos from albums, other events, or your Photo library into your new event.

Create a Slide Show

You can use iPhoto to create slide shows! Click the album you want to display and click the Add button, and then choose Slideshow from the toolbar and click Create; notice that iPhoto adds a Slideshow item in the source list. The same scrolling thumbnail strip appears at the top of the Viewer — this time, displaying the images in the album. Click and drag the thumbnails so that they appear in the order you want (see **Figure 10-6**).

Click and drag thumbnails to put them in the correct order.

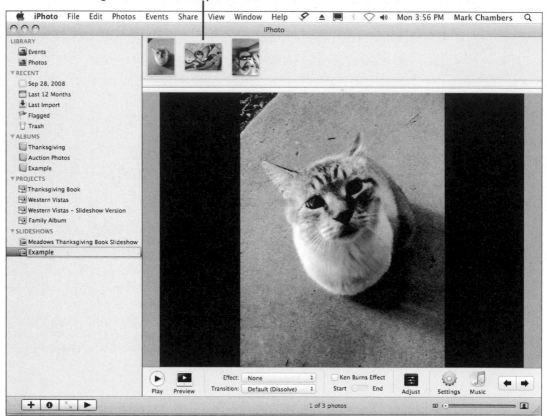

Figure 10-6

To choose background music for your slide show, click the Music button in the Slideshow toolbar to display the tracks from your iTunes library. Drag the individual songs you want to the song list at the bottom of the sheet — you can drag them to rearrange their order in the list as well. Click OK to accept your song list.

 To configure your slide show, click the Settings button on the Slideshow toolbar. You can specify the amount of time that each slide remains on the screen as well as an optional title and rating displays. Wide-screen laptop owners appreciate the Slideshow Format pop-up menu, which lets you choose a 16:9 widescreen display for your slide show.

When you're ready to play your slide show, click the Play button, and iPhoto switches to Full Screen mode. You can share your completed slide show by choosing iPhoto⇨Share, where you can send the slide show to iDVD (for later burning to a DVD), export it as a QuickTime movie, post it to your MobileMe gallery, or send it by e-mail.

Edit Photos with Panache

The first step in any editing job is to select the image you want to fix in the Viewer. Then click the Edit button on the iPhoto toolbar (as shown at the left of the toolbar in Figure 10-2) to switch to the Edit panel controls, as shown in **Figure 10-7**. Now you're ready to fix problems, using the tools that I discuss in the rest of this section. (If you're editing a photo that's part of an event or album, note the spiffy scrolling photo strip at the top, which lets you switch to another image to edit just by clicking.)

If an image is in the wrong orientation and needs to be turned to display correctly, click the Rotate button to turn it once in a counterclockwise direction. Hold down the Option key while you click the Rotate button to rotate in a clockwise direction.

Does that photo have an intruder hovering around the edges of the subject? You can remove some of the border by *cropping* an image, just as folks once did with film prints and a pair of scissors. (We've come a long way.) With iPhoto, you can remove unwanted portions of an image — it's a helpful way to remove Uncle Milton's stray head (complete with toupee) from an otherwise perfect holiday snapshot.

Follow these steps to crop an image:

1. Click the Crop button in the Edit pane.

2. Select the portion of the image that you want to keep.

In the Viewer, click and drag the handles on the square to outline the part of the image you want. Remember that whatever is outside this rectangle disappears after the crop is completed.

 When you drag a corner or edge of the outline, a semiopaque grid (familiar to amateur and professional photographers as the nine rectangles from the rule of thirds) appears to help you visualize what you're claiming. If you haven't heard of the rule of thirds, don't worry: Just try to keep the subject of your photos aligned at one of the grid intersections, or running along one of the lines.

3. (Optional) Choose a preset size.

If you want to force your cropped selection to a specific size — such as 4 x 3 for an iDVD project — select the Constrain check box and choose that size from the Constrain pop-up menu.

4. Click the Apply button.

Oh, and don't forget that you can use the iPhoto Undo feature if you mess up and need to try again — just press ⌘+Z.

 iPhoto features multiple Undo levels, so press ⌘+Z several times to travel back through your last several changes.

If a photo looks washed out, click the Enhance button to increase (or decrease) the color saturation and improve the contrast. Enhance is automatic, so you don't have to set anything.

Unfortunately, today's digital cameras can still produce the same "zombies with red eyeballs" as traditional film cameras. *Red-eye* is caused by a camera's flash reflecting off the retinas of a subject's eyes, and it can occur with both humans and pets.

Use the buttons to edit photos.

Figure 10-7

iPhoto can remove that red-eye and turn frightening zombies back into your family and friends! Click the Red-Eye button and then select a demonized eyeball by clicking in the center of it. To complete the process, click the X in the button that appears in the image.

Add Photos to Your E-Mail

If you need to send a photo or two of your new car to your relatives, iPhoto can help you send your images by e-mail by automating the process. The application can prepare your image and embed it automatically in a new message.

To send an image by e-mail, select it and then click the Email button on the toolbar. The dialog box, shown in **Figure** 10-8, appears, allowing you to choose the size of the images and whether you want to include their titles and comments.

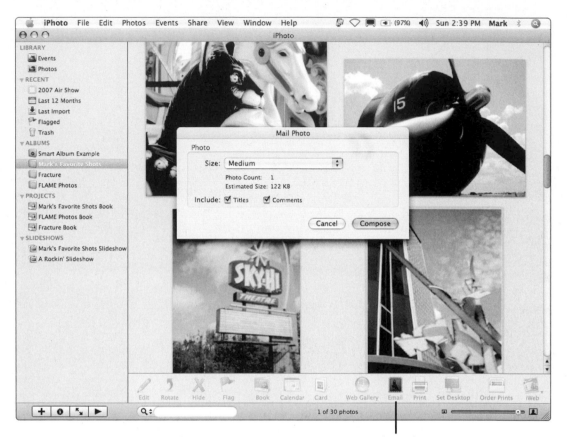

E-mail a photo.

Figure 10-8

 Keep in mind that most ISP (Internet service provider) e-mail servers don't accept an e-mail message that's more than 1MB or 2MB, so watch that Size display. If you're trying to send a number of images and the size exceeds 2MB, you might have to click the Size pop-up menu and choose a smaller size (reducing the image resolution and size of the file) to embed them all in a single message.

When you're satisfied with the total file size and you're ready to create your message, click the Compose button. iPhoto automatically launches Apple Mail (or whichever e-mail application you specify) and creates a new message containing the images, ready for you to click Send!

Enjoying Music, Video, and Podcasts

Chapter 11

*W*hether you like classical, jazz, rock, rhythm and blues, folk, or just talk programs, I can guarantee you that you won't find a better application than iTunes to fill your life with your music. iTunes gives you music that's easy to play, easy to search, and easy to transfer from place to place.

You can use iTunes to

➠ Play all sorts of digital media, including music, video, TV shows, podcasts (audio journals), and Internet radio.

➠ Burn (record) music to your own, custom audio CDs.

➠ Rip (transfer) music from an audio CD to your iTunes library.

➠ Buy music and video from the iTunes Store.

➠ Organize your music into playlists.

To open iTunes, simply click its icon in the Dock. See Chapter 3 for help with opening programs from the Dock.

Set Up Speakers

If you're using a MacBook laptop or an iMac, you probably already know that your computer has built-in speakers. However, you can add external speakers to any Macintosh:

1. Connect the audio cable from the speakers to the Headphone or Line Out audio jack on your computer, as shown in Figure 11-1.

 If you have a set of USB speakers, connect them to your Mac by plugging the USB cable into any open USB port on your Mac. For more information on connecting USB cables, check out Chapter 2.

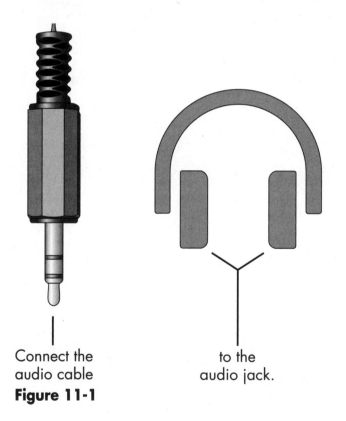

Connect the audio cable

to the audio jack.

Figure 11-1

2. Plug the speakers into a wall outlet (if necessary) and turn them on.

 3. Click the System Preferences icon in the Dock — it looks like a collection of gears. The System Preferences window appears.

4. Click the Sound icon in the System Preferences window, and then click the Output tab, as shown in **Figure 11-2**.

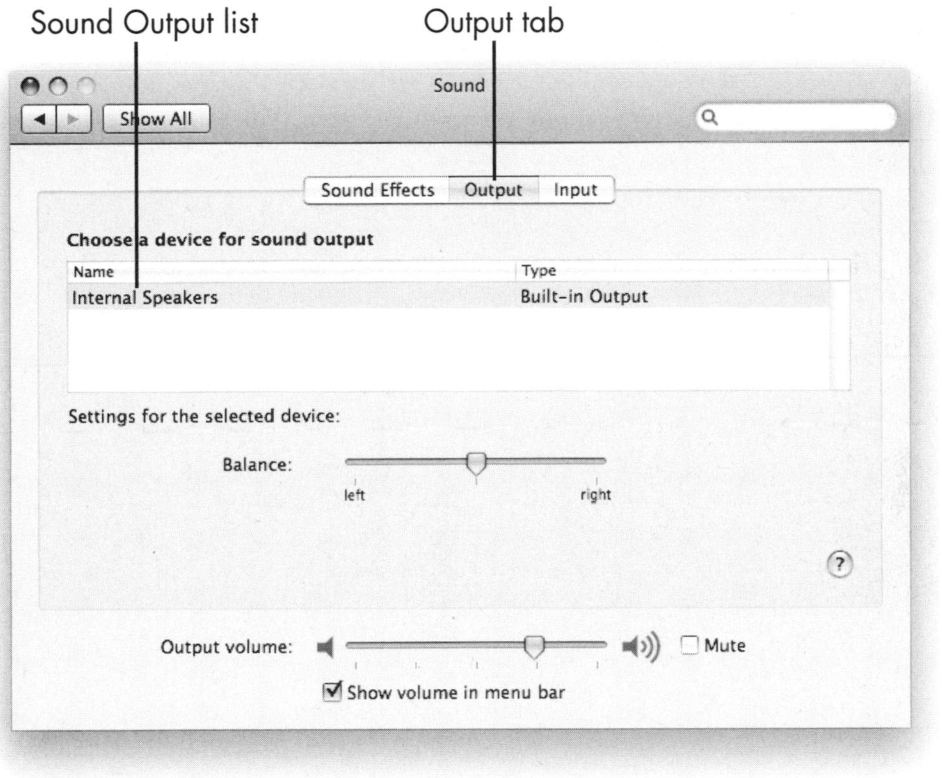

Sound Output list   Output tab

Choose a device for sound output

Name	Type
Internal Speakers	Built-in Output

Settings for the selected device:

Balance: left   right

Output volume: Mute

☑ Show volume in menu bar

Figure 11-2

5. Click the Line Out or USB item in the Sound Output list (depending on the type of speakers you have).

6. Click the Close button in the upper-left corner of the System Preferences window to close the window and save your changes.

Control the Volume

In iTunes, you can control the volume by clicking and dragging the Volume slider, shown in **Figure 11-3**:

➠ **To lower the volume,** drag to the left.

➠ **To raise the volume,** drag to the right.

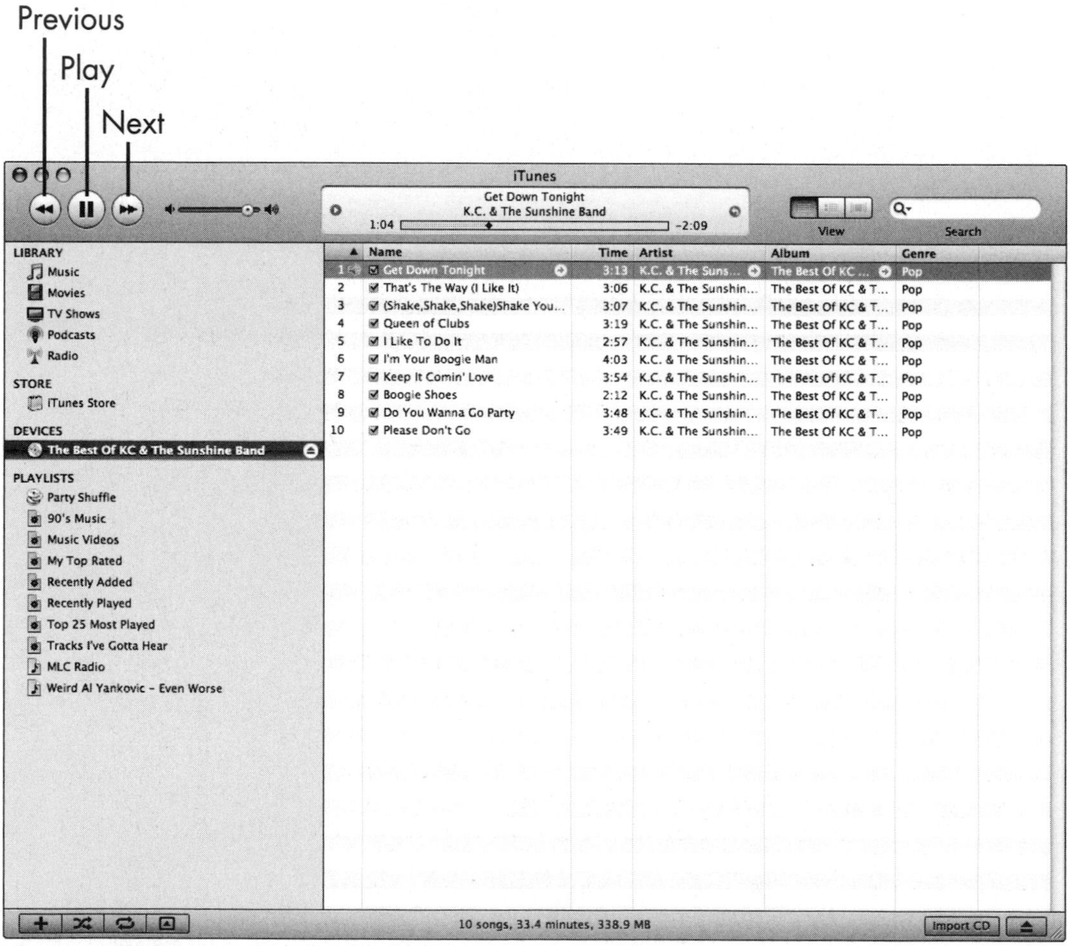

Figure 11-3

Your Mac also has a volume control that affects all your applications. To change the volume for your system as a whole, click the Volume icon on the Finder menu bar (which looks like a speaker) and drag the slider up or down. Because this setting affects all applications, if you change the volume on your system, the volume of the selections you hear in iTunes changes as well.

Add Music from a CD to iTunes

You can easily *rip* (copy) music from an audio CD to your iTunes Music Library. By ripping a song, you create a copy of the song as a digital music file on your Mac.

 1. Launch iTunes by clicking its icon on the Dock.

2. Load an audio CD into your Mac's optical drive. If you have an active Internet connection, the CD title shows up in the iTunes source list, which is on the left side of the iTunes window. The CD track listing appears on the right side of the window, as shown in **Figure 11-4**.

 If iTunes asks whether you want to import the contents of the CD into the Music Library, you can click Yes and skip the rest of these steps. However, if you disabled this prompt, just continue with the remaining two steps.

3. Clear the check box of any song that you don't want to import from the CD. All songs on the CD have a check box next to their titles by default. Unmarked songs aren't imported.

4. After you select the songs you want to add to the library, click the Import CD button. iTunes displays a progress bar showing you how many songs remain to import. The songs you've imported appear in your Music library — click the Music item in the source list to see all your songs.

CD title   CD track list

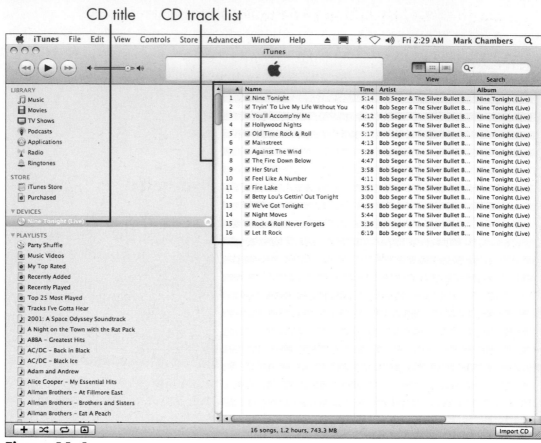

Figure 11-4

Play an Audio CD in iTunes

To play a CD, follow these steps:

1. Load the CD into your Mac. By default, iTunes launches automatically, but you can also click the iTunes icon in the Dock to launch it manually.

2. Click the Play button (refer to Figure 11-3).

 The buttons in iTunes are just like those on a home CD player. Click the Next button to advance to the next song, and click Previous to return to the beginning of a song. To pause the music, click the Play button, and click it again to restart the music.

Play Digital Music, Video, and Podcasts in iTunes

To play digital music files that you added to iTunes from a CD or bought at the iTunes Store (as explained later in this chapter), follow these steps:

1. In the source list on the left, click the media category you want to play. Your choices are Music Library, Movies, TV Shows, Audiobooks, and Podcasts. Clicking a category displays media that you downloaded from the iTunes Store or otherwise added to iTunes.

2. Double-click a specific item to play it, or to display individual episodes, if you're working with TV shows or podcasts.

 iTunes can display your Music Library in three ways. List view displays each song as one entry. Click the second View button (at the top of the iTunes window) to display cover thumbnails grouped by album, artist, genre, or composer. Click the third View button (Cover Flow) to browse by album cover, complete with reflective surface, as shown in **Figure 11-5**.

Cover Flow view   Click a view button

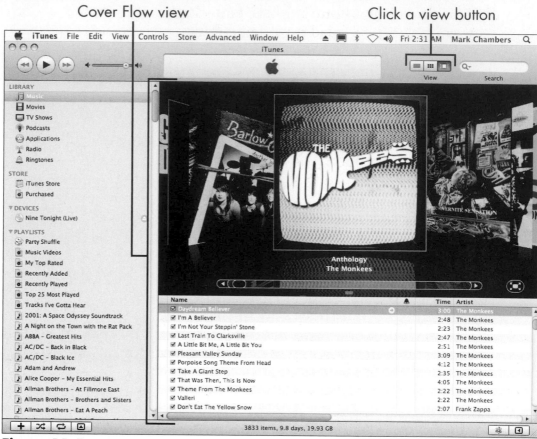

Figure 11-5

Create an iTunes Playlist

A *playlist* is a collection of songs you create that are played within iTunes. Playlists are useful for listening to an entire album and for creating the musical background for your next party or road trip.

The best way to familiarize yourself with playlists is to create one. Here's how:

1. Choose File⇨New Playlist to create a newly created empty playlist (the toe-tappin' *untitled playlist*) in the source list on the left.

2. To help organize your playlists, you should, well, *name* them. (Aren't you glad now that you have this book?) Give your playlist a name by selecting it in the source list. Click the playlist entry in the source list again and then you can type a new name for the playlist.

3. Add a song from the library to your new playlist by clicking the Music entry in the source list and finding the song you want to include. Then drag it to a playlist entry in the source list, as shown in **Figure 11-6**.

4. When your playlist is complete, you're ready to play your songs in iTunes. Simply click a playlist in the source list (if it isn't already selected) to display the songs, and then double-click the first song in the playlist.

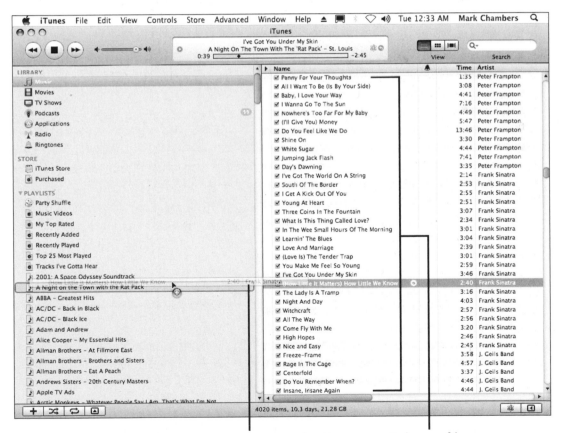

Drag a song to your playlist.   Select a file.

Figure 11-6

After you're familiar with a basic playlist, check out these playlist tips:

➡ iTunes offers multiple ways to create playlists. You may find it easier to first select the songs you want for a playlist and then choose File⇨New Playlist from Selection. This action creates a new playlist and automatically adds any tracks selected in the Music Library. iTunes also attempts to name the playlist automatically for you.

➡ You can add the same song to any number of playlists because the songs in a playlist are simply pointers to songs in your Music Library — not to the songs themselves. Add them to, and remove them from, any playlist at will, secure in the knowledge that the songs remain safe in the library.

➡ As for removing playlists themselves, that's simple, too. Just select the playlist in the source list and press Delete.

➡ Click the Party Shuffle playlist, and you encounter a random selection of songs taken from your iTunes Music Library — perfect for your next party! You can change the order of the songs in the Party Shuffle playlist, add songs from your library, or delete songs that don't fit the scintillating ambience of your gathering. Enjoy!

Burn an Audio CD By Using iTunes

Besides being a fantastic audio player, iTunes is adept at creating CDs. iTunes makes copying songs to a CD as simple as a few clicks of the mouse. Follow these steps:

1. With iTunes open, click to select an existing playlist that you want to copy. If necessary, you can also create a new playlist and add to it whichever songs you want to have on the CD.

2. Click the Burn Disc button at the bottom of the iTunes window. The Burn Settings dialog box appears.

3. In the Burn Settings dialog box, choose Maximum Possible from the Preferred Speed menu. Then click to select the Audio CD disc format, as shown in **Figure 11-7**.

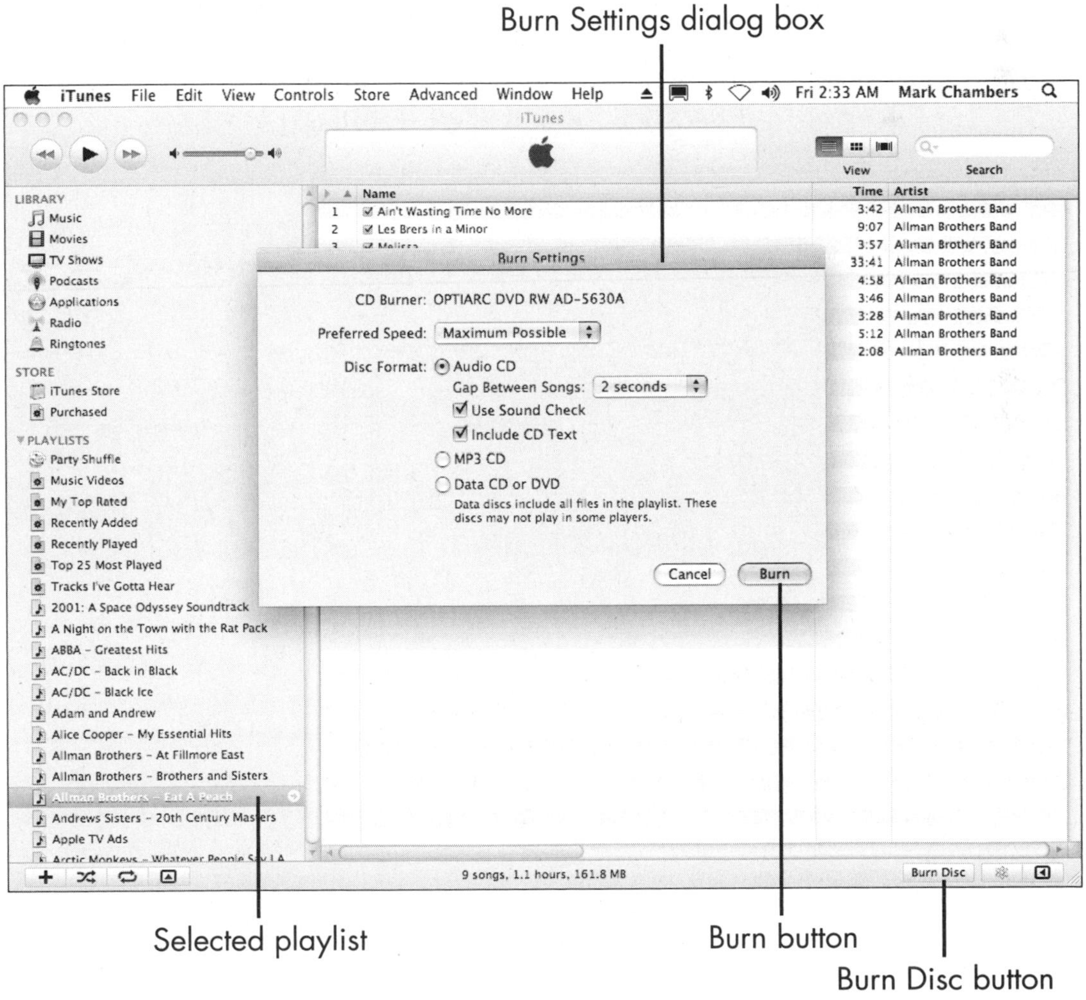

Burn Settings dialog box

Selected playlist

Burn button

Burn Disc button

Figure 11-7

4. Click the Burn button to commence the disc burning process. iTunes lets you know when the recording is complete.

Watch Visualizations

By now, you know that iTunes is a feast for the ears, but did you know that it can provide you with eye candy as well? With just a click or two, you can view mind-bending graphics that stretch, move, and pulse with your music.

1. With your favorite music playing in iTunes, choose View⇨ Turn On Visualizer (or press ⌘+T).

2. To switch to full-screen graphics, press ⌘+F. To escape from Full Screen mode, click the trackpad button or press Esc.

Set up an iTunes Store account

"Why do I need a separate account to buy something from the iTunes Store?" Good question, and there is a good answer: Apple securely stores your payment method, e-mail address, and contact information so that you can purchase things easily, without having to re-enter all that stuff every time you buy an album or a movie. Also, Apple can use the Apple ID you set up during registration, or during your MobileMe signup — less hassle, less confusion.

Depending on what you've already set up, just click the Buy button and iTunes leads you step-by-step through the account setup process (or whisks you right to the payment selection process). Remember, all the information you send is over an encrypted connection — way to go, Apple.

Note that some songs (and most podcasts) are free to download. Apple always clearly indicates whether a download is free, and you get a receipt in an e-mail for every purchase. . . yet another reason for the account!

3. To stop the visual display, choose View⇨Turn Off Visualizer (or press ⌘+T again).

Find Music, Video, Audiobooks, and Podcasts Online

Let me mention the hottest spot on the Internet for downloading music, video, audiobooks, and podcasts: the iTunes Store, which you can reach from the cozy confines of iTunes. (That is, as long as you have an Internet connection. If you don't, it's time to turn the page to a different chapter, because you need Internet access to reach the iTunes Store.) **Figure 11-8** illustrates the lobby of this online audio-video store.

Search for a specific item.

Click to display details.

Figure 11-8

You can search for a specific item (or browse to your heart's content) within the iTunes Store by following these steps:

1. To go to the iTunes Store, click the iTunes Store item in the source list. After a few moments, you see the home screen, which features the latest offerings.

2. Browse the items at the store or search for an item that you already know you want to buy or download. You can do so from the home screen:

 ⟹ Click a link in the Store list to browse according to media type.

 ⟹ Click a featured artist or album thumbnail to jump directly to that artist or album.

 ⟹ Click the Power Search link to search by song title, artist, album, or composer.

3. To display the details of a specific album, song or audiobook, just click it. iTunes allows you to preview a 30-second sample of any audio or video for free — just double-click the entry or click on the Preview button for movies and music videos.

4. To add an item you want to your iTunes Store shopping cart, click the Add Song/Movie/Album/Video button. (The name of the button changes depending on the type of media you want to buy.) If you're interested in buying just certain tracks (for that perfect road warrior mix), you would add just a song; if you want a whole album, click Add Album. To buy an audiobook, just click on the Buy Book button — there's no Add Book button to press.

 Note that you can download individual episodes of a podcast, but you can also subscribe to a podcast. When you subscribe, iTunes automatically downloads future episodes and adds them to the Podcasts item in your source list.

5. When you're ready to buy, click the Shopping Cart item in the source list and then click the Buy Now button. The items you download are saved to the separate Purchased playlist.

6. After the download is finished, access your purchased file or files by clicking the Purchased playlist on the left. From there, you can play them or move them to other playlists just like any other item in your iTunes library.

Although the stuff you buy remains in the Purchased category in the source list, each item is also automatically moved to the proper category as well. For example, any songs you buy are added automatically to the Music category in the source list, while any movies you buy are added to the Movies category.

 The Back and Forward buttons at the top of the iTunes Store window operate much like those in Safari, moving you backward or forward in sequence through pages you've already seen. Clicking the Home button (which, through no great coincidence, looks like a miniature house) returns you to the Store's main page.

Play Online Radio Stations

Although it's not a radio tuner in the strictest sense, iTunes Radio can locate virtual radio stations all over the world that send audio over the Internet — a process usually dubbed *streaming* among the "in" Internet crowd. iTunes can track down hundreds of Internet radio stations in a variety of styles with only a few clicks. Whether you like Elvis (or those passing fads, like new wave, classical, or alternative), something's here for everyone. The Radio also offers news, sports, and talk radio.

1. To begin listening to Internet radio with iTunes, click the Radio icon, located beneath the Library icon in the source list. The result is a list of more than 20 types of radio stations, organized by genre, as shown in **Figure 11-9**.

Expanded category

Click the Radio icon   Radio stations

iTunes	File	Edit	View	Controls	Store	Advanced	Window	Help	▲ 💻 ⚹ ♡ ◀)) Fri 2:35 AM

iTunes

Stream	▲	Bit Rate	Comment
LIBRARY			
♫ Music	▶ Alternative		
🎬 Movies	▶ Ambient		
📺 TV Shows	▼ Blues (28 streams)		
🎙 Podcasts	Absolute Blues Hits(1.FM TM)	128 kbps	1.FM's " Classic Blues and Rock blues cha...
🅐 Applications	Bar Rockin' Blues (clubfmra...	128 kbps	As close to Chicago's blues clubs as you ca...
Radio	Bar Rockin' Blues (clubfmra...	64 kbps	As close to Chicago's blues clubs as you ca...
🎵 Ringtones	Blues Classics	128 kbps	American blues classics of the 30s to the 7...
	Blues Classics	64 kbps	American blues classics of the 30s to the 7...
STORE	Cajun Fest	128 kbps	Cajun, Zydeco and Bayou favorites.
🎵 iTunes Store	Cajun Fest	65 kbps	Cajun, Zydeco and Bayou favorites.
🎵 Purchased	Chittlin Circuit Radio	128 kbps	The Chittlin Circuit is where The Blues and...
PLAYLISTS	Chittlin Circuit Radio	32 kbps	The Chittlin Circuit is where The Blues and...
🎵 Party Shuffle	GotRadio Bit O Blues	128 kbps	Blues, Blues...Nothing but the Blues!
🎵 Music Videos	HellHound Radio	128 kbps	Best of the 80s and below.
🎵 My Top Rated	IcebergRadio.com – Blues ...	56 kbps	Blues greats new and old: BB King, Etta Ja...
	jazz89 KUVO	64 kbps	Jazz, Blues & Latin Jazz on Public Radio
	jazz89 KUVO	32 kbps	Jazz, Blues & Latin Jazz on Public Radio

Figure 11-9

2. When you expand a Radio category by clicking its triangle, iTunes displays the name of several radio stations for that category.

3. After iTunes fetches the names and descriptions of radio stations, double-click one that you want to hear. iTunes immediately jumps into action, loads the station, and begins to play it.

Playing Games in Leopard

Chapter 12

Although Mac OS X is already supplied with at least one game — a good version of chess, which I cover in the next section — the Macintosh has never been considered a true gaming platform by most computer owners. Until recently, many popular Windows games were never released in versions for the Mac, and only the most expensive Mac models had the only important component that determines the quality of today's games: a first-rate 3D video card.

However, within the past few years, all that has changed dramatically. *All* of today's Mac models feature muscle-car-quality video cards that use the NVIDIA GeForce or ATI Radeon chipsets; they can handle the most complex 3D graphics with ease. Match that capability with the renewed popularity of the Macintosh as a home computer and the performance of the current crop of Intel-based processors, and — wham! — suddenly the Mac is quite the game machine.

In this chapter, you

➠ Play 3-D chess with your Mac.

➠ Burn a little time with an old-fashioned sliding tile puzzle.

➡ Download new games for your Dashboard widget collection.

➡ Find out more about online gaming.

Play Chess

It has no flashy weapons and no cities to raze — but chess is still the world's most popular game, and Mac OS X even includes a little 3D. **Figure 12-1** illustrates the Chess application at play; you can find it in your Applications folder.

As you might expect, moving pieces on this board is as simple as clicking a piece and dragging it to its (legal) ending position.

Click and drag a piece to move it.

Figure 12-1

The game features take-back (or undo) for your last move — just press ⌘+Z if you need a second chance. You can also list your games in text form and save games in progress from the Game menu. Maybe it's not a complete set of bells and whistles like commercial chess games have, but the price is right and the play can be quite challenging when you set it at the higher skill levels.

To configure Chess to your liking, choose Chess⇨Preferences. Then you can

➡ **Change the appearance of your board and pieces.** Try a set of fur pieces on a grass board — jungle chess at its best!

➡ **Turn on spoken moves and voice recognition.** Click to select the Speak Computer Moves check box, and then click the Computer Voice pop-up menu to select the voice your Mac uses. If you select the Allow Player to Speak Moves check box, the round Speech Recognition window appears. Press the Esc key and speak your move (in standard chess notation).

➡ **Set the computer's skill level.** The Computer Plays slider determines whether your Mac plays a faster or smarter game.

 If you're like me, a hint at midgame isn't really cheating — especially when I'm behind by several pieces! When it's your turn, choose Moves⇨Show Hint and watch Chess suggest the best move.

Play the Tile Game Widget

Apple also provides a digital version of that old standby, the sliding tile game. The Tile Game is a dashboard widget, so you can display it at any time by clicking the dashboard icon to the left of the Dock. (It looks like a speedometer.) You can also display dashboard applications by clicking the scroll button on your mouse or pressing the correct function key (either F4 or F12, depending on the keyboard your Mac uses). **Figure 12-2** illustrates my dashboard showing the Tile Game widget.

If you haven't played this game, just click the Tile Game window once to randomize the tiles, and then click again to start playing. To move a tile to the free space, click the tile. Of course, the object of the game is to restore the image to its original pristine condition!

You can return to your applications and your Leopard desktop at any time by clicking the scroll button on your mouse a second time or by pressing the dashboard function key again.

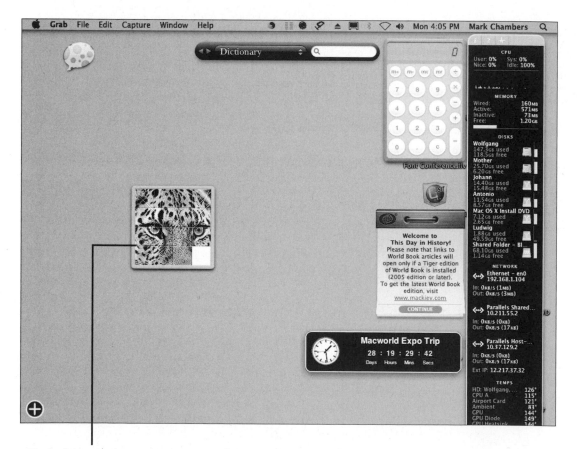

Click the window once to randomize the tiles.

Figure 12-2

One nice thing about dashboard game widgets is that most of them save the current game (or position) when you close the dashboard. That way, you can easily resume the game after you, well, get real work done.

Install New Widget Games from Apple

Looking for a new gaming challenge for your dashboard? No problem. Apple offers additional game widgets that you can download on the Mac OS X download site (www.apple.com/downloads) by using Safari. Third-party software developers also provide both freeware and shareware games. When Safari completes the download, Leopard automatically prompts you for confirmation before installing the new widget.

After you download a new game, you can easily add it to your dashboard:

1. Display your dashboard by pressing the dashboard function key or clicking the scroll button on your mouse.

2. Click the Add button (which bears a plus sign, naturally) in the lower-left corner of the dashboard screen. A scrolling menu strip appears at the bottom of the dashboard display (including any game widgets you downloaded and installed). **Figure 12-3** illustrates this phenomenon.

3. Drag new widgets directly onto your dashboard from this menu.

4. Click the Add button again (now it looks like an X) to return to your dashboard.

 Don't forget to set any options that your new game offers — look for a tiny circle with a lowercase letter *i*. Click this information icon and you can set the options that are available for the game.

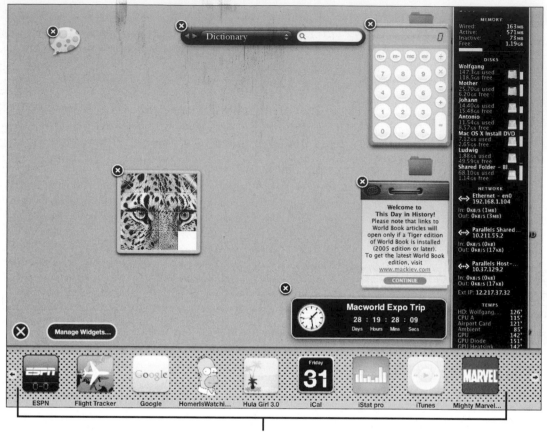

Drag new widgets onto your dashboard.

Figure 12-3

Play Games Online

Some of today's hottest games aren't limited to your Mac — online games use your Internet connection to match you against thousands of other players, in real-time, across the world!

 In my opinion, online gaming is truly enjoyable only if you have a broadband connection to the Internet (either DSL, cable, or satellite). Playing today's 3D online games (or even Web-based games) using a dial-up modem connection is a lesson in frustration.

Probably the most popular online game for the Mac is the online megahit *World of Warcraft* (and the latest expansion to the original game, *Wrath of the Lich King*). This massive multiplayer online role-playing game, or MMORPG, is another wrinkle in the popular *Warcraft* game series. *World of Warcraft* puts the character you create in the boots of human princes, Orc battle generals, undead champions, trolls, gnomes, and elfin lords. In fact, you can create multiple characters and play them as you choose. My recommendation: Stick with the Undead, my friend.

Combat, however, is only half the job. By finishing quests and killing various nasties, you earn experience, upgrade your armor and weapons, and build your reputation with various groups throughout the land. You can take to the air, buy goods from mercenaries, or even discover a trade such as leatherworking or enchanting. Spells abound, and you can join a guild and chat with the new friends you make online. I've played for more than three years, and I'm still excited by this incredible game (see **Figure 12-4**).

Control is by both keyboard and mouse; the game is easy to understand, but you always find someone to kick your posterior in battle-grounds or dungeons.

You pay about $50 online for *World of Warcraft* and then you're charged a set fee for each month's subscription — and it's worth every single penny you spend. (Remember that this program is one you buy on your own; it doesn't come with your Mac or with Leopard.) For all the details and some fancy desktop backgrounds, check the official site at www.blizzard.com.

Other popular online games include

➟ Bridge (OKBridge.com)

➟ Poker (www.fulltiltpoker.com)

➟ Pool (www.flyordie.com)

Some games are free and display advertisements, and others are subscription-based. Visit the Download area on the Apple Web site for more information on the latest online games.

Play World of Warcraft

Figure 12-4

Part III
Exploring the Internet

The 5th Wave   By Rich Tennant

"Awww, cool — a Web Cam! You should point
it at something interesting to watch. The
fish bowl! The fish bowl!"

Understanding Internet Basics

Chapter 13

1'll be honest: The Internet is a terribly complex monster of a network. If you tried to fathom all the data that's exchanged on the Internet and everything that takes place when you check your e-mail for your cousin Joan's fruitcake recipe, your brain would probably melt like a chocolate bar in the Sahara Desert. (I know my brain is overheating just thinking about it.)

Luckily for regular folks like you and me, Mac OS X Leopard closes the trapdoor on all these details, keeping them hidden (as they *should* be). You don't have to worry about them, and the obscure information you need in order to establish an Internet connection is kept to a minimum. You need to know only the basics about the Internet, and that's what I provide in this chapter!

I discuss how to

➠ Evaluate different types of Internet connections.

➠ Connect to the Internet.

➠ Use the Apple MobileMe service.

➠ Add an antivirus program.

➠ Follow common-sense rules to stay safe on the Internet.

Get ready to . . .

Understand How the Internet Works

Many of the Mac and PC owners I talk to are convinced that the Internet is a real substance. They're not quite sure whether it's animal, vegetable, or mineral, but they're sure that they either *have it* or *want it* inside their computers. (It's probably a tiny, glowing ball: a cross between Tinker Bell and St. Elmo's fire.)

Seriously, though, you don't need to know what the Internet is in order to use it. From a Mac owner's standpoint, you would be correct (in a way) if you said that the Internet begins at the phone connection or the cable modem. Therefore, if you want to skip to the next section and avoid a glance underneath the hood, be my guest.

Still here? Good. Here's a brief description of what happens when you connect to the Internet and visit a Web site:

1. You open your Safari Web browser (a *browser* is a program used to display pages from the World Wide Web), and your Mac connects to an Internet service provider (ISP).

An *ISP* is simply the company you pay to connect to the Internet. You might contract with a cable company, such as Comcast, Bright House, or RoadRunner, or you might use a service such as AOL, Juno, or Earthlink. All these are ISPs. Your ISP account usually includes reserved space on its computers for you to create a personal Web site, as well as giving you one, two, or more e-mail addresses.

2. Your ISP locates the Web site across the Internet.

When you ask to open a specific Web site, your ISP uses that Web site's name to locate the computer it resides on. In the Internet world, the Web site *name* is its Web address or URL (which stands for Universal Resource Locator, but you don't need to remember that). When the Web site is located, your ISP opens a sort of pathway between your Mac and the server. For example, if you request the URL www.mlcbooks.com, my personal Web site is displayed.

3. After you connect to a Web site, a Web page is displayed. On this page, you can click *links*, which generally consist of text shown in a different color, and the text is often underlined. Sometimes, however, the link is an image rather than text. Clicking the text or image link opens another page on the same Web site, or it might even open a completely different Web site.

This is the essence of everything you do on the Internet: Computers connect with other computers (no matter where on the planet they might be) and exchange information of various types, such as e-mail messages, photos, Web pages, videos, and music.

So how does your ISP know how to find the particular Web site you want to visit? Every computer on the Internet is assigned a unique address called an *Internet Protocol* or IP address. That address identifies that computer to other computers on the Internet. This IP address takes the form of four groups of numbers separated by periods, as in this example: 192.168.1.100. Sophisticated computers on the Internet keep track of who has which IP address and also which English-language Web address, like Apple.com, is tied to which IP address.

See? It's beautifully organized chaos, and I'm the proud owner of three or four of the billions of Web sites on the planet!

Explore Internet Connections

Consider the types of connections that are available under Leopard to link your Mac to the ISP I describe in the preceding section. You can choose from four pathways to digital freedom:

⟹ **A broadband connection:** Whether it's by way of DSL (which uses a standard telephone line) or cable (which uses your cable TV wiring), *broadband* Internet access is many times faster than a dialup connection. Plus, both technologies are *always-on* — your computer is auto-matically connected to the Internet when you turn it on and the connection stays active. With DSL or cable, no squeaky whine accompanies your modem making a connection each time you want to check your movie listings Web site. Both DSL and cable require a special piece of hardware commonly called a *modem*. This box is usually thrown in as part of your ISP charge. A broadband connection usually requires professional installation.

 Not every Internet connection requires an ISP. For example, some mobile phone providers can equip your laptop with a cellular modem that delivers the Internet wherever you have mobile service. Many larger cities now offer free city-wide public wireless access (not to mention the free wireless access provided by coffee shops and restaurants).

➡ **A satellite connection:** If you're *really* out there — miles and miles away from any cable or DSL phone service — you can still have high-speed Internet access. The price for a satellite connection is usually much steeper than a standard DSL or cable connection, but it's available anywhere you can plant your antenna dish with a clear view of the sky. Plus, a satellite connection is faster than other types of broadband access. Older satellite technologies required you to also use a dialup connection — and the antenna could only receive, not send — but most ISPs that can handle satellite connections now offer satellite systems that send *and* receive through the dish.

➡ **A dialup connection:** Old-fashioned, yes. Slow as an arthritic burro, indeed. However, an *analog* (or telephone modem) connection is still a viable method for computer owners to reach the Internet. It's the cheapest method available, and all you need for this type of connection is a standard telephone jack and a modem (and a contract with a service provider, such

as AOL, Juno, or Earthlink). Apple used to include a
modem with every computer, but no longer — these
days, you have to buy an external USB modem to
make the dialup connection. (Apple makes one, or
any USB modem that's compatible with Mac OS X
works fine.)

➡ **A network connection:** This type of connection concerns Mac models that are part of a local-area network
(LAN) either at the office or in your home. If your
Mac is connected to a LAN that already has Internet
access, you don't even need an ISP and no other hardware is required: Simply contact your network administrator, buy that important person a steak dinner, and
ask to be connected to the Internet. On the other
hand, if your network has no Internet access, you're
back to Square One: You need one of the three types
of connections noted in the preceding bullets.

Set Up a Broadband Internet Connection

Okay, so you sign up for Internet access and your ISP sends you a sheet
of paper covered with indecipherable settings that look like Egyptian
hieroglyphics. Don't worry: Those settings are the ones you need in
order to connect to your ISP. After you transfer this information to
Leopard, you should be surfing the Web like an old pro.

Follow these steps to set up your Internet connection if you're using a
cable modem, DSL connection, or network:

1. Click the System Preferences icon on the Dock and choose
Network.

2. Select Ethernet from the list on the left side of the pane to
display the settings you see in **Figure 13-1.**

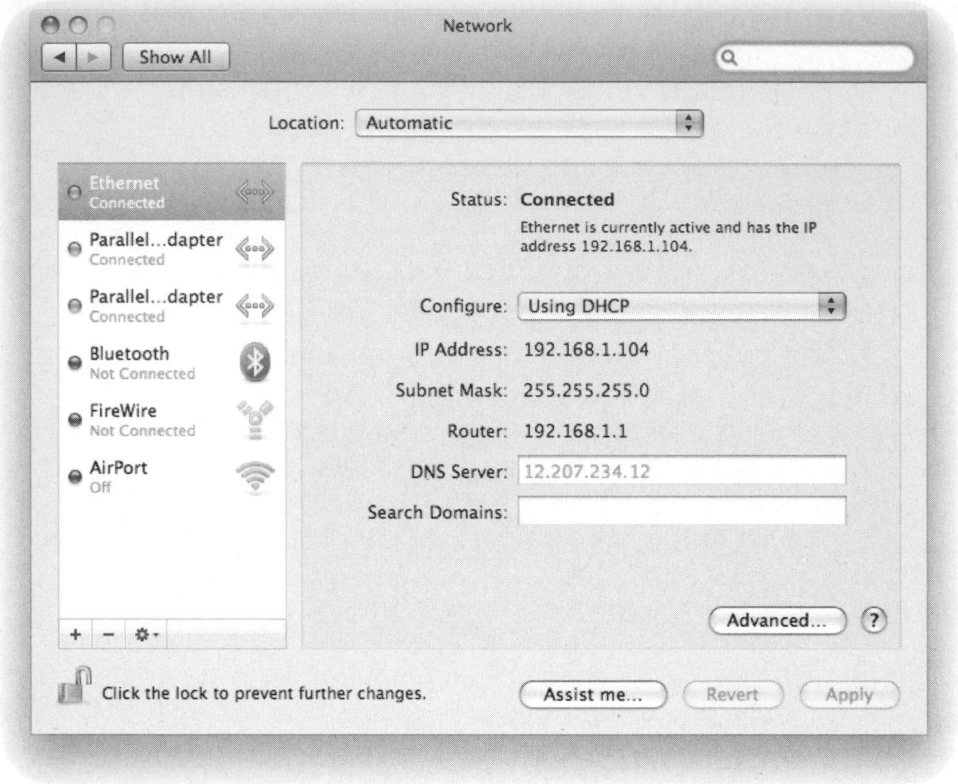

Figure 13-1

3. Refer to the paperwork you received from your ISP and then enter the settings for the type of connection your ISP offers:

- *If your ISP tells you to use Dynamic Host Configuration Protocol (DHCP):* Choose Using DHCP from the Configure pop-up menu, and your ISP can automatically set up virtually all the TCP/IP settings for you! (No wonder DHCP is so popular these days.)

- *If your ISP tells you that you won't use DHCP:* Choose Manually from the Configure pop-up menu. Then enter the settings provided by your ISP in the IP Address, Subnet Mask, Router, and DNS Servers fields.

4. If your ISP uses PPPoE (Point-to-Point Protocol over Ethernet), click the Configure pop-up menu and choose Create PPPoE Service. (If your ISP doesn't use PPPoE, skip to Step 8.)

5. Type an indentifying name for the PPPoE service into the Service Name text box.

6. Click Done.

7. Enter the password for your PPPoE connection.

8. Press ⌘+Q to close System Preferences and save your changes.

 Leopard can get down and dirty in the configuration trenches! To launch a wizard to help with the configuration process, click the Assist Me button and then click Assistant on the wizard's welcome screen.

Set Up a Wireless Internet Connection

If you're within range of a wireless Ethernet network, you can use your Mac's built-in wireless hardware to connect. Most public networks offer Internet access, so this option is an advantage for MacBook owners on the go (those who visit coffee shops, libraries, and schools, for example).

Likewise, if you're using a broadband connection at home with an AirPort Extreme wireless router, your desktop Mac can connect to that wireless network and reach the Internet that way.

Follow these steps to connect to a wireless network:

1. Click the System Preferences icon on the Dock.

2. Click the Network icon.

3. From the Connection list on the left, click AirPort.

4. Click to select the Show AirPort Status in Menu Bar check box.

5. Click the Apply button.

6. Press ⌘+Q to close System Preferences and save your settings.

7. Click the AirPort status icon (which looks like a fan) on the Finder menu bar.

8. From the AirPort menu, choose an existing network connection that you want to join.

The network name is usually posted for public networks. If you're joining a private wireless network, ask the person who set up the network for the name you should choose.

9. If you're joining a secure network, enter the password and click Join.

Again, if the public network you're joining has a password (most don't), it should be posted. If you're joining a private wireless network, ask the good person who set up the network for that all-important password.

Set Up a Dialup Connection

Follow these steps to set up your Internet connection if you're using a standard phone line and either your Mac's internal modem (for older Macs) or an external USB modem (for the current crop of Macs):

1. Click the System Preferences icon on the Dock and choose Network.

2. Choose Internal Modem or External Modem from the Show pop-up menu.

3. Click the TCP/IP tab and enter the settings for the type of connection your ISP provides:

- *If your ISP tells you to use PPP (Point-to-Point Protocol):* Click the Configure IPv4 pop-up menu and choose Using PPP. If your ISP provided you with DNS Server or Search Domain addresses, type them now in the corresponding boxes.

- *If you're using AOL:* Click the Configure IPv4 pop-up menu and choose AOL Dialup. If AOL provided you with DNS Server or Search Domain addresses, click in the corresponding box and type them now.

- *If your ISP instructs you to set up the connection manually:* Click the Configure IPv4 pop-up menu and choose Manually. Then click in the IP Address, DNS Servers, and Search Domains fields and enter the respective settings provided by your ISP.

4. Click the PPP tab.

5. In their respective fields, enter the account name, password, telephone number, and (optional) the service provider name and an alternative telephone number provided by your ISP.

6. Press ⌘+Q to close System Preferences and save your changes.

Find Out about MobileMe

What if you could reach a hard drive with 20GB of your files over any Internet connection — anywhere in the world — and it just *showed up* on your desktop automatically?

That's Apple's MobileMe online hosting service. In this section, I save you the trouble of researching all the benefits of MobileMe. Heck, that's one of the reasons you bought this book, right?

I begin with a definition. The online hard drive offered to MobileMe subscribers (read about subscribing in the following section) is an *iDisk,* and it's well integrated into Mac OS X. In fact, if you didn't know its background, you might think that iDisk was simply another internal hard drive. **Figure 13-2** illustrates the iDisk icon on my desktop. The Finder window displays the contents; notice the folders visible there. (I tell you more about these folders later in the chapter.)

Figure 13-2

The files I add to my iDisk are stored on an Apple server, location unknown — literally. The physical storage (a massive file server that holds uncounted gigabytes of data) might be in California or it might be in Timbuktu. There's a whole bunch of them, too. You and I don't need to care about the *where* part because

➡ **Your iDisk is almost always available.** Oh, yes — 24/7, your files are waiting for you. (Apple takes down the system for scheduled maintenance, though.)

➡ **Your iDisk is secure.** Apple goes to great lengths to guarantee the security of your data, encrypting the transfer of files and folders whenever you use your iDisk. (*Encrypted* data is encoded so that it's much harder for someone to intercept.) You can also password-protect any data you want to offer to others, just in case.

➡ **Your iDisk works even when you aren't on the Internet.** Yep, you read that right — you can create new documents and modify files to your heart's content while you're on a flight or relaxing on the beach. The next time you connect to the Internet, iDisk automatically updates whatever changes you made.

Now that I've piqued your interest (and answered the most common question about iDisk), return to the MobileMe service for a moment so that I can show you how to set up your account.

Although iDisk is the primary attraction, MobileMe also offers a number of other features:

➡ **A Web-based e-mail system:** You can check your MobileMe e-mail on the road.

➡ **Your own, personal Web page:** You can customize it using iWeb, which is part of the iLife program suite.

➡ **A personal photo gallery:** Other people can visit it on the Web and check out your pictures.

➡ **The ability to synchronize multiple Mac computers with the same data:** Contacts and calendars are two examples.

Join the MobileMe Crowd

You have a chance to sign up for MobileMe when you turn on your Mac for the first time. However, if you decide to pass up MobileMe at that time, you can always join in the fun by following these steps:

1. Click the System Preferences icon on the Dock.

2. Click the MobileMe icon.

3. Click the Learn More button.

This step launches Safari and displays the Apple MobileMe Web site (www.me.com). Safari is the Apple Web browser, similar to Internet Explorer in Windows, that displays pages from the World Wide Web. (I discuss Safari in detail in Chapter 14.)

4. Click the Sign Up for a Free Trial button and then follow the onscreen instructions to choose a member name and password.

You need a credit card to sign up, but you can cancel at any time during the 60-day trial period.

5. When you're done with the clicking and are rewarded with your login information, close Safari and enter your name and password into the text boxes in the MobileMe System Preferences pane. Click Sign In to start using MobileMe.

Figure 13-3 illustrates a login example I created.

Figure 13-3

Like the convenient operating system it is, Leopard handles all your MobileMe login chores automatically from this point on.

If you're a dialup Internet user, you may have been dreading this moment; but here it is. I'm truly sorry, but in my opinion, a high-speed broadband connection is a real requirement in order to take full advantage of a MobileMe subscription. You can certainly still use all the functionality of MobileMe with any type of Internet connection, but you're going to spend from now until the next *Iron Man* sequel waiting for files to copy and things to happen.

Here's a bit of good news: Other than the 60-day limit, there's almost no difference between a MobileMe trial account and a full $100 yearly subscription, so you can try out all the MobileMe features, exactly as though you were already paying for them. *Sweet!*

A MobileMe subscription also lets you synchronize your e-mail, Address Book contact information, Gallery photos, and Safari book-marks between multiple Macs, as well as between your iPhone and iPod Touch. What a boon if you spend time on the road with a member of the MacBook species!

Both trial and subscriber MobileMe users can read MobileMe e-mail on the MobileMe Web site by using the Safari browser. That's neat, certainly, and you can use Web mail from any computer with an Internet connection. However, you can also send and receive MobileMe e-mail seamlessly from the Leopard Mail program, which is the preferred method of checking messages. In fact, Leopard automatically creates a matching Mail account for your trial MobileMe account. Unadulterated *cool!*

After you play around with the trial version, if you like what you see, it's easy to subscribe. When you open the MobileMe pane within System Preferences and click the Account button, Leopard displays a countdown reminder telling you how many days remain on your trial period. To upgrade to a full subscription, visit the MobileMe Web site at www.me.com, mentioned earlier, at any time and click the Join Now button.

Keep in mind that MobileMe is many things, but it isn't an ISP. You need an existing Internet connection to use the services and features included in MobileMe membership. This requirement makes a lot of sense, considering that most of us already have Internet access.

MobileMe works with the ISP you already have, so you don't have to worry about AOL or EarthLink conflicting with MobileMe. However, I can't guarantee that your system administrator at work allows MobileMe traffic across his or her pristine network. Perhaps a steak dinner would help your argument.

Open Your iDisk

How do you open your iDisk? Leopard gives you a number of different avenues:

➡ **Choose Go➪iDisk from the Finder menu and then choose My iDisk from the submenu.**

If you're a keyboard type, press ⌘+Shift+I instead.

➡ **Click the iDisk icon in the Finder window Sidebar.**

➡ **Click the iDisk button on your Finder toolbar.**

You can easily add an iDisk button. Open a Finder window, click View, and then click Customize Toolbar. Drag the iDisk icon up to the toolbar and then click Done.

After you open your iDisk, an iDisk volume icon also pops up on your desktop. You can open the little scamp later in your computing session by simply double-clicking the Desktop icon. The desktop iDisk icon hangs around until you log out, restart, eject the iDisk, or shut down your Mac.

Understand the iDisk Storage Folders

Your iDisk contains a number of different folders. Some of them are similar to the subfolders in your Home folder, and others are unique to the structure of your iDisk. In this section, I provide the details on the iDisk folder family.

Although you can store files and create folders in the *root* (or top level) of an iDisk, the same organizational tips apply as in the root of your laptop's internal hard drive. In other words, most items that you copy to or create on your iDisk should be stored in one of these six storage folders (refer to **Figure 13-2**):

➡ **Documents:** Store in this folder the documents you create with your applications (such as a letter you composed in Pages or a spreadsheet you developed in Numbers), which only you can access.

➡ **Movies:** This folder stores your QuickTime movies.

➡ **Music:** You store iTunes music and playlists here.

➡ **Pictures:** The digital images you store in this folder can be used with other MobileMe services (such as your online Photo Gallery) or within iPhoto.

➡ **Public:** The files you store in this folder are meant to be shared with other people. You can also allow other people to copy and save files to your Public folder.

➡ **Sites:** You can use iWeb to create Web pages in this folder.

You can open these iDisk folders in a Finder window just like you can open any typical folder on your Mac's internal hard drive. You can also open and save documents to your iDisk folders using all your applications. In other words, these six iDisk folders act just like normal, everyday folders. Pretty doggone neat!

Your iDisk contains another folder that you *can't* use to store stuff (directly, anyway): the Software read-only folder is a special case. Apple stuffs this folder full of a wide variety of the latest in freeware and shareware as well as commercial demo software. You can copy whatever you like from the Software folder to your Mac's desktop and then install your new software toy from that local copy. (Oh, and the contents of the Software folder don't count against your total storage space limit.) Enjoy!

Keep Your Mac Secure Online

I know that you've heard horror stories about hacking: Big corporations and big government installations seem to be as open to hackers as a public library. Often, you read that even entire identities are being stolen online. When you consider that your Mac can contain extremely sensitive and private information from your life — such as your Social Security number and financial information — it's enough to make you nervous about turning on your computer long enough to check your eBay auctions.

How much of this is Hollywood-style drama? How truly real is the danger, especially to Mac owners? In this section, I continue a quest that I've pursued for almost 15 years — to make my readers feel comfortable and secure in the online world by explaining the truth about what can happen and telling you how you can protect your system from intrusions.

 One quick note: This section is written with the home and small-business Mac owner in mind. Macs that access the Internet over a larger corporate network are likely already protected by that knight in shining armor, the network system administrator. (Insert applause here.) Check with your system administrator before you attempt to implement any of the recommendations I make here.

As a consultant, I run Web sites and squash virus attacks for a number of companies and organizations, so I've seen the gamut of Internet dangers. With that understood, here's what can happen to you online *without* the right safeguards, on *any* computer:

⟶ **Hackers can access shared information on your network.** If you're running an unguarded network, it's possible for others to gain access to your documents and applications or wreak havoc on your system.

⟶ **Your system could be infected with a virus or dangerous macro.** Left to their own devices, these misbehaving programs and macro commands can delete files or turn your entire hard drive into an empty paperweight. (Although Mac viruses are few and far between as I write this, I don't think we'll enjoy such luxury for long. Plus, if you dual-boot your Intel Mac into Windows XP or Vista, you suddenly enter a veritable minefield of PC viruses and spyware.)

⟶ **Unsavory individuals can attempt to contact members of your family.** This type of attack can take place over iChat (the Apple instant messaging and conferencing program, which I describe in Chapter 16), e-mail, or Web discussion boards, putting your family's safety at risk.

⟶ **Hackers can use your system to attack others.** Your computer can be tricked into helping hackers when they attempt to knock out Web sites on the Internet.

⟶ **Criminals can attempt to con you out of your credit card or personal information.** The Internet is a prime tool used by people trying to steal identities.

To be absolutely honest, some danger is indeed present every time you or any user of your Macintosh connects to the Internet. However, here's the good news: If you use the proper safeguards, it's literally impossible for most of those worst-case scenarios to happen on your Mac; and what remains would be so difficult that even the most diehard hacker would throw in the towel long before reaching your computer or network.

I want to point out that virtually everyone reading this book — as well as the guy writing it — really doesn't have anything that's worth a malicious hacking campaign. Information in the form of Quicken data files, saved games of *Sims 2*, and genealogical data might be priceless to us, of course, but most dedicated hackers are after bigger game. Unfortunately, the coverage that the media and Hollywood give to corporate and government attacks can make even Aunt Harriet more than a little paranoid. It's not really necessary to consider the FBI or Interpol every time you poke your Mac's power button. A few simple precautions are all that's required.

Because this book focuses on Mac OS X Leopard, I don't spend much time covering Windows. For a comprehensive guide to Windows XP, Vista, and the PC world, however, I can heartily recommend the sister volume to this book, *PCs All-in-One Desk Reference For Dummies*, 4th Edition, published by Wiley. Why the strong recommendation? Well, I wrote that book!

Interested in the technical side of computer security? Then visit a favorite site of mine on the Web: www.grc.com, the home of Gibson Research Corporation. There you'll find the free online utility ShieldsUP!, which automatically tests how susceptible your Mac is to hacker attacks.

Know the Antivirus Basics

It's time to consider your antivirus protection (under both Leopard and Windows, if you're running an Intel-based Mac). *Viruses* are malicious computer programs that originate at an outside source and can infect your computer without your knowing it. The virus, which is generally activated when you run an infected program on your computer, can then take control of your system and cause lots of trouble. You need to closely monitor what I call the Big Three:

➡ **Web downloads:** Consider every file you receive from the Internet as a possible viral threat.

➡ **Removable media:** Viruses can be stored on everything from CD-ROMs and DVD-ROMs to USB flash drives.

➡ **E-mail file attachments:** An application sent to you as an e-mail attachment is an easy doorway to your system.

Horrors! Mac OS X has no built-in antivirus support. (Then again, neither does Windows XP or Vista.) However, a good antivirus program takes care of any application that's carrying a virus. Make sure that the antivirus program you choose offers *real-time scanning*, which operates when you download or open a file. Periodic scanning of your entire system is important, too, but only a real-time scanning application such as Norton AntiVirus can immediately ensure that the file or the application you just received in your e-mail Inbox is truly free from viruses. Keep in mind that Apple periodically releases software updates for Leopard that are intended to plug security holes as the holes are discovered. So if you get into the habit of grabbing these updates whenever they're available, you can help keep your Mac safe. (Chapter 17 covers how to set up automatic updates to Leopard.)

Virus technology continues to evolve over time, just like more beneficial application development. For example, a recently discovered virus was contained in a JPEG image file! With a good antivirus application that offers regular updates, you can continue to keep your system safe from viral attack.

I heartily recommend both Norton AntiVirus from Symantec (www.symantec.com, available in versions for Leopard and Windows XP) and VirusBarrier X from Intego (at www.intego.com and available only for Leopard). Both programs include automatic updates delivered while you're online to make sure that you're covered against the latest viruses.

Follow Common Sense: Things Not to Do Online

Practicing common sense on the Internet is just as important as adding an antivirus application to your Mac.

With this statement in mind, here's a checklist of things you should *never* do while you're online:

➡ **Never download a file from a site you don't trust.** Make sure that your antivirus software is configured to check downloaded files before you open them.

➡ **Never open an e-mail attachment before it's checked.** Don't give in to temptation, even if the person who sent the message is someone you trust. (Many macro viruses now replicate themselves by sending copies to the addresses found in the victim's e-mail program. Of course, this problem crops up regularly in the Windows world, but it has been known to happen in the Macintosh community as well.)

➡ **Never enter personal information in an e-mail message when you don't know the recipient.** Sure, I send my mailing address to friends and family, but no one else. In fact, even e-mail can be intercepted by a determined hacker, so if you're sending something truly important, use an encryption application, such as PGP Personal Desktop (www.pgp.com).

➡ **Never enter personal information on a Web site provided as a link in an e-mail message.** Don't fall prey to phishing expeditions. *Phishing* is a recently coined Internet term that refers to the attempt that con artists and hackers make to lure you in by creating

Web sites that look just like the sites used by major online stores — including big names such as eBay, PayPal, and Amazon. These turkeys then send out junk e-mail messages telling you that you must log on to the Web site to refresh or correct your personal information. As you no doubt already guessed, that information is siphoned off and sold to the highest bidder — *your* credit card, *your* password, and *your* address. Luckily, if you follow the tips I give you in this section, you can avoid these phishing expeditions!

Some of these e-mail message and Web site combinations look authentic enough to fool anyone! No reputable online company or store will demand or solicit your personal information by using e-mail or a linked Web site. In fact, feel free to contact the company at its *real* Web site and report the phishing attempt!

➡ **Never include personal information in an Internet newsgroup post.** (If you aren't familiar with the term, a *newsgroup* is a public Internet message base, often called a *Usenet group*. Most ISPs offer a selection of newsgroups that you can download.) Newsgroup posts can be viewed by anyone with a newsgroup account, so there's no such thing as privacy in a newsgroup.

➡ **Never buy from an online store that doesn't offer a secure, encrypted connection when you're prompted for your personal information and credit card number.** If you're using the Apple Safari browser, the padlock icon appears in the upper-right corner of the Safari window. When the padlock icon appears in the window, the connection is encrypted and secure.

➡ **Never divulge personal information to others over an iChat connection.** I tell you more about iChat in Chapter 16.

➠ **Never use the same password for all your electronic business.** Use different passwords that include both letters and numbers and change them often, and never divulge them to anyone else.

Browsing the Web with Safari

*N*avigating the Web is easy, but you need a browser to visit your favorite sites. That's Safari, of course, and it just keeps getting better with each new version of Mac OS X. It doesn't matter whether you're working wirelessly from a hotel room or the comfort of your home: Safari delivers the Web the right way.

By using Safari, you can

➡ Search for information, display sites you visited, and navigate immediately to your favorite sites.

➡ Download files and print documents.

➡ Block irritating pop-up windows.

➡ Customize the program to match your preferences.

Navigate the Web

To begin your travels around the Internet, follow these steps:

1. Launch Safari by clicking the Safari compass icon on the Dock.

2. Click in the Toolbar text box, shown in **Figure 14-1**, type the address for the Web site you want to visit, and then press Return. The page appears in the Content window, which occupies most of the Safari window.

Most Web site addresses still begin with the www. prefix and end with the .com suffix, but you may encounter addresses that begin or end differently. Make sure to enter the Web address exactly as it appears in advertisements, e-mail messages, or news reports — and yes, capitalization does matter!

Type Web address here

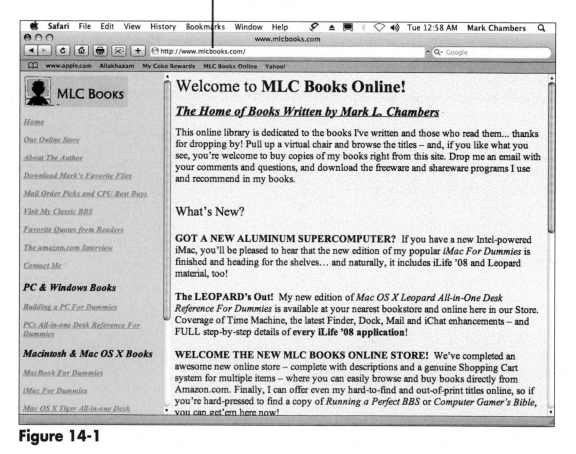

Figure 14-1

3. On the resulting Web page, click an underlined (or high-lighted) link to continue Web surfing. You can also jump directly to another page by returning to Step 2.

Safari also launches automatically when you

➠ Click a page link in Apple Mail or another Internet application.

➠ Click a Safari Web page icon in the Dock, the desktop, or in a Finder window.

➠ Click a Web site within the Address Book.

A typical Web surfing session is a linear experience — you move from one page to the next, absorbing the information you want and discarding the rest. However, after you visit a few sites, you might find that you need to return to a site you just visited or head to the familiar ground of your home page. Safari offers these navigational controls on the toolbar:

➠ **Back:** Click the Back button (the left-facing arrow) on the toolbar to return to the last page you visited. Additional clicks open previous pages, in reverse order. The Back button is disabled if you haven't visited at least two sites.

➠ **Forward:** If you clicked the Back button at least once, clicking the Forward button (the right-facing arrow) opens the next page (or pages) where you were, in forward order. The Forward button is disabled if you haven't used the Back button.

➠ **Stop/Reload:** Click the Reload button (which has a circular arrow) to *refresh*, or reload, the contents of the current page. Although most pages remain static, some pages change their content at regular intervals or after you fill out a form or click a button. By clicking

Reload (look for the curvy arrow), you can see what's changed on these pages. (I use Reload every hour or so on CNN.com, for example.) While a page is loading, the Reload button turns into the Stop button — with a little X mark on it — and you can click it to stop the loading of the content from the current page.

The Safari toolbar also includes four other buttons that I discuss in more detail later in this chapter:

➡ **Home:** Click this button (look for the little house) to return to your home page.

➡ **Add Bookmark:** Click this toolbar button (which carries a plus sign) to add a page to your Bookmarks bar or Bookmarks menu.

➡ **Print:** Click this button (which bears a printer icon) to print the contents of the Safari window.

➡ **Google Search:** Type text in this box to search Google for a specific subject that's available on the Web. (People use Google to find everything from used auto parts to former spouses.)

 A tiny padlock icon appears in the upper-right corner of the Safari window when you're connected to a secure Web site. This is A Good Thing! A *secure site* encrypts the information you send and receive, making it much harder for other people to steal credit card numbers and personal information, for example. *Never* — I mean *never* — enter any valuable personal or financial information on a Web page unless you see the secure-connection padlock symbol.

Search the Web

1. Launch Safari.

2. Click in the Google Search box and type the text that you want to find on the Web.

3. Press Return to display the results, as shown in **Figure** 14-2.

You can click any of the underlined links on the Google results page to jump to that Web site.

 To repeat a recent search, click the down arrow in the Google Search box and select it from the pop-up menu.

 You can search for a specific name or phrase by enclosing it within quotes, such as "Louis Armstrong" or "combustion engine."

Click any link.   Type your search term.

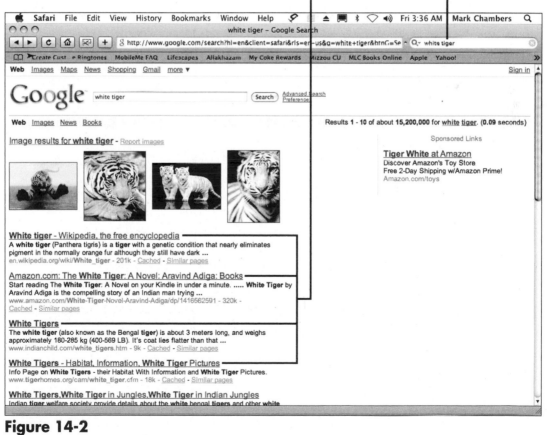

Figure 14-2

Find Content on a Web Page

1. After displaying in the Safari window the Web page you
want to search, press ⌘+F (or choose Edit➪Find➪Find).

2. Safari displays the Find bar (which appears directly under
the toolbar).

3. Type the word or phrase you're looking for in the Find
box — no need to press Return. Safari highlights any
matches it finds, as shown in **Figure 14-3**.

Safari highlights matching words.

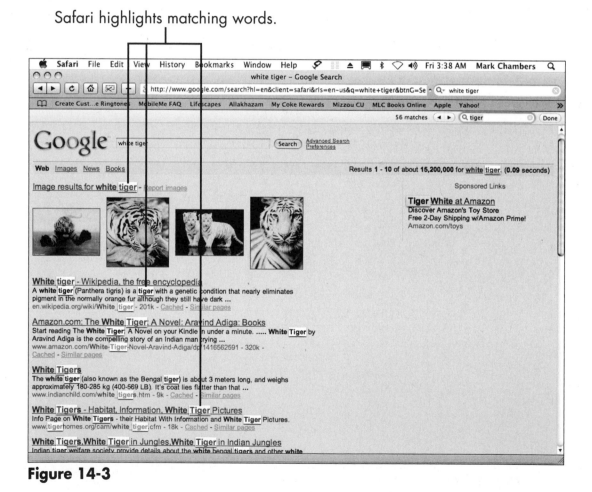

Figure 14-3

4. Click the Next button on the Find bar to advance to each spot within the page in order, all the way to the bottom of the page. To search upward to the top of the page, click Previous.

5. When you're finished searching, click the Done button.

Set Up a Home Page

1. Display the Web page you want as your new home page in Safari. (I recommend selecting a page with few graphics or a fast-loading popular site.)

2. Choose Safari⇨Preferences or press ⌘+, (comma).

3. Click the General button, shown in **Figure** 14-4.

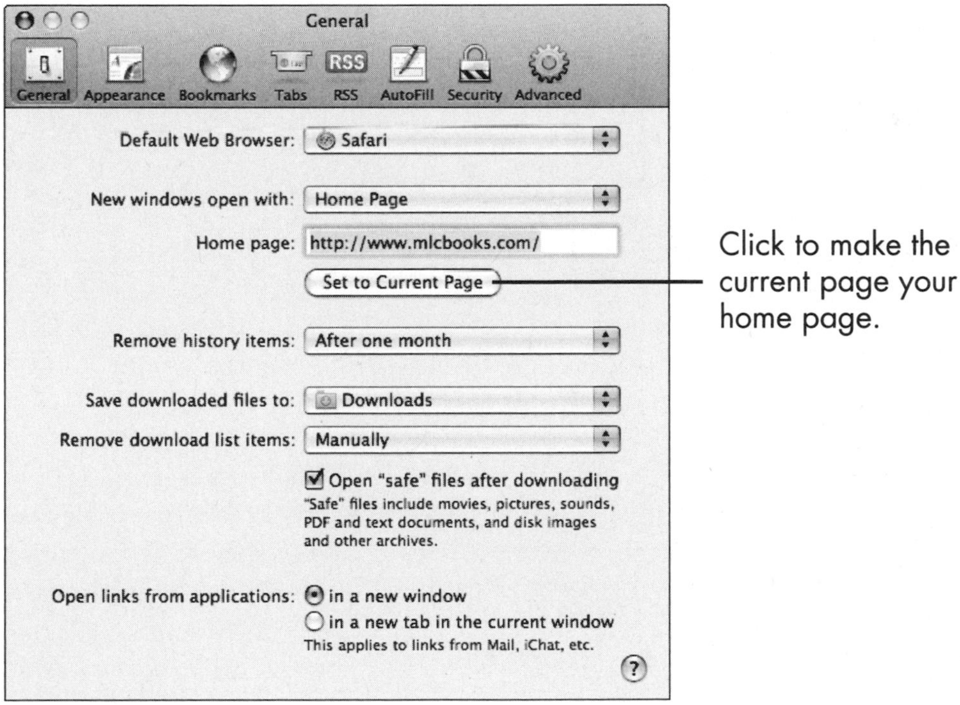

Click to make the current page your home page.

Figure 14-4

4. Click the Set to Current Page button.

 To set a blank page (for the fastest window display), click the New Windows Open With pop-up menu and choose Empty Page.

5. Click the Close button to close the Preferences dialog box.

Bookmark a Web Site

You can set up bookmarks within Safari that make it easy to jump directly to your favorite pages. To bookmark a Web site, follow these steps:

1. Launch Safari and navigate to a page.

2. Choose Bookmarks⇨Add Bookmark or press the ⌘+D keyboard shortcut.

3. Safari displays a sheet where you can enter the name for the bookmark and also select where it appears (on the Bookmarks bar or the Bookmarks menu at the top of the window). Type a name and choose where to store the bookmark from the drop-down menu.

4. Click Add.

The Bookmarks bar appears just below the toolbar. The Collections pane, shown in **Figure 14-5**, opens in a separate pane on the left side of the Safari window. Display it by clicking the Show All Bookmarks button (which carries an open book icon) on the Bookmarks bar.

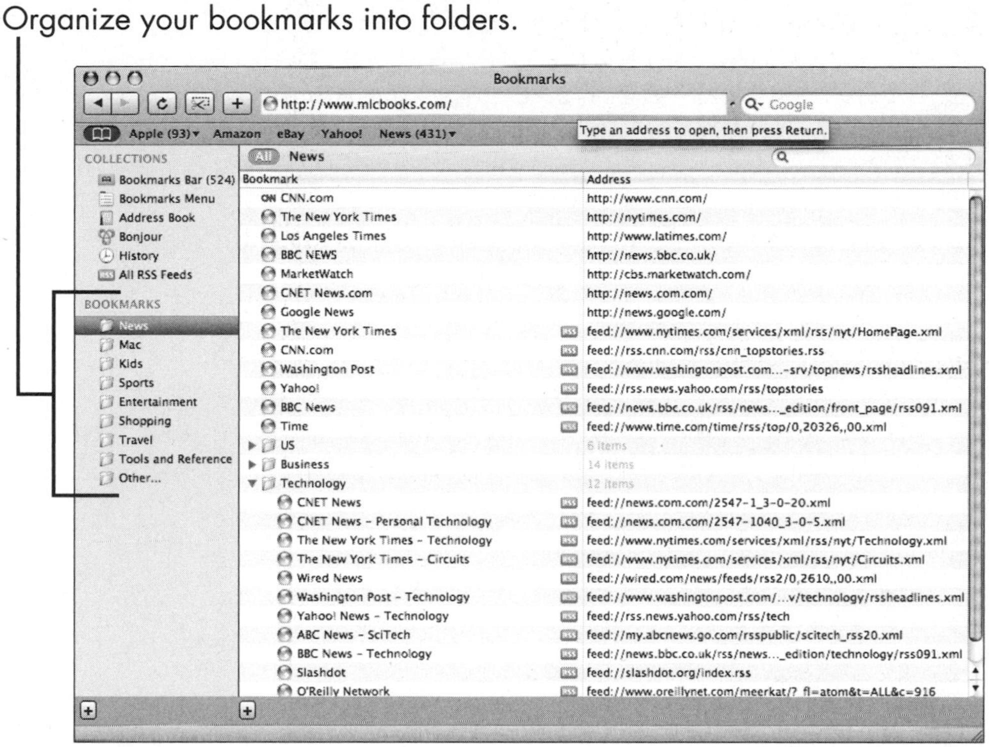

Organize your bookmarks into folders.

Figure 14-5

Organize Bookmarks

The more bookmarks you add, the more unwieldy the Bookmarks menu and the Collections pane become. To keep your bookmarks organized, follow these steps:

1. With Safari open, choose Bookmarks➪Add Bookmark Folder.

2. Type a name for the new folder.

3. Drag bookmarks into the new folder to help reduce the clutter.

4. To delete a bookmark or a folder from the Collections pane, click it and then press Delete.

View Your Browsing History

To keep track of sites you've visited, you can display the History list.

1. With Safari open, click History.

2. To return to a page in the list, just choose it from the History menu.

3. Hover your mouse pointer over past dates to display the sites you visited on those days, and click to jump to a page, as shown in **Figure 14-6**.

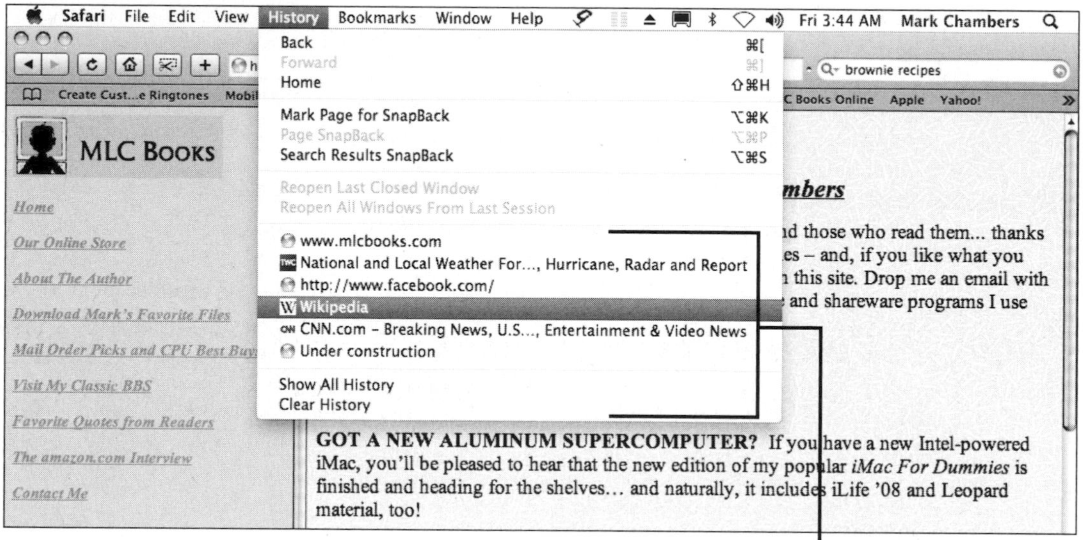

Choose a page.

Figure 14-6

Use Tabs

Safari also offers *tabbed browsing*, which many folks use to display (and organize) multiple Web pages at one time. For example, if you're doing a bit of comparison shopping for a new piece of hardware between different online stores, tabs are ideal.

1. With Safari open, hold down the ⌘ key and click a link or bookmark to open a tab for the new page (which appears under the Bookmarks bar).

 You can also choose File⇨New Tab or press ⌘+T to work the same magic.

2. Click a tab at any time to switch to that page, as shown in **Figure 14-7**.

3. You can remove a tabbed page by clicking the X button next to the tab's title.

 To change settings for tabbed browsing, choose Safari⇨Preferences to display the Preferences dialog box and then click Tabs.

Click a tab to switch pages.

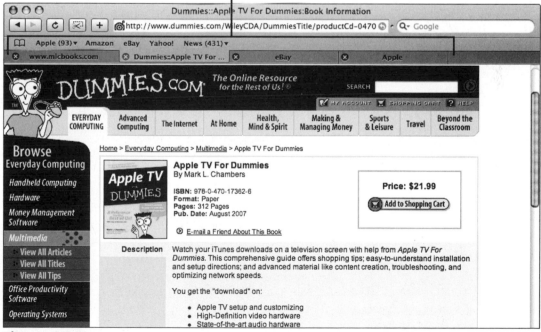

Figure 14-7

Download Files

If you visited a site that offers files for downloading, you typically just click the Download button or the Download File link and Safari takes care of the rest. You see the Downloads status window, which keeps you updated on the progress of the transfer. While the file is download-ing, feel free to continue browsing or even download additional files; the status window helps you keep track of what's going on and when everything will finish transferring.

 By default, Safari saves any downloaded files to your Mac OS X Downloads folder on the Dock.

To download a picture that appears on a Web page, move your mouse pointer over the picture and right-click. Then choose Save Image As from the shortcut menu that appears. Safari prompts you for the loca-tion where you want to store the file.

Maintain Your Privacy

Safari speeds up the loading of Web sites by storing often-used images and multimedia files in a temporary storage, or *cache,* folder. Naturally, the files in your cache folder can be displayed, which can lead to assumptions (hint, hint) about the sites you've visited.

Luckily, Safari makes it easy to dump the contents of your cache file. Just choose Safari⇨Empty Cache; then click Empty to confirm that you want to clean up your cache.

In a similar fashion, your History file leaves a clear set of footprints indicating where you've been on the Web. Maybe you don't want every-one to know you've been spending all your free time checking out *World of Warcraft* online. If so, you can clear out your browser history. To do so, choose History⇨Clear History.

The latest version of Safari also allows you to specify a length of time to retain entries in your History file. Choose Safari⇨Preferences, click the General tab, and then click the Remove History Items pop-up menu to specify a length of time. Items can be rolled off daily, weekly, biweekly, monthly, or yearly.

Print a Web Page

Many Web pages have a button you can click to print the page. If you want to print a page and it doesn't have a Print button or link, follow these steps:

1. Click the Print button on the toolbar, choose File⇨Print from the menu, or press ⌘+P.

2. Click the Printer pop-up menu to select the printer you want to use, as shown in **Figure 14-8**.

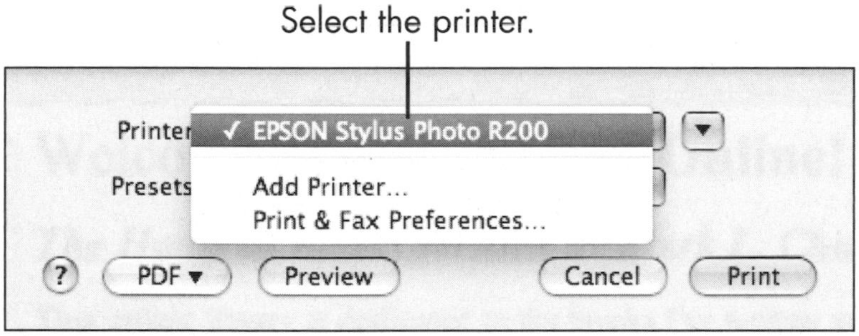

Select the printer.

Figure 14-8

3. To see how the printed pages will look, click Preview. (When you're done with the Preview window, choose Preview⇨Quit Preview to return to Safari.)

4. When you're ready to print the pages, click Print.

Keeping in Touch by E-Mail

Mac OS X includes quite a capable and reliable e-mail client — Apple Mail (affectionately called Mail by everyone except Bill Gates). Mail provides all you need in order to

➠ Send and receive e-mail messages.

➠ Screen junk mail from your Inbox.

➠ Receive attachments.

➠ Update your Address Book with new e-mail contacts.

➠ Organize your mail using folders.

Set Up an Internet E-Mail Account

Most Mac owners choose one of three sources for an Internet e-mail account:

➠ **An existing Internet service provider (or ISP).** If you're signed up with an ISP, that company almost certainly will provide you with at least one e-mail address as part of your service. Contact your ISP for your e-mail account information.

➡ **Apple's MobileMe online service.** MobileMe members receive free e-mail service from Apple. Your MobileMe e-mail address should be yourname@ me.com, where yourname is the username you chose when you subscribed. (I go into more detail on MobileMe in Chapter 13.)

➡ **A Web-based e-mail provider.** Many sites on the Web offer free e-mail services, such as Google Gmail, Yahoo! Mail, and Microsoft Hotmail. You can sign up for these e-mail accounts online. (I use and recommend Google GMail, which you can access at www. google.com. Just click the GMail link in the upper-left corner to start the sign-up process.)

Apple Mail can accommodate most e-mail services, no matter where they're hosted.

 If you already have an existing e-mail account that you use with Windows Mail, Microsoft Outlook, or Outlook Express on your PC, you can use that account easily under Apple Mail.

Note that MobileMe e-mail accounts are set up automatically for you within Apple Mail, so you typically don't have to follow this procedure.

Set Up an Apple Mail Account

After you set up an e-mail account with your ISP or another provider, you need to add that account so that Mail can access it.

Follow these steps to add an account to Apple Mail:

1. Launch Mail from the Dock by clicking the icon that looks like a postage stamp.

2. If the Add Account Wizard doesn't automatically appear, as shown in **Figure 15-1**, choose File⇨Add Account to display it.

Fill in each field and then click Create.

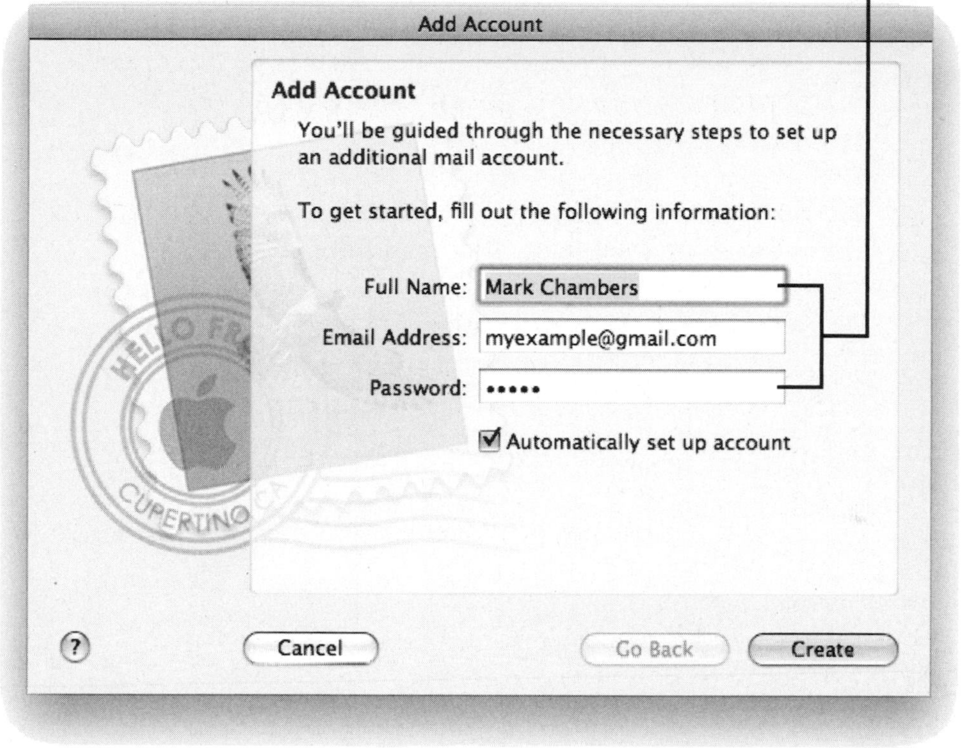

Add Account

Add Account

You'll be guided through the necessary steps to set up an additional mail account.

To get started, fill out the following information:

Full Name: Mark Chambers

Email Address: myexample@gmail.com

Password: •••••

☑ Automatically set up account

Cancel   Go Back   Create

Figure 15-1

3. Type your full name and then your e-mail address and the password you use to log in to your e-mail account.

4. Click Create.

Here's a neat trick: If Mail can immediately recognize an e-mail service, such as Google Mail, it attempts to automatically set up that account for you. If the setup and testing are successful, you don't need to follow the rest of this procedure.

5. Click the Account Type box, choose the type of account you're using, and then click in the Incoming Mail Server text box and type your incoming server address, as shown in **Figure 15-2**. (Your e-mail provider should provide you with this information.)

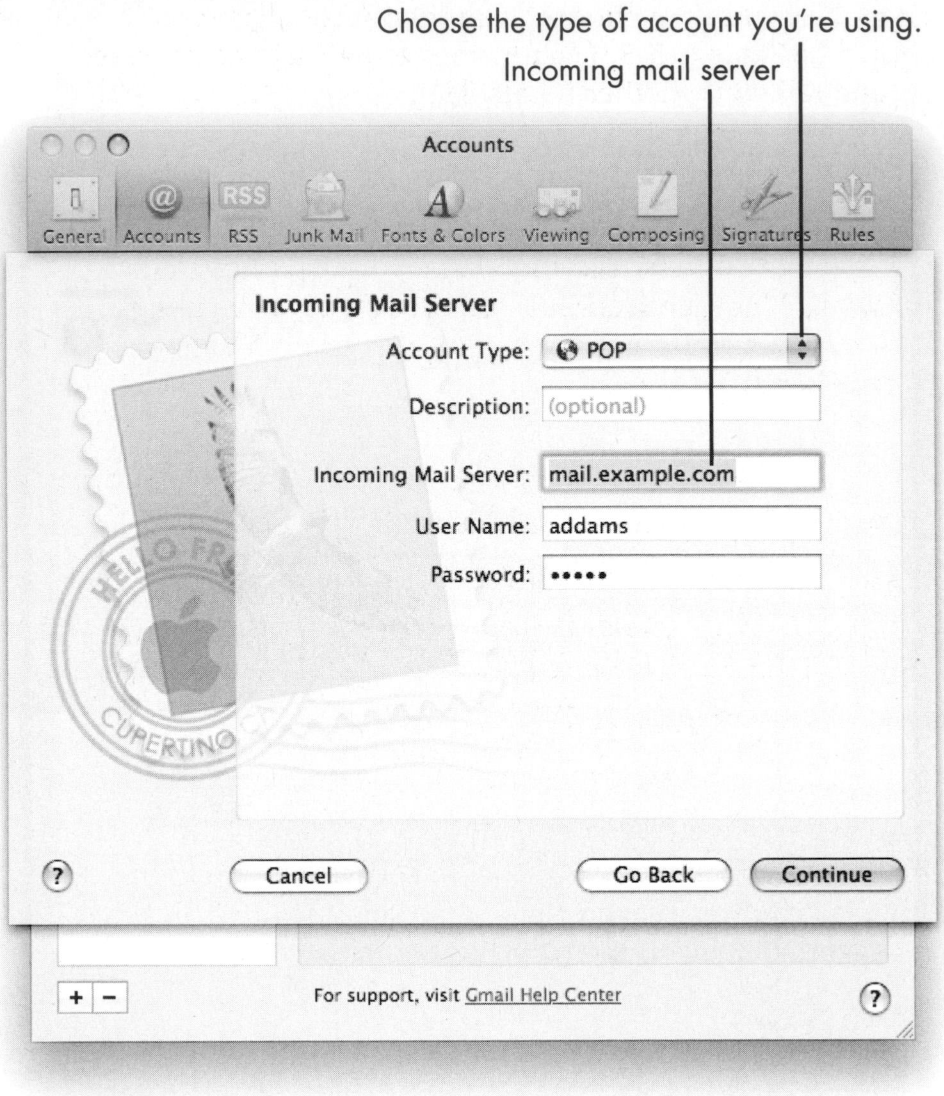

Choose the type of account you're using.

Incoming mail server

Figure 15-2

 To help keep track of multiple e-mail addresses, you can type a description for this account, such as work or home.

6. Click Continue.

7. If your e-mail service uses SSL security, which encrypts your e-mail communications and makes it harder for someone else to read, select the Use Secure Sockets Layer check box and then choose an authentication type, as shown in **Figure** 15-3. (Again, your e-mail service provider should tell you whether it uses SSL.)

8. Click Continue.

9. Click in the Outgoing Mail Server text box, type your outgoing server address, and then enter your username and password if authentication is required. (Yep, you guessed it — only your Internet service provider can tell you what to type here.)

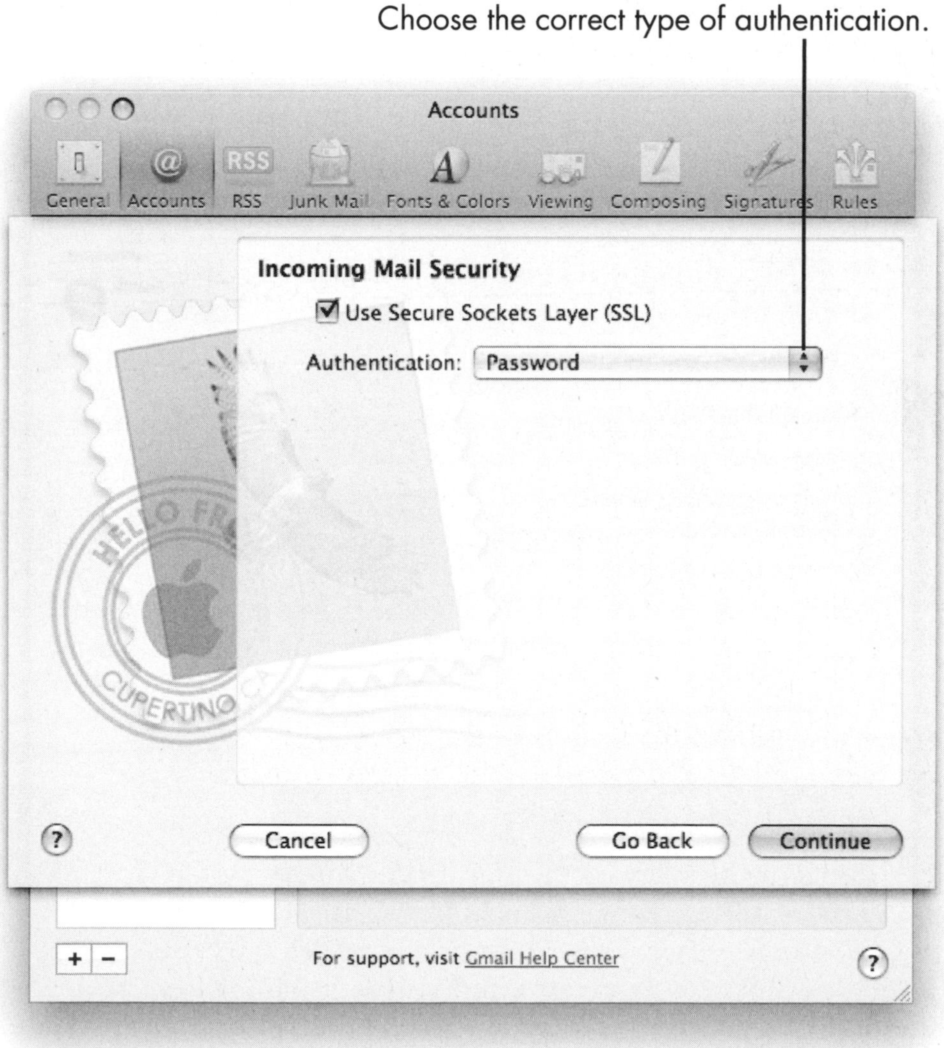

Choose the correct type of authentication.

Figure 15-3

10. Click Continue.

11. Click Create on the wizard's Summary screen to create your account within Apple Mail.

Get to Know Apple Mail

Figure 15-4 illustrates the Mail window. Besides the familiar toolbar, which naturally carries buttons specific to Mail, you find these elements:

➡ **Status bar:** This heading bar at the top of the Mail window displays information about the current folder — typically, how many messages it contains, but other data can be included.

➡ **Message list:** This box contains all the messages for the chosen folder. To resize the list larger or smaller, drag the handle on the bar that runs across the window. You can also resize the columns in the list by dragging the edges of the column heading buttons.

 To specify which columns appear in the message list, choose View⇨Columns. From the submenu that appears, you can toggle the display of specific columns. You can also sort the messages in the message list from the View menu.

➡ **Mailboxes:** The column to the left of the main Mail window is the Mailboxes list. Click any of the folders to switch the display in the message list. The Mailbox list can be hidden or shown from the View menu by choosing the Show Mailboxes option.

➡ **Preview box:** This resizable list box displays the contents of the selected message, including both text and any graphics or attachments that Mail recognizes.

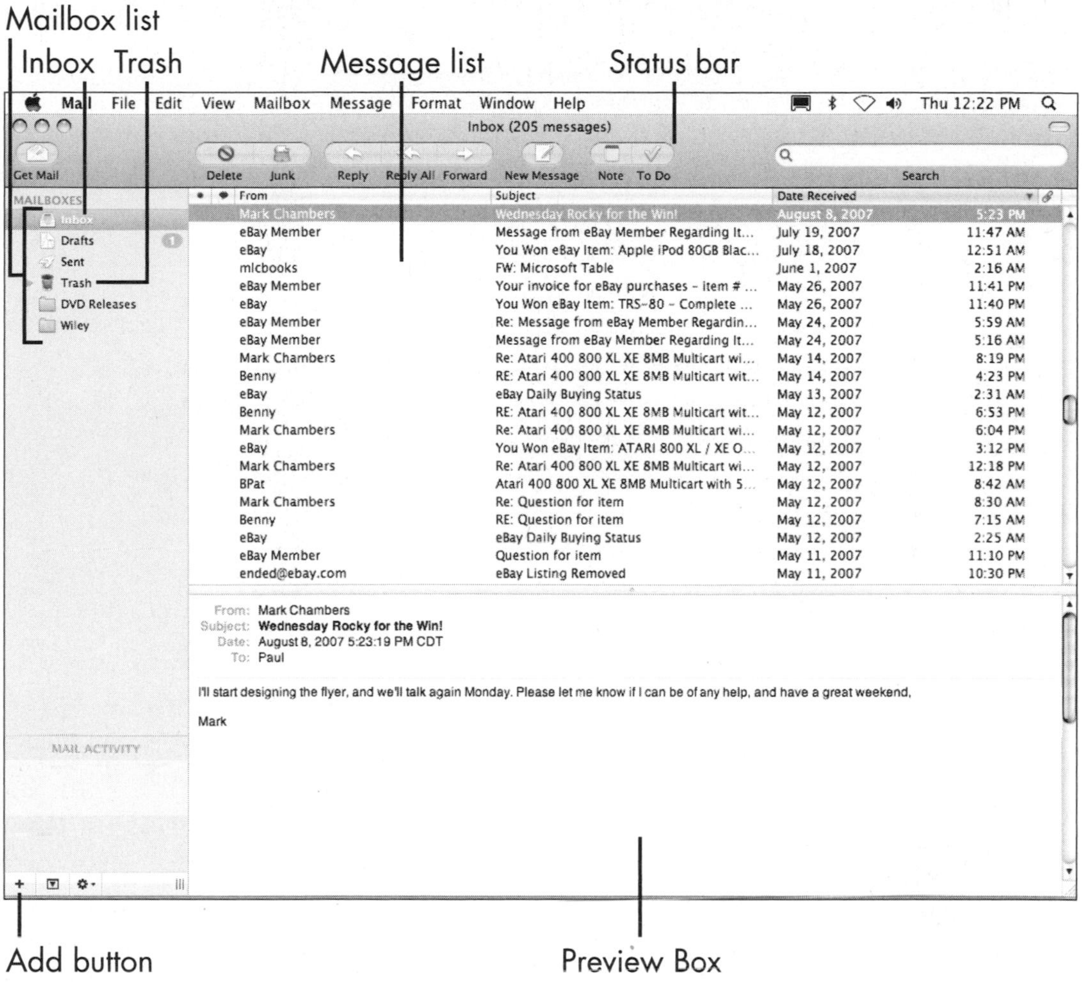

Mailbox list

Inbox Trash   Message list   Status bar

Add button   Preview Box

Figure 15-4

Mail uses the following folders (some of which appear at only certain times):

➠ **Inbox:** Mail you received already.

➠ **Outbox:** Messages that Mail is waiting to send.

➠ **Drafts:** Draft messages waiting to be completed.

➠ **Sent:** Mail you sent already.

➡ **Trash:** Deleted mail. As with the Trash in the Dock, you can open this folder and retrieve items that you realize you still need. Alternatively, you can empty the contents of the Trash at any time by pressing the ⌘+K shortcut or by choosing Mailbox➪Erase Deleted Messages.

➡ **Junk:** Junk mail. You can review these messages or retrieve any that you want to keep by choosing Message➪Move To. After you're sure that nothing of value is left, you can delete the remaining messages straight to the Trash. (Junk mail filtering must be enabled before you see this box; more on this later in this chapter.)

Manage E-Mail Accounts

Choose Mail➪Preferences and click the Accounts button to display the Accounts dialog box, shown in **Figure 15-5**. From there, you can add an account, edit an existing account, or remove an account from Mail. Although most folks still have only one e-mail account, you can use a passel of them. For example, you might use one account for your personal e-mail and one account for your business. To switch accounts, just click the account that you want to use from this list to make it the active account.

You can also edit any field on the Account Information tab. For example, if you decide to change your e-mail "From" name, click in the Full Name text box, press the Delete key to erase the existing name, and then type a new name. Similarly, if you have to change your password for your e-mail user account, click in the Password box and delete your current password, and then type your new password. (Note that the contents of the Password box are always displayed as dots, just to keep your password secure.)

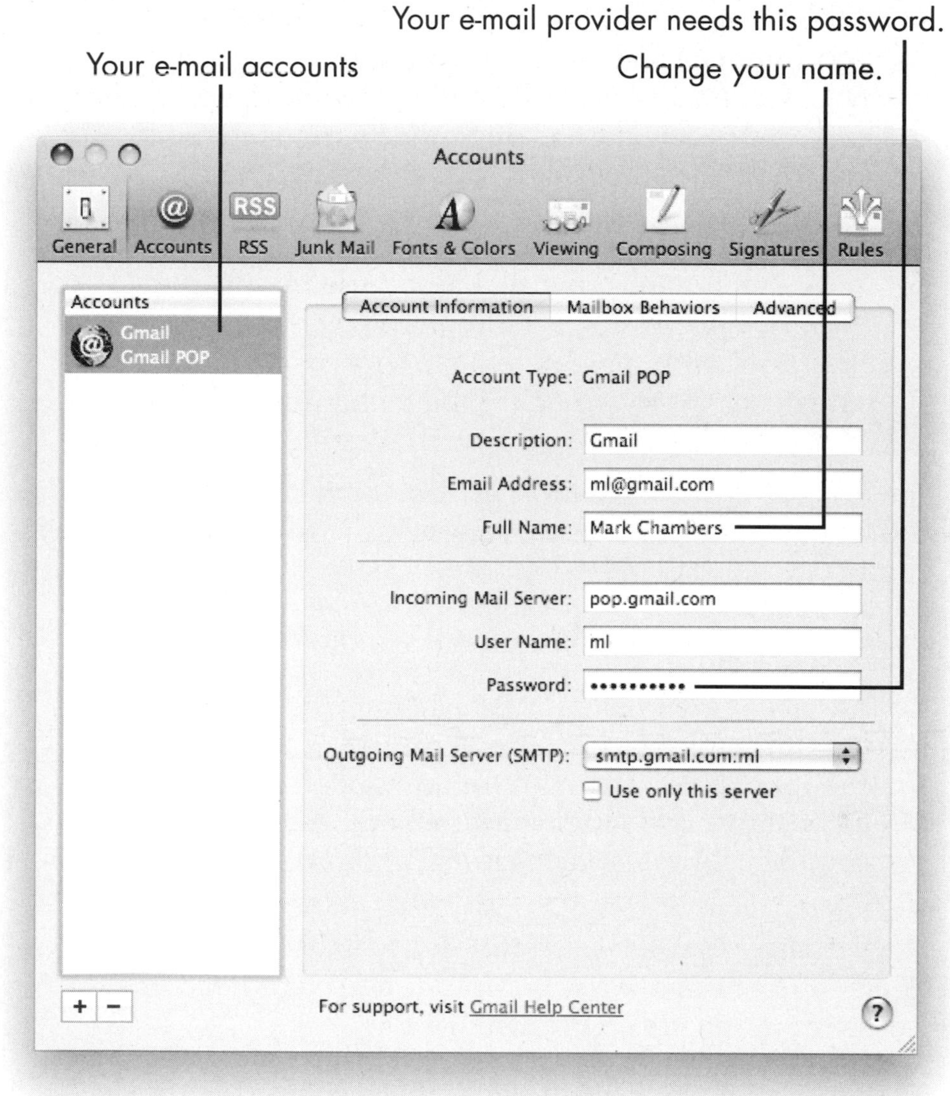

Your e-mail provider needs this password.

Your e-mail accounts   Change your name.

Figure 15-5

Sometimes you can't reach one of your accounts. For example, maybe you're vacationing with your MacBook and you can't access your ISP's mail server directly. To avoid all the error messages and futile attempts to connect to an e-mail provider you can't reach, Apple Mail lets you enable and disable specific accounts without enduring the hassle of deleting an account and then adding it again.

To disable or enable an account, choose Mail⇨Preferences to open the Preferences dialog box and click the Accounts button. Click to select an account, click the Advanced tab, and then select (or deselect) the Enable This Account check box as necessary.

 If you disable an account, you should also deselect the Include When Automatically Checking for New Mail check box to make sure that Mail doesn't display an error message.

Read and Delete E-Mail

The heart and soul of Mail — at least the heart, anyway — is receiving and reading stuff from your friends and family. After your account is set up, use any of these methods to manually check for new mail:

➠ Click the Get Mail button on the toolbar.

➠ Choose Mailbox⇨Get All New Mail or press ⌘+Shift+N.

➠ Choose Mailbox⇨Get New Mail and then choose the specific account to check from the submenu.

 The last method is a helpful way to check for new mail in another account without having to make it active in the Preferences window.

If you have new mail in the active account, the mail appears in the Message list. New, unread messages are marked with a snazzy blue dot in the first column. The number of unread messages is displayed next to the Inbox folder icon in the Mailboxes list.

 Mail also displays on its Dock icon the number of unread messages you received. If you hid the Mail window or sent it to the Dock, you can perform a quick visual check for new mail just by glancing at the Dock.

To read any message in the message list, you can either click to select an entry (which displays the contents of the message in the preview box) or double-click the entry to open the message in a separate window.

To quickly skim your mail, click the first message that you want to view in the list and then press the down-arrow key when you're ready to move to the next message. Mail displays the content of each message in the preview box. To display the previous message in the list, press the up-arrow key.

 If your vision isn't what it once was, why not let Mail *read* you your mail? Simply select one message or a group of messages and then choose Edit➪Speech➪ Start Speaking. *Wowsers!*

To delete a message from the message list, click an entry to select it and then click the Delete button on the toolbar (or press the Del key). To delete a message from within a message window, click the Delete button on the toolbar.

Reply to a Message

Replying to a message you receive is easy. Follow these steps:

1. Click to select a message entry in the Message list and then click the Reply button on the toolbar.

 To respond to a message that you opened in a message window, click the Reply button on the toolbar for the message window.

If a message was addressed not just to you but also to a number of different people, you can send your reply to all of them. Rather than click the Reply button, click the Reply All button on the Mail window toolbar. (This technique is a useful way to quickly facilitate a festive gathering, if you get my drift.)

Mail opens the Reply window, shown in **Figure** 15-6. Note that the address has been added automatically and that the default Subject is Re: *<the original subject>*. Mail automatically adds a separator line in the message body field that reads On *<day><date>*at*<time>*, *<addressee>* wrote:, followed by the text of the original message. The original text is indented and prefaced by a vertical line to set it apart.

If you like, you can click in the Subject line and change the default Subject line; otherwise, the cursor is already sitting on the first line of the text box so that you can simply start typing your reply.

2. After you complete your reply, you can select text in the message body and apply different fonts or formats. (See the task "Format E-Mail Messages," later in this chapter, for more information.)

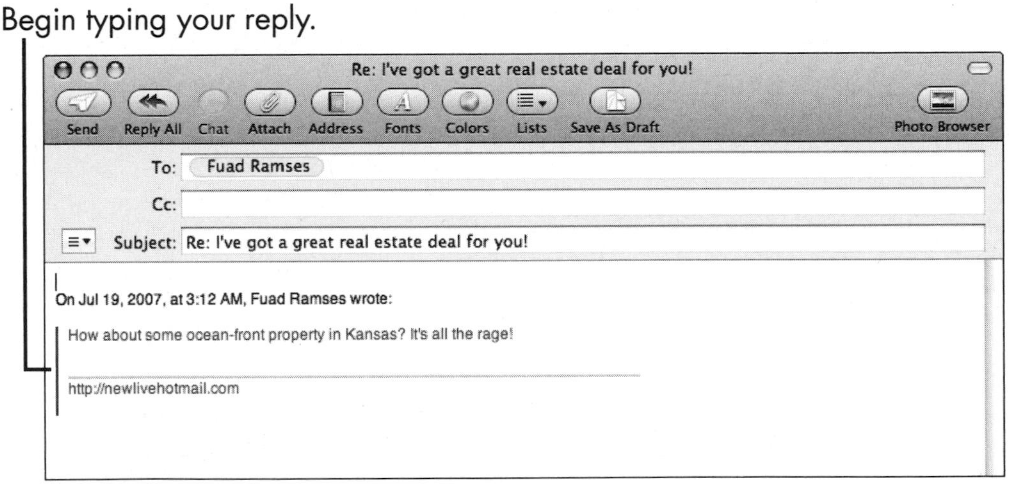

Begin typing your reply.

Figure 15-6

3. To add an attachment, click the Attach button on the toolbar. See the tasks "Send an Attachment" and "Save an Attachment That You Receive," later in this chapter, for the full lowdown on attachments.

4. When you're ready to send your reply, you have two
options:

- *Click the Send button to send the message immediately.*

- *Click the Save as Draft button to store it in your Drafts
  folder for later editing.*

Saving the message to your Drafts folder isn't the same as sending it.
You can save the message for a while so that you can later come back
and finish it. To send a message held in your Drafts folder, click the
Drafts folder in the Mailboxes list and then double-click the message
you want to send. Mail displays the message window — you can make
edits at this point, if you like — and then click the Send button on the
message window toolbar.

 When you reply to a message, you can also *forward*
your reply to another person (rather than the original
sender). The new addressee receives a message containing both the text of the original message you
received and your reply. To forward a message, click
the Forward button rather than Reply or Reply All on
the Mail toolbar.

Create and Send E-Mail

To compose and send a new message to someone else, follow these
steps:

1. Click the New Message button on the Mail toolbar. You
can also choose File⇨New Message (or avail yourself of
the handy ⌘+N keyboard shortcut).

Mail opens the New Message window, shown in
Figure 15-7.

Send your message.

Attach a file.

Open the Addresses window.

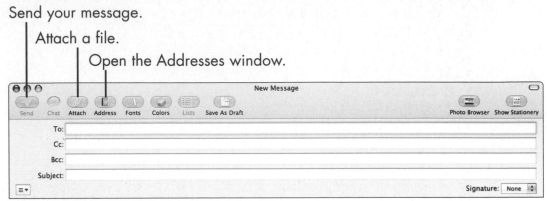

Figure 15-7

2. Enter the recipient's (To) address by taking one of these actions:

- Type it in directly.

- Paste it in after copying it to the Clipboard.

- Drag an e-mail address from your Address Book.

- Click the Address button, which shows you the Addresses window, shown in **Figure 15-8**. Click to select the address you want to use and then click the To button. To pick multiple recipients, hold down the ⌘ key while you select the multiple addresses. Click the Close button in the Addresses window to close it.

Click to select the address you want.

Click to add addresses to your message.

Figure 15-8

3. If you want to send optional "carbon" copies of the message to additional recipients, click in the Cc field. Again, you can type the addresses directly, use the contents of the Clipboard, or display the Addresses window.

If you use the Addresses window, select the addresses you want to use and click the Cc button. Then click the Close button in the Addresses window.

4. Click in the Subject field, enter the subject of the message, and then press Tab.

The text cursor now rests in the first line of the message text box — type your message, my friend!

5. Click the Show Stationery button on the toolbar to display the Stationery strip above the message text box, where you can choose one of the many e-mail message backgrounds that Apple supplies.

Stationery isn't required, but it truly packs a visual wallop! Double-click a thumbnail in the strip to add it to your message; to display a different stationery category, such as a Greeting or Invitation, click the category buttons on the left side of the Stationery strip.

 Not all e-mail applications on other computers correctly display a message with a stationery background.

6. After you finish typing your message, you can select text in the message body and apply different fonts or formats. (I cover formatting in the "Format E-Mail Messages" task, later in this chapter.)

7. To add an attachment, click the Attach button on the toolbar. (Attachments are described in the following next task.)

8. If you're ready to send, click the Send button to immediately send the message, or click the Save As Draft button to store the message in your Drafts folder.

Send an Attachment

Attachments are a fun way to transfer files by e-mail. However, you must remember these three vital caveats:

➡ **Attachments can contain viruses.** Even a message attachment that was sent by your best friend can contain a virus — either because your friend unwittingly passed one along or because the virus took control of your friend's e-mail application and replicated itself automatically. (Ugh.)

 Never — I mean never — send or receive attachments unless you have an up-to-date antivirus scanning application running.

➡ **Corpulent attachments don't make it.** Most ISP mail servers have a 1–3MB limit for the total size of a message, and the attachment counts toward that final message size. Therefore, I recommend sending a file as an attachment only if it's less than 2MB. If the recipient's e-mail server sends you an automated message saying that the message was refused because it was too big, this is the problem. To display a file's size before you send it, right-click the file's icon and choose Get Info from the shortcut menu.

➡ **Not all e-mail applications accept attachments.** Not all e-mail programs support attachments in the same way, and others are simply set for pure text messages. If the message recipient receives the message text but not the attachment, these are the likely reasons.

With that said, it's back to attachments as a beneficial feature.

While replying to a message (or creating a new message), you can add an attachment by clicking the Attach button on the toolbar.

Mail displays a File Open dialog box. Navigate to a file, select it, and click the Open button to add the file to the message.

If the recipient is running Windows, make sure that the Send Windows–Friendly Attachments check box is selected. This results in a slightly larger e-mail message, but helps ensure that PC e-mail programs, such as Outlook and Windows Mail, can correctly open your attachments.

Save an Attachment That You Receive

Sometimes, you don't *want* to save attachments that people send to you. For example, if Cousin Fred sends you a funny cartoon that you chuckle at but don't really need to save, you can safely delete it. But what if someone sends you an attachment, such as a picture of your grandkids, that you truly want to hang on to? Follow these steps to save an attachment that you receive in a message:

1. Click the message with an attachment in your message list.

 If you're having trouble determining which messages have attachments, choose View⇨Columns and then click the Attachments option from the submenu that appears, to toggle it on. Now every message with an attachment appears with a tiny paper clip icon displayed in its entry.

If Mail recognizes the attachment format, it displays or plays the attachment in the body of the message; if not, the attachment is displayed as a file icon.

2. To open an attachment that's displayed as a file icon, right-click the icon and choose Open Attachment from the shortcut menu.

3. To save an attachment, right-click the attachment (however it appears in the message) and then choose Save Attachment from the shortcut menu.

In the Save dialog box that appears, navigate to the location where you want to save the file and then click Save.

Format E-Mail Messages

Why settle for a boring, plain-text message when you can add special fonts and colors? Mail makes it easy to format your messages, much like you format text in a Pages document.

To change text formatting, click the Fonts button on the message window toolbar. From the window that appears, you can choose the font family, type size, and formatting (such as italic or bold) for the selected text. Click the Close button on the Fonts window to continue.

To apply color to selected text, click the Colors button on the message window toolbar and then click anywhere in the color wheel that appears to select that color. You can also vary the hue by moving the slider bar to the right of the Colors window. After you find the color that expresses your inner passion, click the Close button in the Colors window to continue.

Add Address Book Contacts

If you receive a message from your niece Harriet and she isn't in your Address Book yet, you can easily add her to your Address Book contacts from within Apple Mail.

With the message selected in the message list, choose Message➪Add Sender to Address Book. Mail automatically creates a new contact, and the person's name and e-mail address are added automatically to your Address Book.

Customize Apple Mail

Like all other Apple software, Mail is easily customized to your liking from the Preferences window (shown in **Figure 15-9**).

To choose a sound that plays whenever you receive new mail, choose Mail➪Preferences and click the General button. Either click the New Mail Sound pop-up menu and choose one of the sounds that Apple provides or choose Add/Remove from the pop-up menu to choose a sound file from the Sounds folder (which, in turn, is located within your Library folder). Choose None from the pop-up menu to disable the new mail sound altogether.

By default, Mail automatically checks for new mail every five minutes. To change this delay period, display the General panel in the Preferences window, click the Check for New Mail pop-up menu, and then choose one of the time periods.

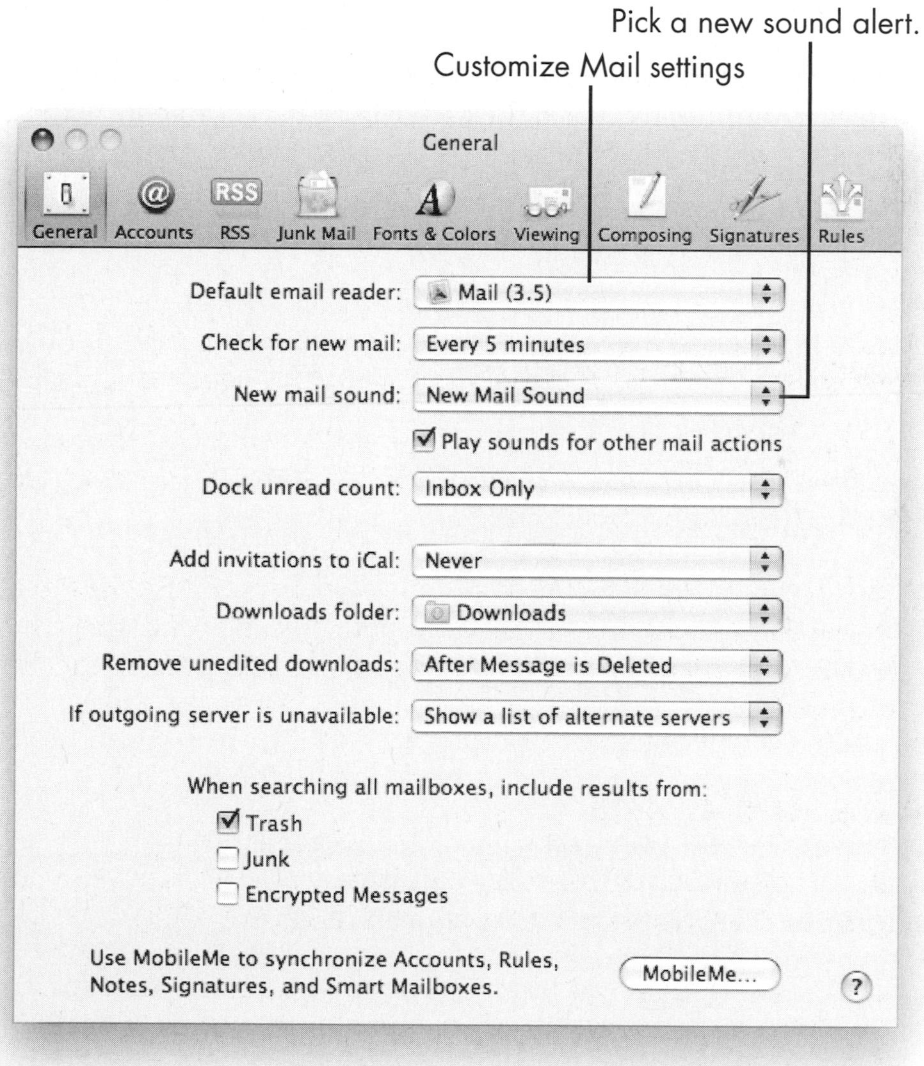

Pick a new sound alert.

Customize Mail settings

Figure 15-9

To disable automatic mail checking, choose Manually; you can click the Get Mail toolbar button to manually check your mail anytime you like. (For example, if you're using a dialup analog modem connection, you may not fancy Mail taking control of the telephone line every five minutes.)

If you like, Mail can be set to automatically delete sent mail (and permanently erase messages that you relegate to the Trash). To configure these settings, display the Accounts list in the Preferences window, click to select an account, and then click the Mailboxes Behaviors tab.

To delete sent messages automatically, click the Delete Sent Messages When pop-up menu and choose a delay period or action. You can choose to delete mail after a day, a week, a month, or immediately after quitting Mail. Alternatively, you can leave this field set to Never, and Mail never automatically deletes any messages from the Sent folder.

To delete junk messages automatically, click the Delete Junk Messages When pop-up menu and choose a delay period or action. (These options are the same as the ones available for sent mail.) I discuss junk mail later in this chapter.

To delete messages from the Trash, click the Erase Deleted Messages When pop-up menu and choose a delay period or action. Again, your choices are the same as for sent messages.

Add a Signature to All Outgoing Messages

To add a block of text or a graphical image to the bottom of your messages as your personal signature, follow these steps:

1. Choose Mail⇨Preferences and click the Signatures button.

2. From the Signatures pane that appears, click the Add Signature button (which carries a plus sign) to display the new signature entry you see in **Figure 15-10**.

3. Click the signature name to open an edit box and then type an identifying name.

Press Return to save the new name.

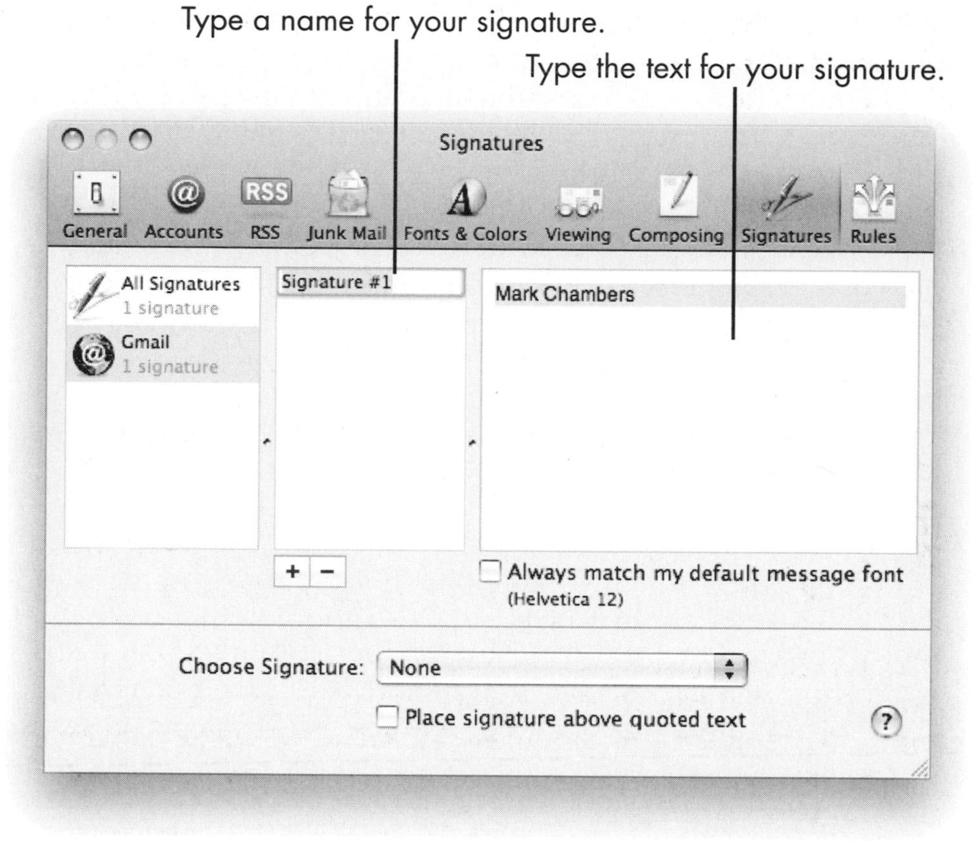

Type a name for your signature.

Type the text for your signature.

Signatures

General Accounts RSS Junk Mail Fonts & Colors Viewing Composing Signatures Rules

All Signatures
1 signature

Gmail
1 signature

Signature #1

Mark Chambers

+ −

☐ Always match my default message font
(Helvetica 12)

Choose Signature: None ⬆⬇

☐ Place signature above quoted text (?)

Figure 15-10

4. Click inside the text entry box to the right to move the cursor.

5. Type the signature itself in the text entry box or copy the signature to the Clipboard and paste it into the text entry box.

 Because downloading a graphical image in a signature takes a long time — and because some folks still use plain-text e-mail — I recommend that you avoid the temptation to include graphics in your signature.

6. If you have multiple signatures, click the Choose Signature pop-up menu to choose which one you want to use or to use them all randomly or in sequence.

If you want your signature to appear above the quoted text in a reply, click to select the Place Signature above Quoted Text check box. (In e-mail jargon, *quoted* text refers to the original message text that's inserted into your reply. Mail adds the quoted text so that your recipient can keep track of the continuing discussion!)

Use Folders

You can add new personal folders to the Mailboxes list to further organize your messages. For example, you can put into a special folder all messages from your quilting club that talk about patterns, making it easy to refer back to them as a group.

To create a new folder, click the Add button in the lower-left corner of the Mail window and choose New Mailbox from the pop-up menu that appears (or choose Mailbox➪New Mailbox from the Mail menu bar). Choose On My Mac as your location and then type the name for your new folder in the Name box. Click OK to create the new personal folder.

Messages can be dragged from the message list and dropped into a folder in the Mailboxes list to transfer them. Alternatively, you can move them from the Message list by selecting the messages you want to move, choosing Message➪Move To, and then clicking to select a destination folder.

Handle Junk Mail

Unfortunately, everyone receives junk e-mail (or *spam*) these days, and because chucking the First Amendment is *not* an option, I guess we'll always have it. (Come to think of it, my paper mailbox is just as full of the stuff.)

Thankfully, Apple Mail has a net that you can cast to collect junk mail before you have to read it. The two methods of handling junk mail are

➠ **Manually:** You can mark any message in the message list as junk mail. Select the unwanted message in the message list and then click the Junk button on the

Mail window toolbar, which marks the message as shown in **Figure 15-11**. (Note that the Junk button turns into a Not Junk button.) If a message is mistakenly marked as junk but you want to keep it, display the message in the preview box and then click the Not Junk button at the top of the preview box.

➡ **Automatically:** Apple Mail has a sophisticated Junk Mail filter that you can train to better recognize junk. (Keep reading to discover how.) After you train Mail to recognize spam with a high degree of accuracy, turn it to full Automatic mode and it moves all those worthless messages to your Junk folder.

You customize and train the Junk Mail filter from the Preferences dialog box (available from your trusty Mail menu); click Junk Mail to show the settings. I recommend that you first try Training mode, using the option labeled When Junk Mail Arrives, Mark As Junk Mail but Leave It in My Inbox. Junk Mail then takes its best shot at determining what's junk. When you receive more mail and mark more messages as junk (or mark them as not junk), you're teaching the Junk Mail feature how to winnow the wheat from the chaff. In Training mode, junk messages aren't moved anywhere — they're just marked with a particularly fitting, grungy brown color.

After you're satisfied that the Junk Mail filter is catching just about everything it can, display the Mail preferences again and choose the Move It to the Junk Mailbox option. Mail creates a Junk folder and prompts you for permission to move all junk messages to this folder. After you review everything in the Junk folder, you can delete the messages it contains and send them to the Trash folder.

 To save a message from junkdom, click the Not Junk button in the preview window and then drag the message from the Junk folder message list to a folder in the Mailboxes list.

If you don't receive a lot of spam — or you want to be absolutely sure that nothing is labeled as junk until you review it — click to deselect the Enable Junk Mail Filtering check box. (And good luck.)

Undo your Junk marking.

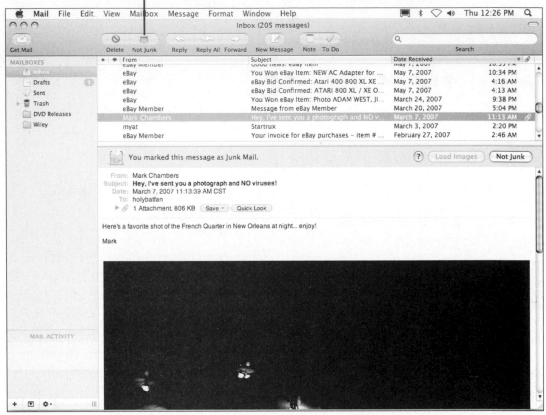

Figure 15-11

 By default, Mail exempts certain messages from Junk Mail status based on three criteria: if the sender is in your Address Book, if you sent the sender a message in the past, or if the message is addressed to you with your full name. To tighten up your Junk Mail filtering to the max, you might want to disable these check boxes as well.

To reset the Junk Mail filter and erase any training you received, visit the Junk Mail settings in Preferences again and click Reset. Then click the Yes button to confirm your choice.

Connecting with People Online

*T*hroughout human history, our drive has been toward communication — from the earliest cave paintings to written language and then to the telegraph, the telephone, and the mobile phone (including newer phones that connect to the Internet, let you check e-mail, take photos, play music, and more). I'm here to tell you that your Mac is the ultimate communications device, no matter whom you need to converse with or what the topic may be!

In this chapter, you find out how to

➠ Chat with someone by typing messages or talking over a microphone and even viewing each other by way of video.

➠ Add to and manage your collection of online friends (otherwise called a Buddy List).

➠ Start audio and video conversations across the Internet (commonly called chats).

➠ Access online journals (blogs) and Web discussion groups (forums).

➠ Start using Web meeting sites (called *social networks*) such as Facebook and MySpace.

Get ready to . . .

Check Your Equipment

Forget that silly mobile phone and your complicated calling plan! By using your Mac, you can easily chat with your friends and family whether they're across the street or halfway across the world. Here's what you need to get started:

➡ **Your Mac:** It comes with the iChat software preinstalled.

➡ **An Internet connection:** (See Chapter 13.) For audio or video chat, make sure that you have a broadband connection.

➡ **A microphone for audio chat and a video camera for video chat:** If you have an iMac computer or a MacBook laptop (the most popular models), you have a built-in microphone for audio chat and a built-in iSight video camera for video chat. You're all set. If you have a MacPro or Mac mini, you need to buy these two devices separately and plug them into the correct port on your Mac.

 When you use video chat, you *see* each other in glorious, full-color video! This fulfills the decades-old promise of the video telephone quite well, thank you. Audio chat is similar to talking on the phone, but without the expense of a calling plan.

Set Up iChat

When you first run iChat, you have a little setup work to do. The following steps walk you through the process:

1. Click the iChat icon in the Dock, and you're prompted to create an iChat account.

2. In the Account Setup dialog box that appears, shown in **Figure 16-1**, select your account type and fill out the boxes, depending on which of the following options best fits your situation:

- *You want to use the MobileMe account that you set up when you first installed Mac OS X:* In this case, your MobileMe account name and password are entered automatically for you, and you're good to go.

- *You don't have a MobileMe account but want one:* You can set up a free iChat account through Apple. Click the Get an iChat Account button and enter the required information on the Apple Web page that appears.

- *You want to use your existing account for AIM, GoogleTalk, or Jabber instead:* Click the Account Type pop-up menu and choose the correct service — and then enter the account information required for that service.

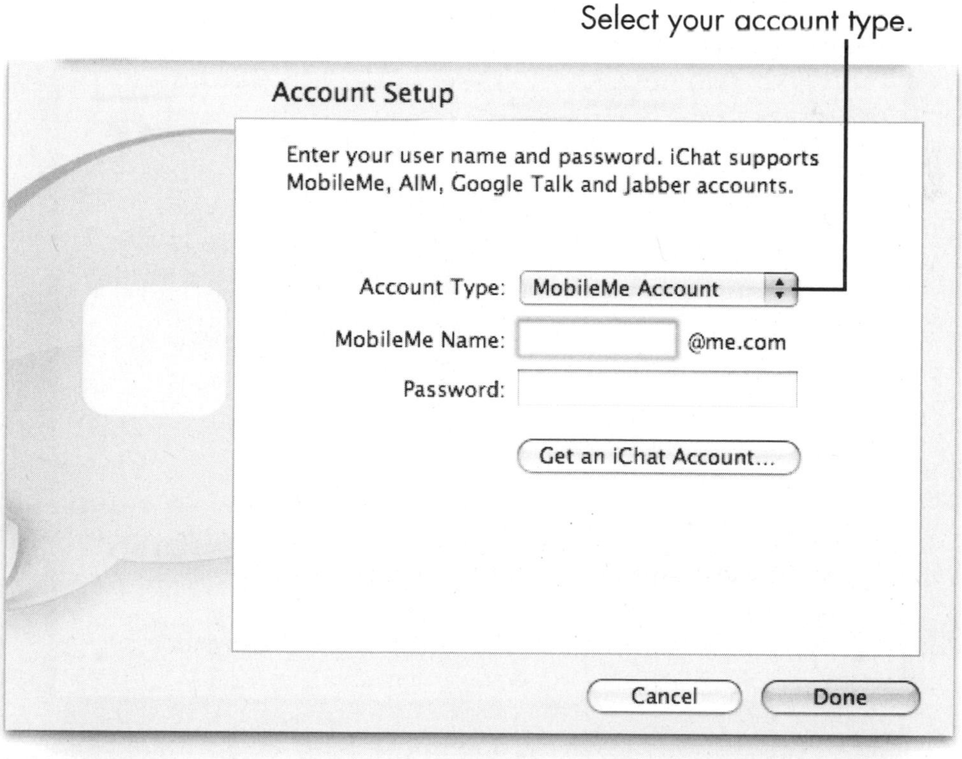

Select your account type.

Account Setup

Enter your user name and password. iChat supports MobileMe, AIM, Google Talk and Jabber accounts.

Account Type: MobileMe Account

MobileMe Name: @me.com

Password:

Get an iChat Account...

Cancel   Done

Figure 16-1

3. Click the Done button in the Account Setup dialog box. iChat displays the Buddy List window, shown in **Figure 16-2**.

 After you configure iChat, you can always run it by clicking its icon from the Dock or double-clicking the iChat application icon (which you find in your Applications folder).

A list of your buddies.

Figure 16-2

Add Friends to Your iChat Buddy List

In iChat, a *buddy* is anyone whom you want to chat with, whether the topic is work related or your personal life. iChat keeps track of your buddies in its Buddy List. To add a new buddy, follow these steps:

1. Open iChat by clicking its icon in the Dock.

2. From the iChat menu bar at the top of the screen, choose Buddies⇨Add Buddy to display the Add Buddy sheet, as shown in **Figure 16-3**.

3. To create a buddy entry from an Address Book contact who has an instant messaging username, click the down-arrow button next to the Last Name box to display the contacts list from your Address Book. Click the entry to select it.

4. To add a brand-new person who isn't already in your Address Book, type the person's instant messaging account name and click the pop-up menu to choose the proper account type (MobileMe, AIM, Google Talk, or Jabber). You can simply ask the person you want to add for this information.

5. Click Add to save the buddy information.

 Even when you add a new buddy and that name appears on the Buddy List, don't be surprised if the name literally fades out after a few seconds — the fading indicates that the person is offline and unavailable. You can also tell when a person is available if her name appears next to a green bullet in the Buddy List. These indicators show a person's status, and your buddies can see your status, too. Find out more about status in the next section.

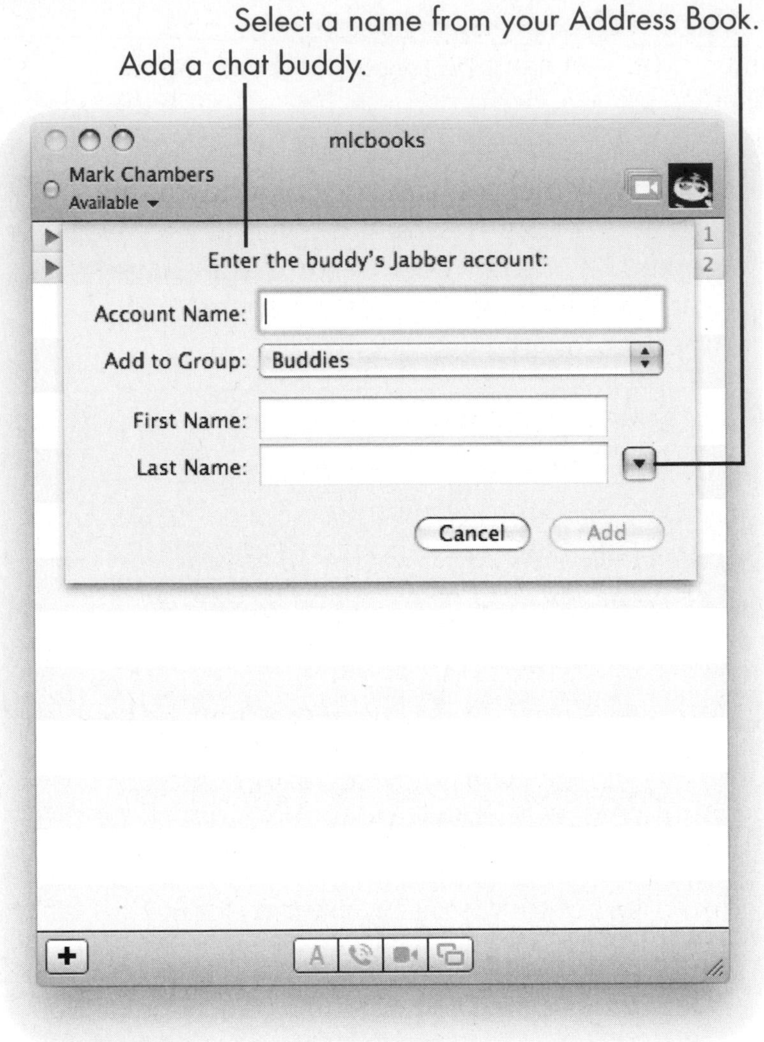

Select a name from your Address Book.
Add a chat buddy.

Figure 16-3

Set Your Status in iChat

Your iChat status lets your iChat buddies know whether you're available to chat. The status options fall into one of two categories:

➡ **Online:** When you're *online,* folks can invite you to chat and communicate with you.

➠ **Offline:** When you're *offline*, you're disconnected — iChat isn't active, you can't be paged, and you can't chat.

 Even when you're offline, you can click a buddy name directly, which automatically switches iChat to online mode and opens the paging window for that buddy. (Naturally, you have to have the proper network or Internet connection first.)

Now that you know what's going on behind the scenes, here's the scoop on the live options you can choose from:

➠ **Available:** You're at your Mac and willing to chat. In addition to plain old Available, Apple provides you with some more specific choices, such as Surfing the Web.

➠ **Away:** You can use *Away* mode whenever iChat is running and you're still online but not available. For example, if I'm away from my Mac for a few minutes, I leave iChat running but switch my status to Away. My buddies see a message saying that I'm away so that they don't bother trying to contact me. Apple also offers a few specific options for Away, too, such as In a Meeting.

➠ **A custom status:** You, too, can create a custom mode — such as Bored Stiff! or Listening to My Significant Other — and use it instead of the somewhat mundane choices of Available and Away. You find out how to create a custom status later in this section.

To choose an existing mode, follow these steps:

1. Click the Mode button in the Buddy List window (which should read either `offline` or `online`). Modes with a green bullet are Available modes, and red bullet modes are Away modes. See **Figure 16-4**.

Choose an existing mode.   Chat modes

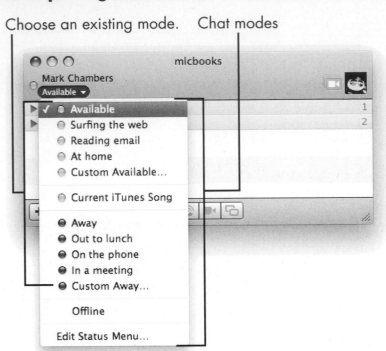

Figure 16-4

2. If you chose an Away mode, when you return to your computer, simply move your mouse, and iChat intelligently inquires whether you want to return to Available mode.

To create a custom status, follow these steps:

1. In the Buddy List window, click the word *Available* beneath your name, and a pop-up menu appears.

2. Click the Custom Available or Custom Away menu entries to create the new mode.

3. In the edit box that appears, type the message you want to appear for the new mode

4. Press Return to automatically add the newcomer to your mode list. You can also switch modes from this pop-up menu.

Chat with a Buddy

A text chat doesn't require a microphone or video camera on both ends — both sides of the conversation just rely on old-fashioned typing. To invite someone to a text chat, follow these steps:

1. Select that person from the Buddy List.

2. Click the Buddies menu, and then choose Invite to Chat. **Figure 16-5** shows a text invitation in progress.

 You can invite additional buddies to enter the chat by clicking the plus button (+) in the lower-left area of the Participants list and choosing another buddy. If the Participants list isn't visible, choose View⇨Show Chat Participants.

3. Type your invitation text into the entry box at the bottom of the window.

 If you want to use bold or italic text, highlight the text and press ⌘+B for Bold (**B**) or ⌘+I for Italic (*I*). You can also add an *emoticon* (a symbol that conveys emotion, in tech-speak, also called a *smiley*) to your invitation text: Click in the text where you want the emoticon to appear, click the Smiley button to the right of the text entry field, and then choose the proper smiley from the list.

4. To send the invitation text, press Return.

If the chat is accepted, iChat displays a message saying that the buddy you invited has joined the chat and you now can begin the chat. You don't have to alternate sending messages back and forth between participants — everyone in a chat can compose and send messages at the same time — but I personally like to alternate when I'm chatting one-on-one.

Invite more buddies to chat.

Type your invitation text.

Figure 16-5

If someone invites you to a chat, you experience the opposite side of the coin: A prompt dialog box appears and you can choose to accept or decline the invitation.

5. Click in the text entry box at the bottom of the Chat window and type a line of text, then press Return to send it.

6. Once you're done with your conversation, click the red Close button at the upper left corner of the Chat window to end the chat.

Start an Audio Chat

 If the green phone icon appears next to both your name and your buddy's name, you can enjoy a two-way audio (or voice) chat.

 If your Mac has a microphone hooked up but you don't see the phone icon, click the Video menu and make sure that the Microphone Enabled menu item is checked.

To invite a buddy to an audio chat, follow these steps:

1. Select that person from the Buddy List.

2. Click the Buddies menu, and then choose Invite to Audio Chat (or One-Way Audio Chat, if only one of you has a microphone). An Audio Chat window opens with a Waiting for Reply message, as shown in **Figure 16-6**.

Inviting a buddy to an audio chat.

Waiting on a chat buddy
Figure 16-6

3. After your buddies accept your invitation, you can begin speaking. (No need to press a button to speak — just talk normally into the microphone.)

To change the volume of your outgoing audio, drag the volume slider under your name in the Audio Chat window to the left. To change the volume of your buddy's voice, drag the volume slider under that name in the Audio Chat window to the left.

4. To end your audio chat, click the red Close button at the top left corner of the Audio Chat window.

Start a Video Chat

When you use iChat, you can jump into a real-time, two-way video chat room, complete with audio. To do so, both you and your buddy (or buddies) must be lucky enough to have iSight or video cameras connected to your Macs. If that's the case, you see video icons next to her name in your Buddy List (as well as next to your own name at the top of the list).

If your Mac has a microphone or video camera hooked up but you don't see the video icon, click the Video menu and make sure that the Microphone Enabled and Camera Enabled menu items are checked.

Starting a video chat is similar to starting an audio chat:

1. Select that person in the Buddy List.

2. Click the Buddies menu and choose either Invite to Video Chat or Invite to One-Way Video Chat, depending on the available hardware. See **Figure 16-7**.

3. If your buddy accepts the chat, a Video Chat window happens and you can begin to talk while also seeing facial expressions, the new baby, and whatever else is going on over the video stream.

To see your buddy

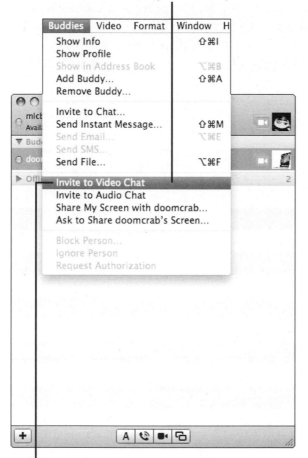

Start a video chat.

Figure 16-7

4. Click the Effects button to choose from a range of optional effects for your outgoing video (like black and white, sepia, x-ray, or thermal camera). Click on a thumbnail to apply that effect to your video. Once you've chosen the appropriate effect, click on the Close button at the top left of the Video Effects dialog to return to the Video Chat window.

5. When you're done chatting, click the red Close button at the top left corner of the Video Chat window.

As with an audio chat, a prompt appears if you're invited to a video chat, and you can accept or decline. (You even see a video preview of the person inviting you.)

Share on a Blog (an Online Journal)

In its purest form, a *blog* is simply an online journal kept on the Web by an individual or group — at least, that's what they started as several years ago. Most blogs are now online podiums, where personal opinion is king. (Remember that, because anyone can put up a blog — no matter how wildly inaccurate or biased the content they present may be.) You can keep up with people you know or your favorite organizations or writers if they keep a blog. The following tips help you understand what a blog is and how it works:

➠ A blog can contain text, photos, audio, and video.

➠ A blog is basically a Web site with a special format. You visit a blog by typing its Web address into your Safari browser. Chapter 14 explains using Safari to check out Web sites.

➠ You can find blogs that focus on any topic that interests you: for example, politics (of course), gardening, travel, and photography are well represented on the Internet.

➠ Some blogs allow you to add a comment to a post. To do so, you'll typically click the Comment button or link next to that post. Keep in mind that whatever you post is public — everyone on the Internet can read it.

➠ You can host a blog by using your MobileMe account — the Apple iWeb program (which is part of the iLife suite) lets you easily design and produce a blog as part of your Web site. iWeb even automatically updates your blog site with your changes! **Figure 16-8** illustrates iWeb at work on one of my Web sites.

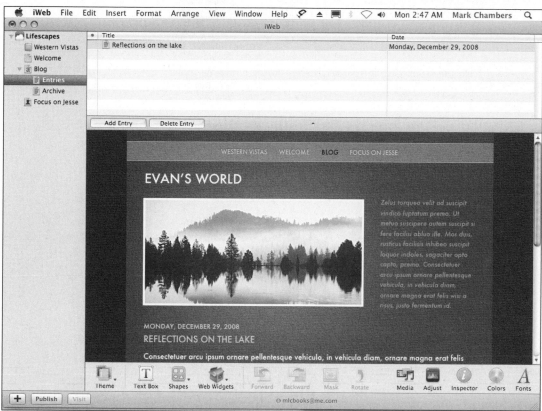

Figure 16-8

Communicate on Message Forums

Unlike a blog, a message forum is more like a conversation — think of a series of public e-mail messages. On a message forum, however, an original topic message leads to replies from multiple forum members. These discussions can last for weeks (I've been part of topics that have spanned months, including literally dozens of replies.)

Forums are known as a source of information and recommendations on a particular topic, like Mac troubleshooting or genealogy. For example, I often use my favorite photography forum to gather opinions on cameras and lenses before I buy — I also enjoy reading the various tips and "spirited" conversations from professional photographers on all sorts of optical topics.

Forum message bases include a number of features, depending on the software used to host the forum. For example, the forum site likely keeps track of the messages you read, enabling you to read just the new messages on the topics you choose. You likely can format your messages as you like, with color, italics, and smiley characters.

Suppose that you need tips on how to fine-tune a slide show within iPhoto. Follow these steps:

1. Visit Apple's iPhoto forums at `www.apple.com/support/iphoto`.

2. Click the Discussion Forums link to display the iPhoto forum page.

3. To read a discussion, just click the topic line (which appears in bold blue type).

 If you don't see the topic you're interested in, you can perform a search. Click in the Search Forum box at the right side of the page and type your search term. - Because I'm interested in a specific iPhoto feature, I would type `slideshow`. Then press Return to display discussions on your particular topic.

4. To start a new discussion, click the Post New Topic link. The Web site prompts you to log in using the Apple ID you created during registration — most forums require you to create a user account before you can reply to a discussion or post a new topic.

Again, anyone can host a forum message base — companies offer them to allow discussions among employees, and it's easy for a club to offer a forum for its members. As with a blog, you find both free and commercial forum hosting sites by making a simple Google search at `www.google.com`.

Network with Others

I'll be honest: I find social networking sites such as Facebook (www.facebook.com) and MySpace (www.myspace.com) simply addictive! That's because they make the following activities so easy:

➡ **Search for friends and family who are also members of the network.** The list includes old friends you lost touch with over the years. For example, you can search for members from your hometown or high school.

➡ **Share photos and commentary with everyone.** These services make it easy to share photos by providing you with your own photo page that other users can see. You can choose the images you want to share with everyone. You can also join in simple discussions with others by posting messages on their pages.

➡ **Play games with network contacts.** Games on a social network site are usually quick to play and involve a lot of users, so competition can be heavy on the more popular games! For example, Facebook offers you the chance to build your own country, or engage in battles with others as a superhero.

➡ **Find fun activities.** I use Facebook to check on local live concerts in my area, as well as throw virtual "snowballs" at others and swap favorite jokes.

➡ **Share your contact list with others.** If you know people who are friends in real life (or went to the same school or worked at the same company), you can recommend them to each other so that they can become friends online as well.

Both Facebook and MySpace are free to join, and you can feel safe knowing that your personal information is secure. (You should never post personal information, however, such as your address or telephone number, in your public member record.)

Part IV

Taking Care of Your Computer

The 5th Wave   By Rich Tennant

AFTER SETTING UP THE COMPUTER, NED AND LORETTA SELECT THE COMPUTER'S BACKGROUND

"Oh — I like this background much better than the basement."

Protecting Leopard

The wise Mac owner is aware of the security issues that surround today's computers — from the Internet and from unauthorized use directly from the keyboard!

If you're wondering whether your Mac is vulnerable to attacks by bad guys, rest assured that your computer is surrounded by defenses that you can't even see. In this chapter, you find out how to

⟹ Keep Leopard current with the latest security updates from Apple.

⟹ Add applications to your Leopard firewall.

⟹ Configure FileVault to protect your home folder.

⟹ Configure your Mac for the tightest login security.

Chapter 17

Get ready to . . .

Understand Computer Security

Computers now face three major security challenges:

➡ **Attacks from the Internet.** A *hacker* (another name for a computer user who wants to take control of your computer) can use your Internet connection to monitor your communications or receive copies of your data.

➡ **Viruses.** You've probably heard of *viruses* — applications that can damage Leopard or your files or slow down your Mac. Although viruses are far less common on Macs than on Windows machines, you can invest in a good antivirus application to ensure that your computer remains pristine. (Leopard doesn't come with a built-in antivirus application, but I use Symantec's Norton AntiVirus for Mac, available from www.symantec.com).

➡ **Unauthorized users.** Whether the user is your niece or someone who has stolen your MacBook laptop, you want to protect your private documents and prevent anyone from using your Mac without your permission.

With the right security safeguards in position, you can rest easy, knowing that your Mac is well protected.

 Although you might not consider a backup of your Mac to be a "security safeguard," it really is. With a full backup safely stored in your home or office, you're protected in case your files and data are damaged or destroyed.

Configure and Run Software Update

I prefer that my Mac take care of cleaning up after itself, so updating Leopard with the latest security fixes should be automatic as well. In

Mac OS X Leopard, operating system updates are performed by the Software Update application.

Software Update uses the Internet, so you need an Internet connection to shake hands with the Apple server and download any updates. (The faster the connection, the better.)

You can find Software Update in two convenient spots:

➡ **On the Apple menu:** Click the Apple menu (🍎) and then choose Software Update, which displays the Update dialog box and alerts you to any new updates that are available.

➡ **In System Preferences:** Click the Software Update icon to display the Software Update pane, shown in **Figure 17-1**.

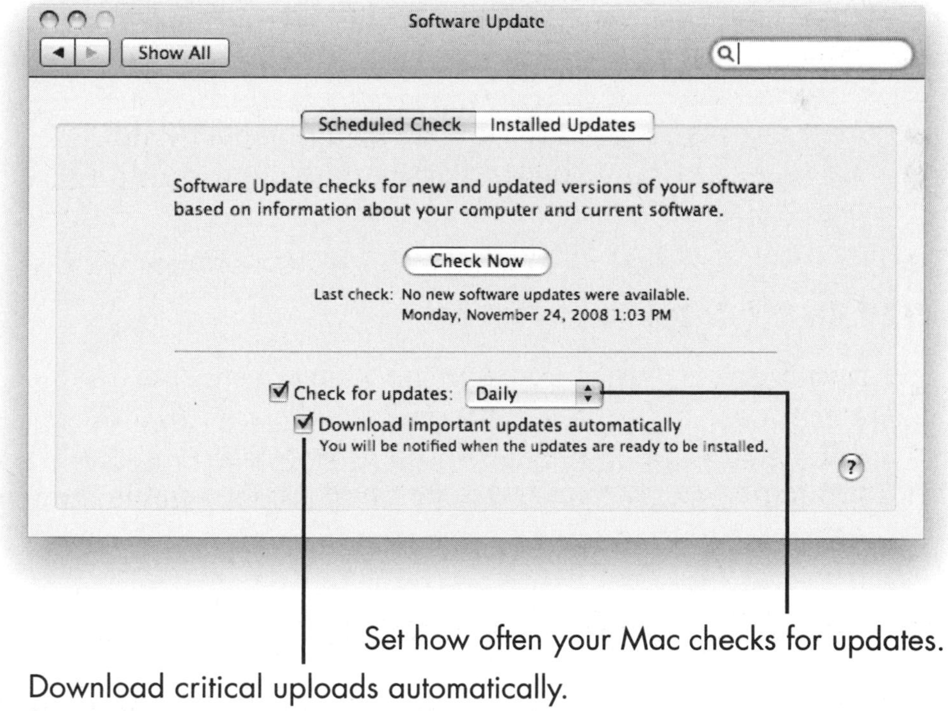

Set how often your Mac checks for updates.

Download critical uploads automatically.

Figure 17-1

If you take the System Preferences route, you can set Software Update to check for updates automatically:

1. Mark the Check for Updates check box to enable it.

2. Choose the frequency from the Check for Updates pop-up menu.

 Software Update covers every Apple application, so I usually configure it to check for updates once a day just to make sure that I don't miss anything.

3. Click to select the Download Important Updates Automatically check box.

If something needs to be updated, the program alerts you. Critical updates are automatically downloaded, and minor updates are displayed for your confirmation before they're downloaded. You're prompted for an administrator account password (typically yours) before the updates are installed.

 You can even also check for updates immediately from the Software Update pane in System Preferences — just click Check Now.

Customize the Leopard Firewall

Leopard's built-in software *firewall* acts as the wall surrounding your castle — I mean, your Mac — by allowing in the communications you want and preventing unknown communications from potential threats. The firewall works with your Internet connection and with any networks you might have joined.

To display the Firewall settings, click the System Preferences icon in the Dock and then click Security to display the Security pane. Click the Firewall tab to display the settings in **Figure 17-2**.

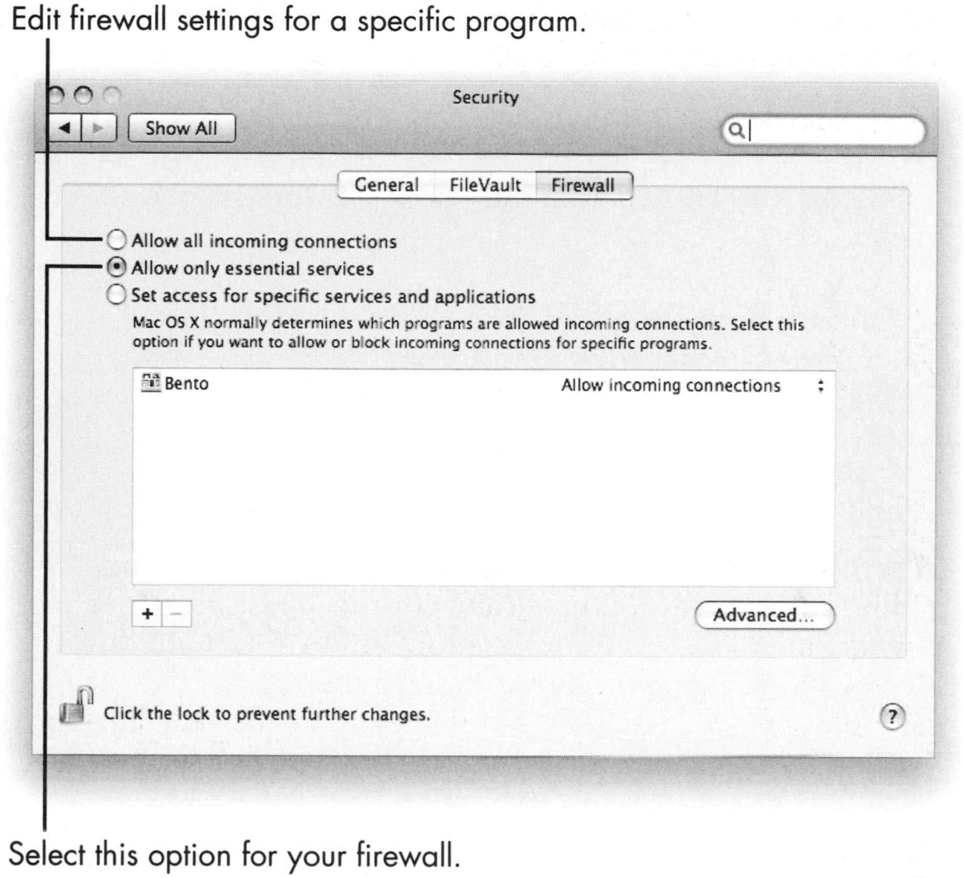

Edit firewall settings for a specific program.

Select this option for your firewall.

Figure 17-2

You have three options for setting your firewall:

- *To turn off the firewall entirely,* click Allow All Incoming Connections. Don't do this. This option is the very definition of Not a Good Thing, and I *always* recommend that any Mac hooked up to a network or the Internet avoid it.

- *To turn on the firewall with minimal exclusions,* click Allow Only Essential Services. The firewall automatically does the best it can to block unusual activity (so some network and Internet communications are stopped), but you can still use common Internet applications such as Safari, iChat, and Mail. (Yes, this option is the correct one for most Mac owners.)

- *To turn on the firewall with exclusions,* click Set Access for Specific Services and Applications. Any connection to a service (such as Web Sharing) or an application (such as iChat) that isn't listed is blocked. If you install any new applications that use the Internet, you'll have to specifically tell your Mac firewall to allow them if you use this option.

  To add an application to those allowed by this last option, click the button with the plus sign at the bottom of the Firewall pane and then navigate to the application that needs to communicate with the outside world. Click the application to select it and then click Add. Remember that only third-party applications that you install yourself will likely need to be added to the list.

  To delete an application and return it to blocked status, select it in the list and click the button with the minus sign.

 You can edit the settings in a specific application by clicking the pop-up menu on the right side of the entry. By default, the setting is Allow Incoming Connections (including both your local network and the Internet). However, you can also choose Block Incoming Connections to prevent that application from receiving any communications.

If you suddenly can't connect to other computers or share files that you originally could share, review the settings that you enabled from this pane: They might be the culprit. You can also verify that the correct sharing services are still enabled in the Sharing pane within System Preferences, as shown in **Figure 17-3**. Open the System Preferences window and click the Sharing icon, and make sure that the services you want to provide are selected.

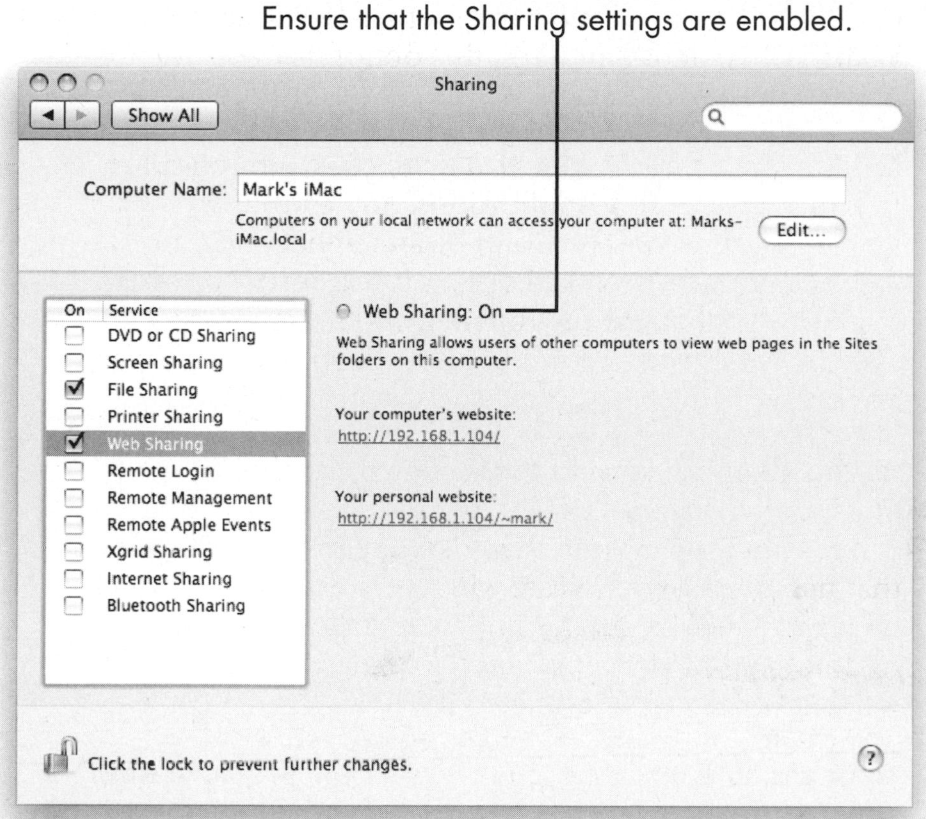

Ensure that the Sharing settings are enabled.

Figure 17-3

Configure and Run FileVault

As I mention earlier in this chapter, every Mac owner should be interested in securing personal files from prying eyes. Granted, this isn't a problem if you're the only one using your Mac. However, if you're sharing a computer with others, you might want a little more protection for those all-important tax records and that journal you're keeping.

Never fear: Leopard offers the *FileVault* feature, which provides Home folder encryption that prevents just about anyone except the NSA or FBI from gaining access to the files in your Home folder. You can enable the FileVault feature from the Security pane in System Preferences, as shown in **Figure 17-4**.

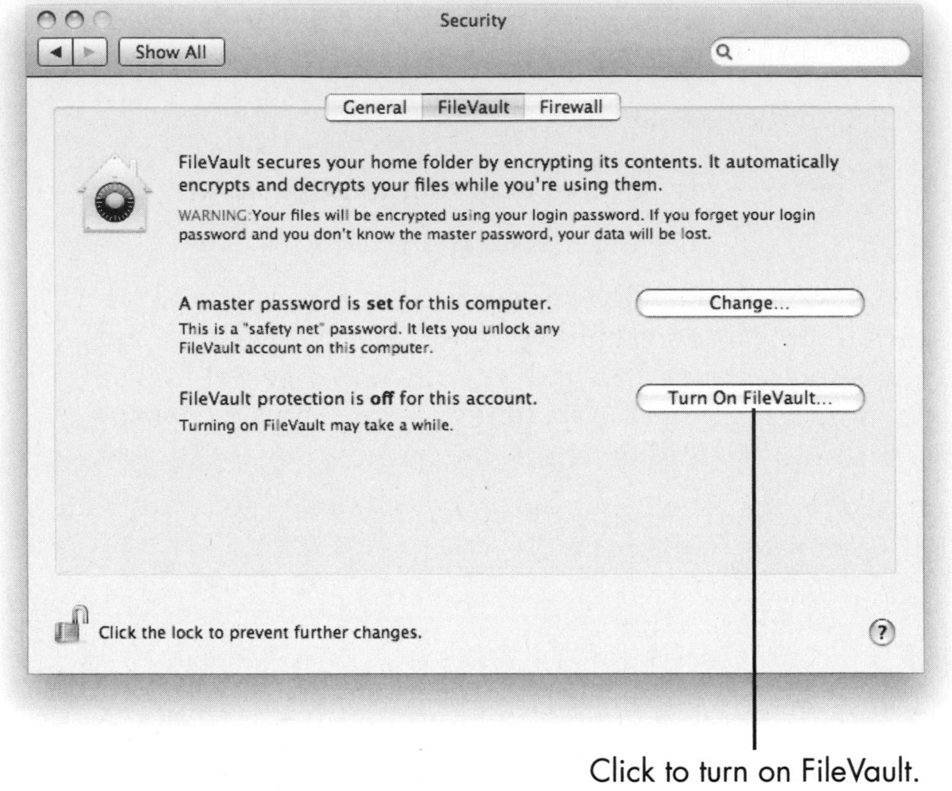

Click to turn on FileVault.

Figure 17-4

Two passwords control access to your Home folder when FileVault is active:

→ **Master password:** Can unlock any Home folder for *any* user. Only someone with an administrator account can set the master password. It must be set before you can turn on the FileVault feature for any account on your system.

→ **Login password:** Unlocks your Home folder.

To configure FileVault, follow these steps:

1. Click the System Preferences icon in the Dock.

2. Click the Security icon and click the FileVault tab.

3. Click the Set Master Password button to display the settings shown in **Figure** 17-5.

4. Type a master password.

5. Click in the Verify box and type your master password again.

6. If you want to provide a hint to your master password, click in the Hint box and type a word or short phrase. This hint should serve to remind you of your password in case you forget it. (I don't use a hint because I think that giving someone a hint rather defeats the purpose of security in the first place!)

7. Click OK.

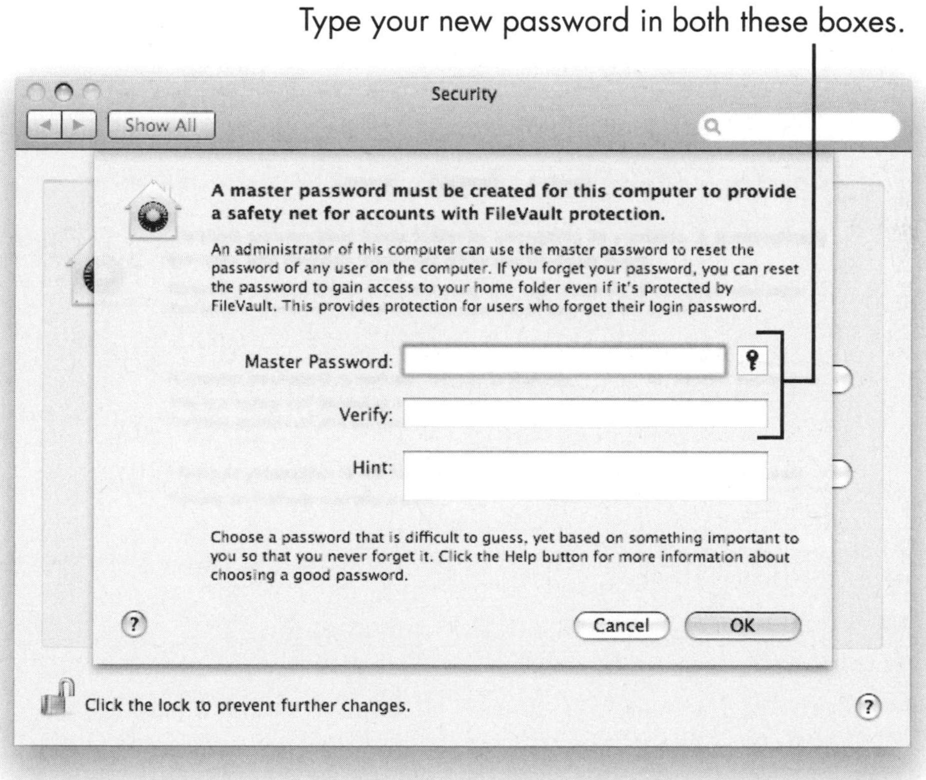

Type your new password in both these boxes.

Figure 17-5

8. Click the Turn On FileVault button to enable FileVault encryption for the user who's logged in.

9. Type your login password and click OK to begin the encryption process. (Remember that the user's login password becomes his FileVault password as well.)

I love this feature, and I use it on all my Macs running Leopard. Yet, a risk is involved (insert ominous chord here). To wit:

> DO NOT forget your login password, and make doggone sure that your admin user remembers that all-important master password!

Mac OS X displays a dire warning for anyone who's considering using FileVault: If you forget these passwords, you can't retrieve *any* data from your Home folder. Period. As Jerry Reed used to say, "It's a gone pecan."

I should also mention that FileVault protection slows things down somewhat when you're loading or saving a very large document — 100MB (megabytes) or more — to your Home folder.

Configure Secure User Options

You can also configure Leopard for tighter login security, making it much harder for anyone to sit down at your Mac and "break in" to your system. The secure login options are found within the System Preferences Security pane, so click the System Preferences icon in the Dock and click the Security icon to display the settings in **Figure 17-6**.

 If you're an admin-level user, you can set the global security features, in the For All Accounts on This Computer section, which affect all user accounts.

For tighter security, I recommend that you enable these options:

⟶ **Require Password to Wake This Computer from Sleep or Screen Saver:** Select this option to add an extra layer of password security to a laptop (or a Mac in a public area). Mac OS X then requires that you enter your login password before the system returns from a sleep state or exits from a screen saver.

➠ **Disable Automatic Login:** Enable this option to force a full login every time you boot your Mac. (Laptop owners, take note: Turn on this option to prevent a thief from accessing your data!)

➠ **Disable Remote Control Infrared Receiver:** Do you have an Apple Remote that you use with your computer? If you don't want small fingers accidentally controlling your Mac, select this option. (Don't forget to turn your IR receiver back on for your next movie night!)

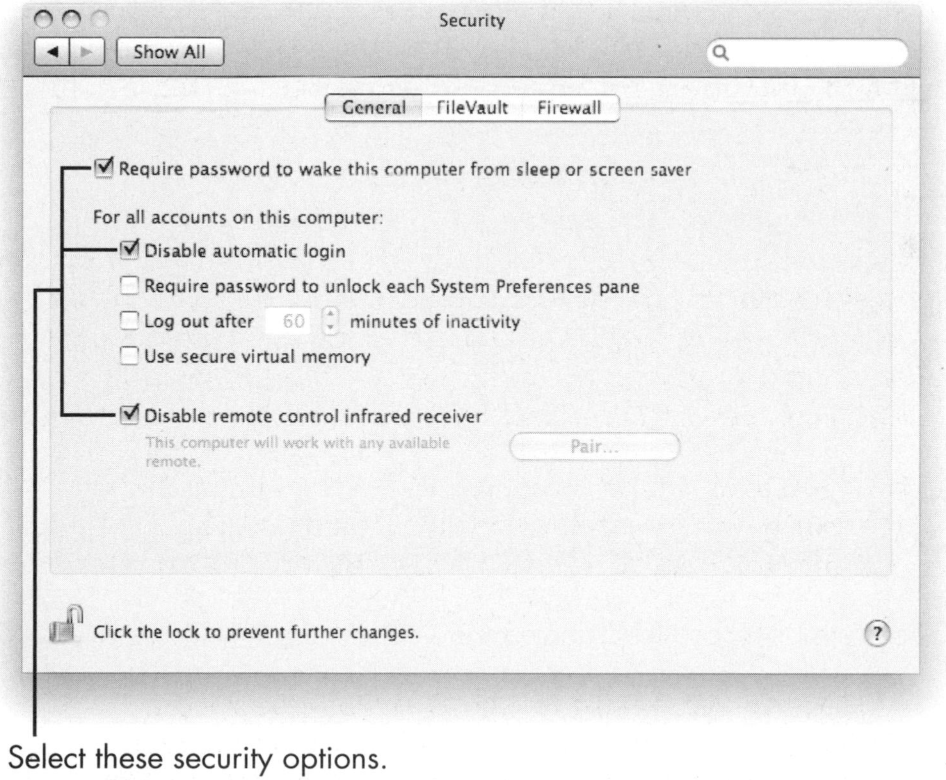

Select these security options.

Figure 17-6

Maintaining Leopard

Chapter 18

Although your Mac doesn't roam the highway like your car does, a computer still needs regular maintenance. Over time, regular use (and unexpected events, such as power outages) can produce problems ranging from hard drive errors to slower browser performance.

Don't worry, there's no oil filter to change! In this chapter, you find out how to

➠ Detect and correct errors in your Mac's file system.

➠ Repair permissions errors that can prevent applications from loading and running properly.

➠ Remove cookies that can slow down your Web surfing.

➠ Trim the Safari browser history and download lists.

Scan a Drive for Errors

Leopard's Disk Utility is a handy tool for troubleshooting and repairing your hard drive. You can find it in the Utilities folder within the Applications folder.

In the left column of the Disk Utility window, you can see

➠ The *physical* hard drives in your system (the actual hardware)

➠ The *volumes* (the data stored on the hard drives)

 You can always tell a volume because it's indented underneath the physical drive entry.

➠ Any CD or DVD loaded on your Mac

➠ USB or FireWire Flash drives. *Flash drives* are external hardware devices that you can add to your Mac for additional storage room or as a secure place to back up your data.

For example, in **Figure 18-1**, I have one hard drive (the 298.1GB entry) and one USB Flash drive (the 3.7GB entry). The hard drive has two volumes (Wolfgang and Mother), and the USB drive has one volume (MLC USB).

Disk Utility can use Verify Disk to check the format and health of both hard drives and volumes, and, if the problem can be corrected, use Repair Disk to fix any error.

Using Disk Utility to repair your hard drive carries a couple of caveats:

➠ **You can't repair the boot disk or the boot volume.** This statement makes sense because you're using that disk and volume right now. (The *boot volume* is usually your Mac's internal hard drive, where Leopard is installed.)

To verify or repair your boot hard drive, you need to boot from the Mac OS X installation disc. Press the Media Eject key on your keyboard and load the

Leopard installation disc, and then reboot and hold down the C key when you hear the boot tone. (You can also boot from an external hard drive that has Leopard installed.) After your Mac boots from the Mac OS X installation disc, click the Utilities menu and choose Disk Utility.

You should be able to select your boot hard drive or volume, and the Verify Disk and Repair Disk buttons should be enabled.

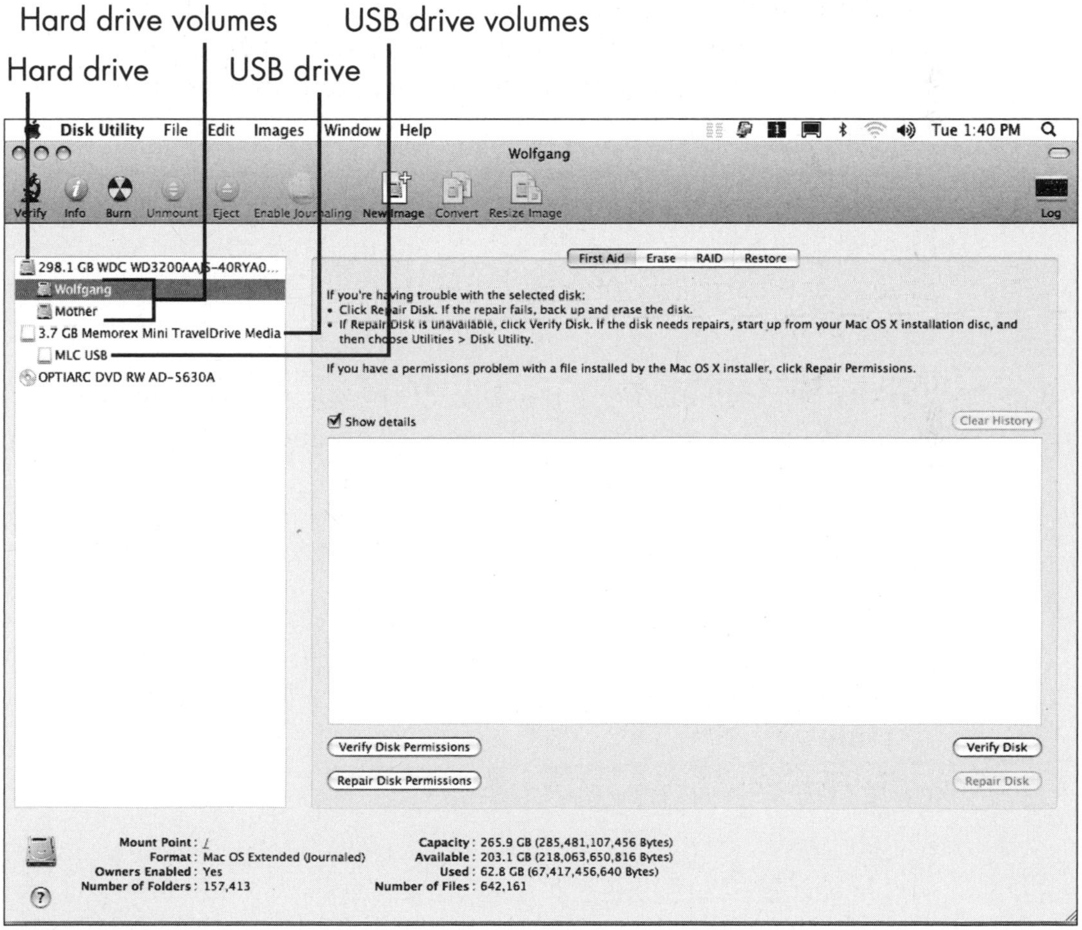

Hard drive volumes   USB drive volumes

Hard drive   USB drive

Figure 18-1

➡ **You can't repair CDs and DVDs.** Because CDs and DVDs are read-only media, they can't be repaired (at least by Disk Utility).

If your Mac is having trouble reading a CD or DVD, wipe the disc with a soft cloth to remove dust, oil, and fingerprints. If that technique fails, invest in a disc-cleaning contrivance of some sort. (If you need to buy a CD/DVD cleaning kit, Best Buy is a good bet.)

If you need to verify and repair a disk or volume, follow these steps:

1. If you need to repair your boot drive and volume, save all open documents and reboot from either an external drive or your Mac OS X installation disc.

 You can choose which drive your Mac boots from by clicking the System Preferences icon in the Dock. Click the Startup Disk icon, select a drive from the list, and then click Restart.

2. Double-click the Disk Utility icon in the Utilities folder.

3. In the list on the left side of the Disk Utility window, click the disk or volume that you want to check.

4. Click the Repair Disk button.

5. If changes were made (or if you had to boot from a disc or external drive), reboot after repairing the disk or volume.

Fix File Permission Problems

Shifty-eyed, sneaky, irritating little problems can bother your hard drive: *permissions errors.* Incorrect disk and file permissions can

➡ Make your Mac lock up

➡ Make applications act screwy (or refuse to run)

➡ Cause strange behavior within a Finder window or
System Preferences

Permission errors are usually introduced on your system by a faulty
application installer — sometimes the application itself has a bug that
produces errors when it tries to open or close files. Fortunately, you
don't have to investigate the cause of a permission error. (That's good
because you and I aren't likely to understand such technogibberish,
anyway.) You just need to know that Disk Utility fixes the errors.

 To keep Leopard running at its best, fix permissions
errors at least once a week.

To fix any permissions errors on your system, follow these steps:

1. Open a Finder window, click Applications, and then click
Utilities.

2. Double-click the Disk Utility icon.

3. Click the volume on the left that you want to check. (In
this case, it's a named partition, such as Macintosh HD,
which appears under your physical hard drive.) **Figure
18-2** illustrates my hard drive Mac volume, musically
named Wolfgang in honor of Mozart.

4. Click the Repair Disk Permissions button.

Disk Utility does the rest and then displays a message
about whatever it has to fix. (When will someone invent a
car with a Repair Me button?)

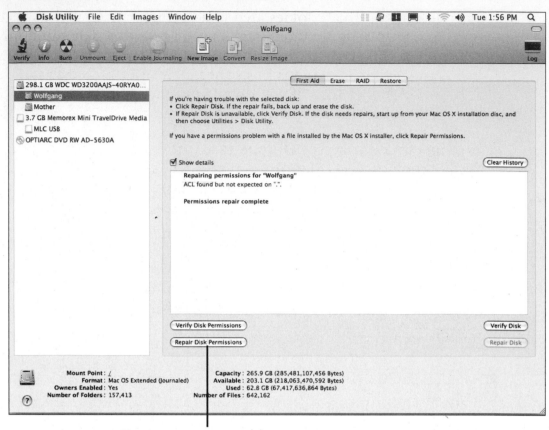

Fix permissions problems.

Figure 18-2

Delete Cookies in Safari

First, a definition of the ridiculous term *cookie:* It's a small file that a
Web site automatically saves on your hard drive, containing information that the site will use on your future visits. Unfortunately, for these
purposes, cookies aren't yummy treats that we make from flour, sugar,
butter, and eggs. For example, a site might save a cookie to preserve
your site preferences for the next time or — in the case of a site such as
Amazon.com — to identify you automatically and help customize the
offerings you see.

In and of themselves, cookies aren't bad things. Unlike a virus, a cookie file doesn't replicate itself or wreak havoc on your system, and only the original site can read the cookie it creates. However, many folks don't appreciate acting as gracious hosts for a slew of little snippets of personal information. Also, if you do a large amount of surfing, cookies can occupy a significant amount of your hard drive space over time.

You can choose to accept all cookies — the default setting — or opt to disable cookies altogether. You can also set Safari to accept cookies only from the sites you choose to visit. To change your *cookie acceptance plan* (or CAP, if you absolutely crave acronyms), follow these steps:

1. Choose Safari⇨Preferences.

2. Click the Security button.

Safari displays the preference settings, as shown in **Figure 18-3**.

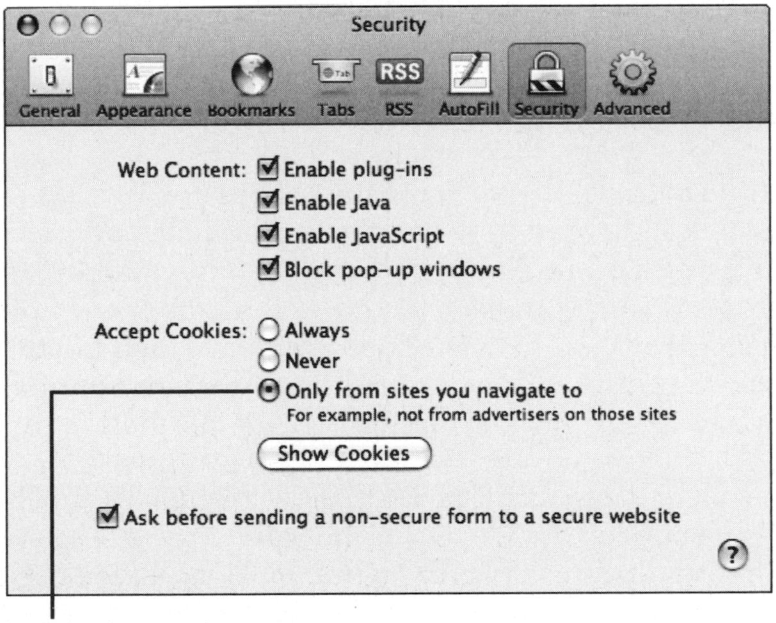

Select this cookie option.

Figure 18-3

3. Choose how to accept cookies by using these radio button choices:

- *Never:* Block cookies entirely.

- *Always:* Accept all cookies.

- *Only from Sites You Navigate To:* I use this option, which allows sites such as Amazon.com to work correctly without allowing a barrage of illicit cookies.

4. To view the cookies now on your system, click the Show Cookies button.

 If you block all cookies, you might have to take care of some tasks manually, such as providing a password on the site that used to be read automatically from the cookie.

5. Click the Close button to save your changes.

Delete the Safari Browsing History

As you might imagine, your Web browsing History file leaves a clear set of footprints indicating where you've been — and it can become downright expansive if you don't clear it from time to time. And hey, maybe you just don't want your grandkids to know about the many hours per day that you spend at the Paris Hilton fan club Web page. To delete the contents of the History menu, launch Safari and choose History⇨ Clear History.

The latest version of Safari also lets you specify a length of time to retain entries in your History file. Open the Safari Preferences dialog box, click the General tab (shown in **Figure 18**-4), and then click the Remove History Items pop-up menu to specify a length of time. Items can be rolled off daily, weekly, biweekly, monthly, or yearly.

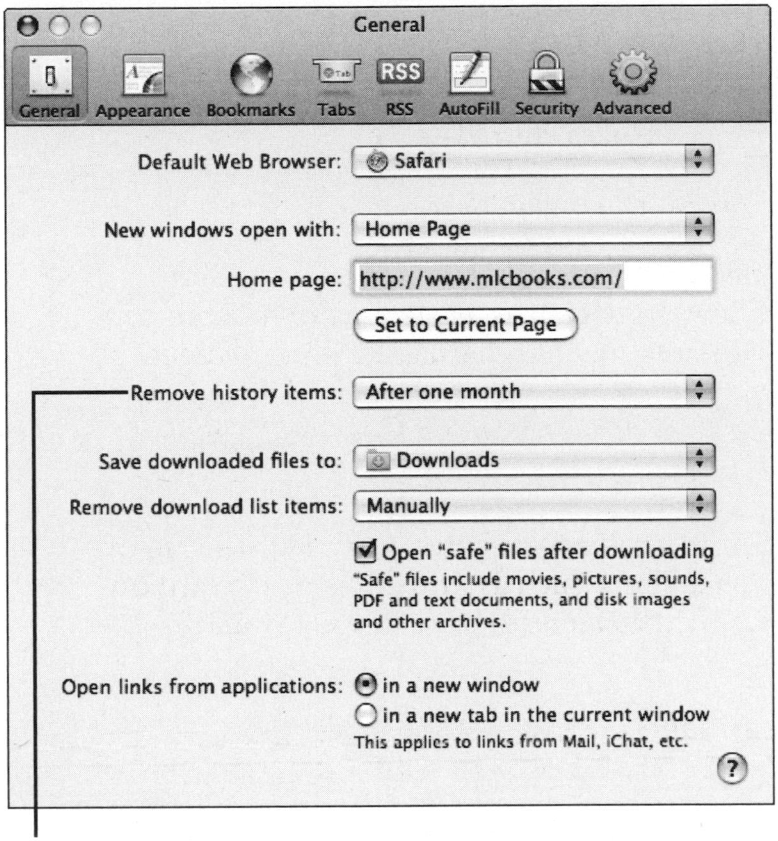

Control how long items stay in History.
Figure 18-4

Delete the Safari Download History

Safari makes it easy to clear the list of files you downloaded over time. The file list is maintained within the "floating" Downloads window, which appears whenever you start a download. (You can also display the Downloads window at any time by clicking Window on the Safari menu bar and then choosing the Downloads item.)

To keep your Safari Downloads window tidy (and prevent other people from seeing what you've been pulling down from the Web), click the Clear button at the bottom of the Downloads window. Safari automatically removes any entries for downloaded items you successfully received.

Index

• N •

Q

• R •

S

scroll balls, Mighty Mouse, 32–33
scroll bars, 71, 163
scroll wheels, 88
scrolling speed, 88
searches
  forum hosting sites, 298
  Google Search, 248
  Help system, 131–133
  image keywords, 185–187
  iTunes Store, 209–211
  Mac support resources, 137–138
  Spotlight, 60–63
  Web page content, 250–251
  Web sites, 249–250
Secure Sockets Layer (SSL) security,
    262–263
security
  AutoFill risks, 175
  backups, 304
  common sense practices, 242–244
  deleting cookies, 320–322
  deleting History files, 322–323
  Desktop screen savers, 83–84
  e-mail encryption, 242
  file permissions, 318–320
  FileVault settings, 309–312
  Firewall settings, 306–309
  hacker attacks, 304
  identity theft, 174–175
  Internet issues, 238–240
  iTunes Store account, 208
  password hints, 40
  phishing attacks, 242–243
  Secure Sockets Layer (SSL), 262–263
  Secure User options, 312–313
  software updates, 305–306
  threat types, 304

unauthorized user risks, 304
  Usenet groups, 243
  virus attacks, 304
  virus risks, 240–242
Security pane, 306–313
selections
  deleting Pages text, 145
  formatting Pages text, 147–148
  items, 110–112
  Pages table cells, 149
  printing, 122
  resizing Pages image, 152–153
  spreadsheet cell data, 163–164
Sent folder, Mail, 265
servers, Internet time, 43–44
shading, spreadsheet cells, 168–169
shapes, Pages background, 153
Sharing pane, 134–137, 239
Show Fax Status in Menu bar, 127
Shut Down command, 45
signatures, Mail, 278–279
Sites folder, 36–37, 237
Sleep command, 44–45
Sleep mode, secure user settings, 313
slide shows, 189–191
Slow Keys, keyboards, 85–86
smileys, text chats, 291
social networking, 298–299
software. *See also* programs
  patches, 12–13
  processing power, 14–15
  system requirement information, 15
  updates, 305–306
  upgrades, 12–13
  version numbers, 13
  versus hardware, 13
Software folder, 238

BUSINESS, CAREERS & PERSONAL FINANCE

Accounting For Dummies, 4th Edition*
978-0-470-24600-9

Bookkeeping Workbook For Dummies†
978-0-470-16983-4

Commodities For Dummies
978-0-470-04928-0

Doing Business in China For Dummies
978-0-470-04929-7

E-Mail Marketing For Dummies
978-0-470-19087-6

Job Interviews For Dummies, 3rd Edition*†
978-0-470-17748-8

Personal Finance Workbook For Dummies*†
978-0-470-09933-9

Real Estate License Exams For Dummies
978-0-7645-7623-2

Six Sigma For Dummies
978-0-7645-6798-8

Small Business Kit For Dummies, 2nd Edition*†
978-0-7645-5984-6

Telephone Sales For Dummies
978-0-470-16836-3

BUSINESS PRODUCTIVITY & MICROSOFT OFFICE

Access 2007 For Dummies
978-0-470-03649-5

Excel 2007 For Dummies
978-0-470-03737-9

Office 2007 For Dummies
978-0-470-00923-9

Outlook 2007 For Dummies
978-0-470-03830-7

PowerPoint 2007 For Dummies
978-0-470-04059-1

Project 2007 For Dummies
978-0-470-03651-8

QuickBooks 2008 For Dummies
978-0-470-18470-7

Quicken 2008 For Dummies
978-0-470-17473-9

Salesforce.com For Dummies, 2nd Edition
978-0-470-04893-1

Word 2007 For Dummies
978-0-470-03658-7

EDUCATION, HISTORY, REFERENCE & TEST PREPARATION

African American History For Dummies
978-0-7645-5469-8

Algebra For Dummies
978-0-7645-5325-7

Algebra Workbook For Dummies
978-0-7645-8467-1

Art History For Dummies
978-0-470-09910-0

ASVAB For Dummies, 2nd Edition
978-0-470-10671-6

British Military History For Dummies
978-0-470-03213-8

Calculus For Dummies
978-0-7645-2498-1

Canadian History For Dummies, 2nd Edition
978-0-470-83656-9

Geometry Workbook For Dummies
978-0-471-79940-5

The SAT I For Dummies, 6th Edition
978-0-7645-7193-0

Series 7 Exam For Dummies
978-0-470-09932-2

World History For Dummies
978-0-7645-5242-7

FOOD, GARDEN, HOBBIES & HOME

Bridge For Dummies, 2nd Edition
978-0-471-92426-5

Coin Collecting For Dummies, 2nd Edition
978-0-470-22275-1

Cooking Basics For Dummies, 3rd Edition
978-0-7645-7206-7

Drawing For Dummies
978-0-7645-5476-6

Etiquette For Dummies, 2nd Edition
978-0-470-10672-3

Gardening Basics For Dummies*†
978-0-470-03749-2

Knitting Patterns For Dummies
978-0-470-04556-5

Living Gluten-Free For Dummies†
978-0-471-77383-2

Painting Do-It-Yourself For Dummies
978-0-470-17533-0

HEALTH, SELF HELP, PARENTING & PETS

Anger Management For Dummies
978-0-470-03715-7

Anxiety & Depression Workbook For Dummies
978-0-7645-9793-0

Dieting For Dummies, 2nd Edition
978-0-7645-4149-0

Dog Training For Dummies, 2nd Edition
978-0-7645-8418-3

Horseback Riding For Dummies
978-0-470-09719-9

Infertility For Dummies†
978-0-470-11518-3

Meditation For Dummies with CD-ROM, 2nd Edition
978-0-471-77774-8

Post-Traumatic Stress Disorder For Dummies
978-0-470-04922-8

Puppies For Dummies, 2nd Edition
978-0-470-03717-1

Thyroid For Dummies, 2nd Edition†
978-0-471-78755-6

Type 1 Diabetes For Dummies*†
978-0-470-17811-9

---

* Separate Canadian edition also available
† Separate U.K. edition also available

Available wherever books are sold. For more information or to order direct: U.S. customers visit www.dummies.com or call 1-877-762-2974.
U.K. customers visit www.wileyeurope.com or call (0)1243 843291. Canadian customers visit www.wiley.ca or call 1-800-567-4797.

INTERNET & DIGITAL MEDIA

AdWords For Dummies
978-0-470-15252-2

Blogging For Dummies, 2nd Edition
978-0-470-23017-6

**Digital Photography All-in-One
Desk Reference For Dummies, 3rd Edition**
978-0-470-03743-0

Digital Photography For Dummies, 5th Edition
978-0-7645-9802-9

**Digital SLR Cameras & Photography
For Dummies, 2nd Edition**
978-0-470-14927-0

**eBay Business All-in-One Desk Reference
For Dummies**
978-0-7645-8438-1

eBay For Dummies, 5th Edition*
978-0-470-04529-9

eBay Listings That Sell For Dummies
978-0-471-78912-3

Facebook For Dummies
978-0-470-26273-3

The Internet For Dummies, 11th Edition
978-0-470-12174-0

Investing Online For Dummies, 5th Edition
978-0-7645-8456-5

iPod & iTunes For Dummies, 5th Edition
978-0-470-17474-6

MySpace For Dummies
978-0-470-09529-4

Podcasting For Dummies
978-0-471-74898-4

**Search Engine Optimization
For Dummies, 2nd Edition**
978-0-471-97998-2

Second Life For Dummies
978-0-470-18025-9

**Starting an eBay Business For Dummies,
3rd Edition†**
978-0-470-14924-9

GRAPHICS, DESIGN & WEB DEVELOPMENT

**Adobe Creative Suite 3 Design Premium
All-in-One Desk Reference For Dummies**
978-0-470-11724-8

**Adobe Web Suite CS3 All-in-One Desk
Reference For Dummies**
978-0-470-12099-6

AutoCAD 2008 For Dummies
978-0-470-11650-0

**Building a Web Site For Dummies,
3rd Edition**
978-0-470-14928-7

**Creating Web Pages All-in-One Desk
Reference For Dummies, 3rd Edition**
978-0-470-09629-1

**Creating Web Pages For Dummies,
8th Edition**
978-0-470-08030-6

Dreamweaver CS3 For Dummies
978-0-470-11490-2

Flash CS3 For Dummies
978-0-470-12100-9

Google SketchUp For Dummies
978-0-470-13744-4

InDesign CS3 For Dummies
978-0-470-11865-8

**Photoshop CS3 All-in-One
Desk Reference For Dummies**
978-0-470-11195-6

Photoshop CS3 For Dummies
978-0-470-11193-2

Photoshop Elements 5 For Dummies
978-0-470-09810-3

SolidWorks For Dummies
978-0-7645-9555-4

Visio 2007 For Dummies
978-0-470-08983-5

Web Design For Dummies, 2nd Edition
978-0-471-78117-2

Web Sites Do-It-Yourself For Dummies
978-0-470-16903-2

Web Stores Do-It-Yourself For Dummies
978-0-470-17443-2

LANGUAGES, RELIGION & SPIRITUALITY

Arabic For Dummies
978-0-471-77270-5

Chinese For Dummies, Audio Set
978-0-470-12766-7

French For Dummies
978-0-7645-5193-2

German For Dummies
978-0-7645-5195-6

Hebrew For Dummies
978-0-7645-5489-6

Ingles Para Dummies
978-0-7645-5427-8

Italian For Dummies, Audio Set
978-0-470-09586-7

Italian Verbs For Dummies
978-0-471-77389-4

Japanese For Dummies
978-0-7645-5429-2

Latin For Dummies
978-0-7645-5431-5

Portuguese For Dummies
978-0-471-78738-9

Russian For Dummies
978-0-471-78001-4

Spanish Phrases For Dummies
978-0-7645-7204-3

Spanish For Dummies
978-0-7645-5194-9

Spanish For Dummies, Audio Set
978-0-470-09585-0

The Bible For Dummies
978-0-7645-5296-0

Catholicism For Dummies
978-0-7645-5391-2

The Historical Jesus For Dummies
978-0-470-16785-4

Islam For Dummies
978-0-7645-5503-9

**Spirituality For Dummies,
2nd Edition**
978-0-470-19142-2

NETWORKING AND PROGRAMMING

ASP.NET 3.5 For Dummies
978-0-470-19592-5

C# 2008 For Dummies
978-0-470-19109-5

Hacking For Dummies, 2nd Edition
978-0-470-05235-8

Home Networking For Dummies, 4th Edition
978-0-470-11806-1

Java For Dummies, 4th Edition
978-0-470-08716-9

**Microsoft® SQL Server™ 2008 All-in-One
Desk Reference For Dummies**
978-0-470-17954-3

**Networking All-in-One Desk Reference
For Dummies, 2nd Edition**
978-0-7645-9939-2

**Networking For Dummies,
8th Edition**
978-0-470-05620-2

SharePoint 2007 For Dummies
978-0-470-09941-4

**Wireless Home Networking
For Dummies, 2nd Edition**
978-0-471-74940-0